After years of bad raps, evangelism has a new lease on life thanks to Will McRaney's wonderful new book, *The Art of Personal Evangelism*. Not only will this new book help individual Christians better share their faith, it will help church leaders better grow their churches. Anyone interested in sharing a timeless message in a timely manner will want to be sure to read this book.

Charles Arn
President, Church Growth, Inc.

Evangelism! Some people love it, while others hate it. Still others think it is an outmoded concept that should be allowed to gather dust in the back rooms of our minds. *The Art of Personal Evangelism* literally blows the dust off such uncritical thinking and challenges us to see evangelism through the lenses of our pluralistic age.

McRaney carefully rebuilds a biblical foundation for evangelism, while providing practical tips on reaching people for Christ in the postmodern environment in which we minister. *The Art of Personal Evangelism* may well become the classic resource on how to share Jesus in a changing culture.

Gary McIntosh
Professor of Christian Ministry and Leadership
Talbot School of Theology, Biola University
President, McIntosh Church Growth Network

Christian leaders are telling us to "Just Do It" when it comes to personal evangelism—and those are Will McRaney's parting words. But McRaney goes beyond what we know we should be doing and tells us how. After grounding us in the biblical foundation for evangelism, McRaney translates it into our postmodern culture and gives steps to take in sharing the gospel. This book will be on your shortlist for evangelism resources. "Just Read It—then do it!"

Bob Reccord
President, North American Mission Board

For over ten years I have taught courses on evangelism. The one glaring need over these years has been for a comprehensive, practical text on personal evangelism. Dr. Will McRaney has provided both the academy and the church an essential tool. In evangelism, personal witnessing lays the foundation for all other approaches; this book provides the essential resource for personal witnessing.

Alvin Reid
Professor of Evangelism
Southeastern Baptist Theological Seminary

THE ART
OF PERSONAL
EVANGELISM

THE ART
OF PERSONAL
EVANGELISM

SHARING JESUS IN A CHANGING CULTURE

WILL McRANEY JR.

NASHVILLE, TENNESSEE

ISBN: 978–0–8054–2624–3

Published by B&H Publishing Group,
Nashville, Tennessee

Dewey Decimal Classification: 248.5
Subject Heading: WITNESSING \ EVANGELISTIC WORK \
CHURCH GROWTH

Unless otherwise noted, Scripture text is from the Holy Bible, New
International Version, copyright © 1973, 1978, 1984 by International
Bible Society. Scriptures marked NASB are from NASB, the New
American Standard Bible © the Lockman Foundation, 1960, 1962,
1963, 1968, 1971, 1972, 1973, 1975, 1977; used by permission.

20 21 22 23 24   18 17 16 15 14

Contents

*especially
good*

Preface

WRITING A PERSONAL EVANGELISM TEXT has been a challenging undertaking. I have discovered much about myself. I discovered many of my limitations as a writer and scholar. I have been humbled by the challenge of putting into words that which will be most helpful to you.

Some of the issues addressed in the book required some serious investigation and reflection. I discovered significant areas that I have not explored. However, I have experienced the grace of God to complete this privileged task in spite of my limitations.

It is much easier to critique books than to write one. I often have my students discuss the strengths and the limitations of a book, not its weaknesses. However, I recognize that this book does have weaknesses for which I assume responsibility.

I have also rediscovered much from writers who have gone before. Much of what I am saying has been written before in some form. I am indeed attempting to stand on the shoulders of people of great faith and skill who have written much on personal evangelism.

No one book could possibly cover all the issues surrounding personal evangelism. I am limited, and the subject is broad. I have not attempted to develop an in-depth book around the biblical basis or particular practices of evangelism, but I am thankful that others have done so. Also, I have not attempted to ask or answer all the theological questions. However, I am glad that others have done extensive work in the theological areas as I have been helped in this project through their significant contributions.

In reviewing my efforts, I have come to discover components that could have been included but were not. It is difficult to leave some things unsaid and other areas only highlighted. My hope is that you will find encouragement, strength, and practical help in the midst of all the limitations of this work.

This book addresses the major foundational and practical issues surrounding personal evangelism in order to assist in reversing the church's decline in the latter part of the twentieth century in many parts of the Western world. A danger is to write about the methods of personal evangelism to the neglect of the foundational principles. It is my desire to be practical and yet give you the basis on which personal evangelism approaches and strategies should be built. Without effective personal evangelism, the church cannot reverse the decline in most every denomination in the United States.

I have attempted to provide a balanced book that takes seriously the foundations and theories from which all of evangelism must flow, while providing principles and practical tips in communicating our rich message. I have intentionally seen my task through the lenses of the pluralistic context in which we live, particularly postmodernism. This shift will have a great impact on the approach of evangelism but not on the foundational principles that are rooted in Scripture.

Many good books cover personal evangelism through the lenses of modernity. Most of the evangelistic questions arising out of modernity have been identified and answered in some form. I also trust that my book will assist you with the foundational issues and provide some assistance to you along your spiritual journey. If you find yourself operating in a culture built primarily around modernity, you can find additional books to support your quest for assistance in evangelism, particularly personal evangelism.

I will touch on many resources that have helped me along the way, but if you are looking for an overview of the subject, I encourage you to read *Introduction to Evangelism* by my friend Dr. Alvin Reid. I will not attempt to duplicate the topics that he and others have covered so well.

Acknowledgments

I GIVE SPECIAL THANKS TO THOSE who have encouraged me through the years of ministry and particularly through completing this often overwhelming task. My wife Sandy is my friend and partner of eighteen years. We share the love of our three girls, Blakeney, Hadley, and Macy, each with a unique personality that brings much joy and excitement to our lives.

I also thank my president, Dr. Chuck Kelley, and my colleagues at New Orleans Baptist Theological Seminary for their encouragement and assistance and for allowing me to chase my dreams in such a wonderful teaching environment. I also thank my students with whom I have learned and, I trust, contributed to their passion and skill in communicating the gospel message to those without Christ.

Several students assisted me in various ways with this book, particularly Myles Brown. In addition to the professional editing by Leonard Goss from Broadman & Holman, my assistant, Carol Bryd, and several colleagues and friends provided input.

Two other people have made this book possible. One is the person who personally taught me to walk with Jesus day by day and challenged me to invest my life in others through the sharing of my faith, within and outside my comfort zone. That person is Rick Stark, who as the Athletes and Action staff member at Mississippi State, walked with me through those critical years of spiritual development. Rick, thank you for investing part of your life in me.

The final person is my mentor in ministry, Pastor Harold Bullock of the Hope Community Church in Ft. Worth, Texas. Through Harold

I was challenged not to do church in a business-as-usual fashion. He did this not only through his words and his church but through his personal example. I cannot count the things I have learned from you, Harold. During and since the writing of the book, it often has been difficult to distinguish what I have personally read or thought from what you taught me. Your fingerprints are found through the pages of this book. Harold, thank you for investing and entrusting your godly wisdom and ministry insights with me.

One of my prayers is that I will be found faithful with the investments so many have made in my life through the years. My prayer for you today is that your discovery and application of your unique, God-given evangelistic personality and passion will increase as a result of reading this book.

Introduction

M Y PRESBYTERIAN NEIGHBOR in Littleton, Colorado, jokingly
called it the "E word" because there are apprehensions in saying
the word. Others cringe at hearing the word. That word is *evangelism*.

The word *evangelism* is not an emotionally neutral word. Much
like the home environment with preschoolers, there are always high
emotions around evangelism. Our reactions to the topic of evangelism
are more often fear, guilt, discouragement, and uncertainty rather than
courage, passion, and excitement. Whether we are comfortable with
the word *evangelism* or choose to use a different word to describe the
task before us, the church has been and forever will be undeniably
linked to personally communicating the hope found only in Christ.

Evangelism need not be seen in a negative light. The word
evangelism comes from a combination of Greek words for "good" and
"messenger." Evangelism involves bringing good news. Kent Hunter
reminded us that "when Christians witness, they tell how Jesus Christ
has changed their own lives. The change in their own lives gives them
the desire to share the Good News with others. But the Good News
isn't about themselves. It is about the Lord who changes them."[1]

A wise man expressed much wisdom and passion, summarizing
what the Christian church needs to hear. He said, "Any religion that
does not consider itself valuable enough to share with nonbelievers
is fated to crumble from within." Was this statement made by a great
Christian? an evangelist? maybe Billy Graham? Was this a warning
to Christians? No, the statement was made by Yosef Abramowitz,
a Jew, in an article "Taking on the Southern Baptists" in his warning to

1

fellow Jews. Southern Baptists at an annual convention had voted to dedicate a year to the evangelization of Jewish people. He also said, "If Jews shrink from the task of proselytizing, it might send a signal that Judaism isn't worth spreading to others."[2] Is it possible with the lack of personal evangelism that evangelical Christians are unintentionally sending the signal that Christianity isn't worth spreading to others?

People across America are searching for meaning and purpose in life. Are we in danger of signaling that Christians have not found the answer? We are in danger of signaling that Christ is not worth sharing with others because He has not made a significant difference in our lives.

Given the tragedy of September 11, 2001, and turmoil in the Middle East, we should think about the signal we are sending if we remain silent about how God broke into history to redeem people through Jesus Christ. Those sacrificial terrorists died for an evil and eternally damning cause. How can we who call ourselves followers of Christ not live with equal passion and sacrifice for a just and eternally life-giving cause?

No book can solve the problem of silence among the people of God. However, a book like this one just might assist readers in knowing how to communicate more effectively the love of Christ. The purpose of this book is to blow the dust off the biblical essentials and help you connect the timeless message of the past with the postmodern culture of the present in which God means everything and nothing. A culture where the local Christian church is out of favor with the person on the street, some antagonistic and others indifferent toward the church. The book is geared more to be instructional than inspirational, all the while knowing that evangelism is primarily an act of passionate obedience rather than intellectual pursuit.

There are many reasons to reexamine the basics of personal evangelism. Personal evangelism is the foundation of all church growth methods. Without personal evangelism there are no churches, no pastors, no worship services. Everything begins with personal evangelism. Nothing much happens in church until some concerned Christian shares the life-changing message of Jesus Christ.

Why another book on personal evangelism? Americans are searching spiritually, but the Christian church is often not connecting with the people they are seeking to reach. According to a George Barna poll, 48 percent of Americans are searching for the meaning and purpose of life.[3] Yet according to American Religious Identification Survey 2001, more than 29.4 million Americans said they had no religion—more than double the number in 1990.[4] Thirty-three percent of Americans describe themselves as "spiritual but not religious."

Rick Richardson summarized the views of many concerning our ineffectiveness in sharing the gospel. He said: "Unfortunately, most of our approaches to proclaiming the gospel are still aimed at the modern scientific, analytical, individualistic mindset. We are ineffective in part because we are building our communication bridge to a mindset and an age that are passing away, or at least being radically transformed. . . . We need to understand and address a new mindset if our proclamation and demonstration of the gospel are to remain relevant and influence the minds and hearts of the next generation. The emerging mindset has been labeled 'postmodern.'"[5]

It is not my intent to criticize past methods of evangelism. Many of them were effective in their given context. We stand on the approaches of the past. I cut my teeth on personal evangelism and still find myself returning to the four spiritual laws. Writers of the past gave us insights into how to reach a people who grew up in a Judeo-Christian culture. So, much of the context has changed and will continue to change. I will be suggesting that our approach to evangelism cannot be our fathers' approach to evangelism.

The reasons are numerous for overhauling our approaches, but I will summarize with the following list.

1. We are failing at our mission.
2. We live in a radically different culture (modernism vs. postmodernism).

3. People no longer share a common story.
4. People now perceive and determine truth in different ways.
5. People no longer believe in absolute truth as determined by others.
6. Lost people are more negative toward church than in the past.
7. Lost people are further from a true understanding of God than in the past.
8. We live in a post-Christian and pre-Christian culture, not a Christian culture (no home court advantage).
9. Christians have an identity and image problem. (Christianity means everything and nothing.)
10. People perceive themselves as spiritual and therefore not in need of the church.
11. The church has little to no perceived value in the lives of many lost people.
12. People's approaches to life have changed and our methods have not.
13. Much of conservative Christianity's evangelism has been built upon one-time encounters and memorized presentations, an approach effective only in a highly homogeneous culture.[6]

We must respond to our changed world with fresh, biblical approaches. I do not want to suggest that any *one* method of evangelism is *the* method of evangelism. Neither do I want to imply that methods created primarily in the mid-twentieth century have no place in an overall strategy to evangelize those under age forty today. However, we do live in a radically different world. Francis Schaeffer asked the question, "How should we then live?" A question for this generation is not only how we shall live but also, how now shall we evangelize in a postmodern culture?

SITUATION AT HAND

The church in America is failing to impact the pool of people who do not claim to possess a personal relationship with Jesus Christ. Indeed, for several successive generations we have experienced great difficulty in retaining our own youth upon graduation from high school, and if the truth were known, we are having difficultly retaining adults who are on our church membership rolls. Somehow the great message and the God-given preferred lifestyle are not being communicated and lived out in a manner that is attractive to those on church rolls, never mind outside the church.

I do not desire to be an alarmist. God is still on His throne and He will be victorious. On the other hand, the long-established, non-missional church is in big trouble in the U.S. According to Bill Easum, 60 percent of the churches in America have a median age of sixty or higher.[7] This does not bode well for the future of the church. Someone needs to sound the alarm, ring the bell, shout from the mountaintops.

Like the *Titanic*, our ship has a huge hole beneath the surface, and we are taking on large amounts of boat-sinking water. Many things above the waterline may look as though all is well, yet much of the church in America is sinking. If we do not pay attention soon, we will not even notice it until it is too late.

We are in a battle, an actual spiritual war where the eternal destiny of generations is at stake. My fear is that in many respects we are acting as though we are in a time of peace. On other fronts we are fighting the wrong enemy. The challenge is to storm the gates of hell with the only message that can rescue people from the most horrific thought and reality—an eternal separation from God.

Several experts suggest that 95 to 97 percent of American Christians do not share their faith with others. If this tragedy continues, the words from the Book of Judges will repeat themselves, "After that whole generation had been gathered to their fathers, another generation grew up, who knew neither the LORD nor what he had done for Israel" (Judg. 2:10).

A spiritual formation professor at a leading seminary compiles the results from testing the spiritual development of first-year seminary master's level students. The new students rate themselves in several facets of the vertical relationship with God and their horizontal relationship and ministry with others. Consistently, entering students assess their development and experience in the area of personal evangelism as the lowest area of their spiritual formation.

From the personal evangelism courses I have taught, I find that seminary students consistently report that they themselves are inexperienced in personal evangelism. Few seminary students taking entry-level evangelism courses rate themselves as experienced, and even fewer indicate a preparation to help train others in personal evangelism.

This fact is disheartening. While teaching an undergraduate evangelism course, Jake Roudkovski, a Ph.D. student and local church pastor, had a student tell him, "I have been in the ministry for five years, and I have not led a single person to Christ."

My own personal evangelism courses are not without some disturbingly honest comments. There is little boring or routine about leading others to discover their role in the expansion of God's kingdom and glory. While discussing the strengths of "servant evangelism" and how this approach would help a novice in evangelism, a student raised her hand and asked, "What about students who did not come here to do evangelism?" It is possible to be a seminary student and miss the vital connection between evangelism and all forms of Christian ministry. However, it is a goal of the course to impact our students' attitudes, values, and actions in regards to sharing their faith. This is done through both classroom and field experiences.

If there is a significant need among seminary students, the need surely exists in the pews as well. Most of us have struggled at points in sharing our faith. The greatest need today in the Christian church just may be the need to equip people effectively and intentionally to share their faith in a way that makes sense to the witness and also makes sense to the person hearing the gospel.

Baptisms never tell the whole story about how well we are equipping people to share their faith and how well they are doing in sharing their faith. However, baptisms do give us some indications. Southern Baptists are known to be evangelistic. In 2000, out of more than forty-three thousand Southern Baptist churches, almost ten thousand churches did not report a single baptism. Recognizing that some churches simply did not complete their annual report, John Yarbrough, vice president of the North American Mission Board in charge of the evangelism team, noted that sixty-seven hundred reporting SBC churches did not baptize one person.

The difficulties are not limited to the SBC. Many estimate that 85 percent of the churches in America are either plateaued or declining. Denominations are struggling to reverse this trend. This trend cannot be turned around without personal evangelism. Eventually, some believer has to share his or her life and Christ's message with a lost person. It is even reported that Billy Graham said there is no such thing as mass evangelism. He was pointing out that for people to respond to Christ in a crusade, Christians have to invest in a relationship and invite someone to the crusade.

We live in a postmodern context where people are no longer looking to the institutional church for answers to their deep spiritual questions and needs as their grandparents and parents did. Therefore, of the three major categories of evangelism—attraction, projection, and media—projection strategies will have to play an increasing role.[8] Just as Jesus depended upon His disciples, the church will become increasingly dependent on members to communicate its message outside the walls of the church.

So then, exactly what is our objective, our marching orders? We will examine this objective to make sure that our efforts are pointed toward a clear target.

THE OBJECTIVE

Our objective is more than just to download or disseminate information to the lost. And our objective is more than just to have people make a statement of faith with only intellectual agreement with facts.

It is not enough to get decisions; we ultimately desire to develop disciples. Oscar Thompson in *Concentric Circles of Concerns* noted some key characteristics of disciples. He reminded us that:

1. A disciple has a personal relationship with the teacher.
2. A disciple is under the total authority of the teacher.
3. A disciple possesses and demonstrates the character of the teacher.
4. A disciple must be prepared to suffer for the teacher.[9]

The father of the modern church growth movement, Donald McGavran, defined church growth in terms of personal evangelism among all the tribes of the world such that they become congregationalized. And, with this target in mind, our approaches to evangelism need to be altered to reflect the target Jesus laid before us.

Many of our approaches to personal evangelism and training for personal evangelism have been *efficient* yet not *effective.* I can just hear Jesus talking with a time management consultant in the first century about His plan to take His message to the world through twelve men. By most human standards Jesus did not appear to be efficient in how He lived; however, history has proven that his approach was effective.

Efficiency need not be the enemy of effectiveness, but little about dealing with people in ways that please and honor God is efficient. People are complex and deserve more than a UPS delivery approach to hearing about Christ. Because of their great value to God, we should treat them with dignity. Based on a given culture, this will mean different things, but it will impact our approaches to sharing Christ and how we motivate and train others to do so.

Regeneration occurs at a moment in time, often a known moment to the believer. For other Christians it is a sure event in their lives without specific knowledge of the particular moment. However, evangelism is in some respects a process. Though there are exceptions, it is generally true that the farther away from God a person is in terms of knowledge of Him and receptivity to the Holy Spirit, the longer the evangelistic process.

Our incremental objective in personal evangelism will be different at various points in the evangelism/conversion process.[10] However, we do have an overall objective to provide the best possible systems, environments, approaches, communication tools, and training to help people become intimate followers of Christ. We are seeking not only to make more disciples but also to disciple a dedicated and missional people.

Usually our approaches and strategies in various facets of life are an overflow of our concept of success. We behave in such a way as to succeed, based on our perspective and values. Therefore it is always good to define success, even in personal evangelism. What is success? What is the target? We want people to come to the Forgiver and Leader of their lives.[11] We want people to seek to live in harmony with God's way of running the universe. This gives life meaning and purpose.

We are ultimately seeking to assist people in moving from being far from God to being close to God through a dynamic relationship with Jesus. This will involve such things as following scriptural commands under the leadership of the Holy Spirit. We are seeking to have people act like Jesus, think like Jesus, possess attitudes like Jesus, and share the financial, time, and prayer priorities of Jesus.

We desire for people's life skills, work habits, family structures, interpersonal relationships, and every other facet of life to be affected by Jesus. We want people to operate out of a Christian worldview with a deep sense of mission, meaning, and purpose. And ultimately the overarching task of evangelism gains impetus as the evangelized becomes the evangelizer. However, we do need to acknowledge that part of the process of evangelism will involve activities of planting seeds, watering, and weeding both before and after regeneration.

Success is often elusive in personal evangelism. It can be small or large. It is both now and in the future. It is eternal and temporal. It is emotional and physical. It is both what God does and what we do. It is natural and spiritual. It is incremental and monumental. It involves both receiving life and giving up one's life.

We are seeking to have people join us in the great journey of walking with Jesus for a lifetime while we rightly relate to those around us. We want people to live in loving obedience to God and thereby enjoy the benefits of following the Creator and Sustainer of the universe who designed how we are to live. We want people to live under the protection and care of God because it expands the glory of God and profits the people themselves.

Our objective is *not* to bag them and leave them. We are not seeking to tally decisions or to baptize a certain number or even make people into good church members but to help people become disciples, knowing that we cannot control the future of a person's life. We want people to operate out of spiritual, mental, emotional, relational, and physical wholeness, recognizing that God blesses and does whatever He pleases.

Our desire is to bring reconciliation between God and all the peoples of the world through Jesus Christ and Him alone. We want to see people restored much like the prodigal son in Luke 15. We want people to have abundant life (John 10:10) and bear much fruit (John 15:8) as they become increasingly pleasing to Jesus with their lives.

Our objective is to see people follow Jesus exclusively. He commands that we place no other gods before Him. According to research by George Barna, people do not see following Jesus as an exclusive matter. In a world of tolerance and pluralism, syncretism is bound to occur. People want to take a little bit of Jesus along with a little bit of whatever else comes along in their spiritual journey. As distinct from other religions of the world, Jesus is an inclusive God who demands exclusive allegiance.

In *Becoming a Contagious Christian,* Bill Hybels reminded us that we never look into the eyes of someone for whom Jesus did not give His life. And lost people really matter to God. Heaven rejoices when one lost sheep is found. Our objective begins to materialize as we start to see others as Jesus sees them and save us, as sheep without a shepherd.

May a desire to see the glory of God expanded into places of darkness drive our efforts to communicate the message of Christ.

THOUGHT PROVOKERS

An ancient philosopher said that the unexamined life is not worth living. It is wise to reflect on things in the past in order to make adjustments to improve the future. As we begin this journey of exploring the issues surrounding evangelism, consider the following observations made by a local pastor and what implications we can draw.

In my home church children were frequently baptized upon their profession of faith. For an adult to come to Christ was a rare event.

I went to an evangelism training weekend in 1971 to look over a major collegiate ministry's adaptation of their survey approach to sharing Christ door-to-door in the community. I took the plan back to our church, which was already doing relational evangelism. We tested the plan for six months. At the end of six months, fifty-four people had prayed to receive Christ through door-to-door witness. Though we tried follow-up in their homes and their neighbor's homes, only one came to church during the six-months period. During the same six months, forty-eight had prayed to receive Christ through relational evangelism, and forty-four became baptized church members.

A denominational person promoting youth work impressed on a gathering of pastors the importance of youth evangelism by saying that, statistically, if people are not saved by age seventeen, the chances of their ever accepting Christ are almost nil. I thought about the successful evangelism of adults in the New Testament. I wondered if the contemporary lack of response from adults was due to closed, unbelieving hearts or inappropriate evangelistic methods.

In a seminary class where we learned the methods of Evangelism Explosion, a fellow about age thirty reported a conversation with a schoolteacher who taught at the same school as his wife. "I asked her, 'If you were to die tonight and were to appear before God and he asked, "Why should I let you into my heaven?" What would you say?' She replied, 'You got the wrong person, baby. I don't believe in no God, and I don't believe in no heaven and no hell.' What do I say to her now, Dr. _____?"

I sat at a pastor's conference luncheon with a pastor of a church of fifteen hundred in attendance and one with three thousand in attendance. They were discussing their failure to incorporate new converts from their Evangelism Explosion programs. "We're only baptizing one or two out of a hundred decisions," complained the pastor of the larger church. "We're doing about the same," replied the other. After some discussion they concluded that they needed to lean harder on their evangelizers to get their converts "down the aisle and get 'em wet."

Studies of the Billy Graham crusade in the Northwest and the "I Found It" evangelistic campaign showed no significant increase in local church attendance.

Evangelism-In-Depth was a program in the 1960s for mobilizing all the church members in a nation to witness over a year's time. Starting from door-to-door witness and revival meetings in villages, the effort moved to towns, then to provincial capitals, and then to the national capital. After a decade, studies showed that in every country where EID had been done, church attendance declined the following year.[12]

The information above does not prove anything. However, it should cause us to pause in serious evaluation of the approaches we have been using to reach America for Christ.

BOOK OVERVIEW

No single book can address all the theology, issues, questions, and methods of evangelism. However, this book is designed to be a fairly comprehensive overview to both the student and the practitioner of personal evangelism. The material is divided into three major sections and an extensive appendix.

The first section addresses the foundational elements of personal evangelism: understanding God's involvement, understanding your role, and understanding content essentials in personal evangelism. It deals primarily with clarifying the gospel message by addressing essential content elements. In a world where people are bombarded with thousands of messages each day, it is vital that the Christian church understand its message. To borrow a phrase from politics, the church must have its message "on point." We cannot afford to send a distorted, confusing, and unfocused message.

The second section addresses the theory of communicating in personal evangelism. My intent is to enable you to help the gospel make sense for others. This section has two major strains of discussion: communicating inside your context and communicating outside your context.

The third section addresses practical aids in personal evangelism. It is designed to provide practical assistance as you seek to communicate the love of Christ. It is subdivided into conversation tips, removing/ addressing internal and external barriers, and the "best of the rest" of personal evangelism. This final chapter addresses gender issues, follow-up, and personal evangelism training in a postmodern context.

The book closes with several appendixes for further investigation into personal evangelism. Included are sections on gospel illustrations, constructing a testimony, personal growth assignments, review and evaluation of personal evangelism training materials, and a selected annotated bibliography for personal evangelism.

CHAPTER 1

Understanding God's Involvement

JUST HOW DO PEOPLE COME to know Christ? Some elements of conversion to Christ are a mystery, while other elements of the process have been revealed. Christians hold different beliefs on the roles that God and mankind play in the process of salvation and evangelism. There are two extreme positions on how people come to respond to Christ. One position is that everything depends on God. From this perspective Christians have no responsibility and play little role in leading others to Christ. The danger in this position is that it can lead to passivity in reaching out to the lost.

The second extreme position is that conversion depends entirely on the schemes and methods of the people who are sharing their faith. The dangers here are threefold.

First, it places too much pressure for conversion on the witness. This can lead to paralyzing fear, self-doubt, and insecurity.

Second, the witness may be tempted to manipulate the spiritually searching to get a verbal decision in order to feel good about themselves or to please God and others. Because God creates people, they should be honored and treated with the same respect that God has assigned to them. Therefore, manipulation is out-of-bounds in God-honoring personal evangelism.

This indicates the third danger, the temptation to use methods that are out-of-bounds. A method such as bait and switch would reflect negatively on Christ and his church, so this approach would be out-of-bounds. Christians are to conduct themselves in every area of their lives in such a way as to reveal the character of God. Additionally, Christians will want to use approaches that operate within the purposes and majesty of God, so that in all things God is glorified (1 Cor. 10:31).

In the next several chapters, we will explore biblical truths about how people come to know and follow Christ as the forgiver of sins and the leader of their lives. In this chapter we will examine God's desire, God's role/activity, and God's tools in the regeneration process. In chapter 2 we will explore the role of the witness and follow with a discussion of the essential elements of the Christian message in chapter 3.

GOD'S DESIRE

When so much of life revolves around our limited perspective, it is easy to forget that God was the designer of the universe and everything in it and thereby has all the rights and privileges to run the universe as He sees fit. This fact should give us great comfort, not fear.

So just what is God up to with His prized creations? From the beginning of humankind, God has been purposeful in His desire and His activities with people. The God who made us has positive desires toward mankind. And, unlike humankind, He also possesses unlimited power to act on His desires.

RELATIONSHIP, RESTORATION, RECONCILIATION WITH PEOPLE

Plants live, die, and exist no more. The same can be said of animals, but this is not true of people. God created people to live for an eternity. People are born to live forever. This demonstrates God's yearning to have an eternal relationship with His people. God could have made us temporal beings with lives like the plants and animals, but He did not. We are created to be blessings to Him and trophies to His grace, power, glory, and honor forevermore.

The Old Testament contains passages that clearly indicate God's plan to bless all people. Although it can be misunderstood and misapplied, God's desire to bless His people is without question. As examples, God blesses by making available to all peoples the opportunity for marriage, family, rain, and other natural resources.

God's desire centers on reconciliation. "Not only is this so, but we also rejoice in God through our Lord Jesus Christ, through whom we have now received reconciliation" (Rom. 5:11). He acted, and we are to act, to reconcile the world to God through Christ Jesus.

God desires to establish a redemptive relationship with all of humankind. The Bible refers to the people of God as family, friends, and a community of faith. People become part of God's family through reconciliation, through a restoration of the severed relationship.

The fact that not all people come to redemption through Christ begs at least two important questions. First, is God capricious by desiring what He refuses to allow? No, the Bible clearly communicates that God is good. "'Why do you call me good?' Jesus answered. 'No one is good—except God alone'" (Mark 10:18). "For it is God who works in you to will and to act according to his good purpose" (Phil. 2:13). Second, is God finite, ultimately unable to do what He says? No, biblical accounts indicate that God is infinite.[1] People fail to receive reconciliation with God because of their sin, their own rebellion.

Paul wrote, "For Christ's love compels us, because we are convinced that one died for all, and therefore all died. And he died for all, that those who live should no longer live for themselves but for him who died for them and was raised again" (2 Cor. 5:14–15). "We are therefore Christ's ambassadors, as though God were making his appeal through us. We implore you on Christ's behalf: Be reconciled to God" (2 Cor. 5:20). Serving as Christ's ambassadors provides us with a purpose, the ministry of reconciliation.

Not only does God desire an eternal relationship through reconciliation, but He also desires a communal relationship with Himself and others. God's call for restoration is not a call to live out the Christian faith in isolation. God desires to restore community and family among the redeemed. God created for Himself a people that would ultimately share His involvement with them to others through evangelism. Making a covenant with His people, He took actions to develop a family relationship, which would be expanded to include the Christian family of faith in the New Testament.

God's purpose for us involves our responding to His invitation to join His family. He extends this desire to all the people of the world. God's desire is open to all who would respond because He desires none to perish, regardless of race or heritage. Like the song "Jesus Loves Me" says, all are precious in His sight. Fisher Humphreys summarized: "God's purpose is to create a community of persons who freely choose to accept God as their God, who receive His love into their lives, and who respond by loving Him with all their hearts and by loving their neighbors as themselves."[2]

OLD TESTAMENT INDICATIONS OF GOD'S DESIRE

The ancient Hebrews readily saw the need to address God's role in the existing world (Gen. 1) as did the early church (John 1). Simply but profoundly, the ancient witnesses understood their existence as an act of God: "In the beginning God created" (Gen. 1:1). God was living in community with Himself as Trinity and created all things to enjoy the benefits of such community. Thus God exists in a communal relationship, although it is somewhat mysterious to man. In Genesis 1:26, God said, "Let us make man in our image, in our likeness."

God Himself was living a form of community, the Trinity, prior to forming mankind in His image. The very nature of God's existence involves community. The Trinity was a forerunning model for the human family, which must live in community. These foundational concepts found in the Old Testament pointed in the direction of the redeemed community God would be creating through Christ.

The act of creation was the first expression of the divine community. The community God created in the garden became a covenant relationship with His people in the exodus. God desired to lead His people, and if they would follow, they would experience His blessing and protection. Moses brought this idea into theological focus in Exodus 19:5–6: "'Now if you obey me fully and keep my covenant, then out of all nations you will be my treasured possession. Although the whole earth is mine, you will be for me a kingdom of priests and a holy nation.' These are the words you are to speak to the Israelites."

As God initially created humankind, He showed His desire to have a lasting relationship, a covenant, with them, and for them to have good relationships with one another. This relationship came with the gift of free will to people. Because of their own desires and the trickery of Satan, man and woman chose to disobey God and thereby severed the once-perfect relationship. Adam and Eve's decision to go their own way had enormous consequences for them and for all of mankind—separation from God.

When mankind's relationship with God was broken by the sinful, freewill choice of His creations, God expressed His desire to restore that relationship by providing them with a covering for their bodies so that they might not be embarrassed before Him. This was God's first act of mission: to seek, cover, and restore His creation; but it would not be His last. This expression of His desire continues to take shape through His intentional efforts to restore a right relationship with His creation that has been broken by sin.

We have lost our first blessing, but Isaiah reminds us that one of God's desires is to be gracious and compassionate toward us in our fallen state. "Yet the LORD longs to be gracious to you; he rises to show you compassion. For the LORD is a God of justice. Blessed are all who wait for him!" (Isa. 30:18).

God acts on His desires by sending messengers to His people. With the Ninevites we see God's desire to be gracious and merciful carried out through a reluctant prophet, Jonah. God is also receptive to granting mercy at the request of His servants. In response to God's plan to destroy Sodom and Gomorrah, Abraham pleaded with God for His mercy. God promised not to destroy the cities if Abraham could locate a few righteous men (Gen. 18–19).

God's intentional purpose is wonderfully implied by His offer of the sacrificial vehicle for reconciliation to Himself. God established the use of blood sacrifices to cover the sins of His people (Exod. 12). God also established worship and the ritual festival, which were fore-running aspects of community. God's desires seen in the Old Testament foreshadow His desires and acts as recorded in the New Testament.

New Testament Indications of God's Desire

The New Testament is filled with demonstrations of God's desire to bring real life to people. As an example, Jesus tells us, "The thief comes only to steal and kill and destroy; I have come that they may have life, and have it to the full. I am the good shepherd. The good shepherd lays down his life for the sheep" (John 10:10–11). Jesus came to bring meaning, purpose, and fulfillment in life based on God's desires and plans.

God's intention and plan was not to condemn the world but to save it. Jesus said, "For God did not send his Son into the world to condemn the world, but to save the world through him. Whoever believes in him is not condemned, but whoever does not believe stands condemned already because he has not believed in the name of God's one and only Son" (John 3:17–18).

The New Testament gives us further insight into the clear desire of God for His people. God's desire is that people come to a saving relationship with Him, the Creator and Sustainer of the universe. From Peter we learn that God is resolute to save all those who enter into a covenant relationship with Him. "The Lord is not slow in keeping his promise, as some understand slowness. He is patient with you, not wanting anyone to perish, but everyone to come to repentance" (2 Pet. 3:9).

Jesus wept over the lostness of the people of Jerusalem. "As he approached Jerusalem and saw the city, he wept over it" (Luke 19:41). His tears moved him to action, ultimately to the deepest sacrifice of death on the cross. Jesus said, "For the Son of Man came to seek and to save what was lost" (Luke 19:10). And once they were found, Jesus referred to some of His followers as "friends," not slaves. Jesus' death and resurrection provided mankind a way out of a desperate and helpless condition. His sacrifice gives hope for our hopeless state. Hope is a deep human need.

Another aspect of God's desire is to bring life, hope, meaning, purpose, justice, love, kindness, and all things which are good to His people.[3] Even the fruit of the Spirit, as revealed in the writings of Paul, demonstrates God's desire for His people. "But the fruit of the Spirit is love, joy, peace, patience, kindness, goodness, faithfulness, gentleness and self-control. Against such things there is no law" (Gal. 5:22–23).

Scripture teaches that evangelism did not and does not begin with the desires or schemes of man. Clearly, from the Old Testament through the New Testament, we see that God desires to have an intimate relationship with His creations, individually and corporately. From Genesis to Revelation we see God creating man for relationship with Him and with one another for His glory (Rev. 5:12–13).

GOD'S INITIATIVE

People have been and are now on the heart of God. However, God moved beyond desires; He acts on our behalf. He has taken and continues to take the initiative in all aspects of salvation, including evangelism.[4] Both the Old and New Testaments reveal the activity of God on our behalf.

OLD TESTAMENT

Many philosophers throughout history have missed an essential aspect of God's interplay with humankind. Although God is distinct from His creatures, He is not distant from them. God is obviously above all of His creation. Only God could create something from nothing. Everything else that has been created was created from something already in existence. Yet God alone was able to create everything from nothing. He did not just create us; He created us in His image and likeness.

We glean from Scripture and nature that God is intimately involved with His people and not just when we follow His commands. After the disobedience of Adam and Eve, we see God *walking with* them. "Then the man and his wife heard the sound of the LORD God as he was walking in the garden in the cool of the day, and they hid from the LORD God among the trees of the garden" (Gen. 3:8). From this point we begin to see God's active involvement with His people when He begins to extend His grace. We see God on mission with His people as He seeks them out in Genesis 3:21. He demonstrated concern about their shame by providing them a covering for their nakedness and the gift of His presence.[5]

God's redemptive character is especially highlighted in His handling of Cain's wrongdoing. Even when Cain persisted in the wrong kind of sacrifice, God confronted him and reminded him of the way. What mercy God showed to Cain! But this mercy was not limited to the Jews; it was also extended to the Gentiles. In Acts 15:15–19, a quotation of Amos 9:11–12, James related how from the beginning God intended to include the Gentiles in His redemption plan. The exodus account testifies to such inclusive mercy: everyone who came out of Egypt became part of God's covenant community (Exod. 19–23).

The two great redemption stories from the Old Testament likewise foreshadow the work of Christ on the cross with the shedding of blood for the remission of sin—the Egyptian sojourn and the Babylonian exile. Events surrounding the return from both Egypt and

Babylon set the stage for the later work of Christ. From the Egyptian exile (sojourn/bondage, not exile or captivity) emerges the Passover lamb. Jesus Christ was the ultimate and final Passover lamb.

After a half century of exile, Daniel recognized the redemptive purpose of God. Daniel realized that it had been God's intention to restore prodigal Israel through the punishment of exile (Dan. 9:1–20). The use of seventy sevens is found in Daniel 9:24–25. In the New Testament Jesus told Peter that he must forgive seventy-seven times, the complete number for forgiveness (Matt. 18:21–22).[6]

In several spots in the Old Testament we see God's desire for all peoples of the world. His plan was rooted in His unique relationship with the people of Israel. In Jonah we see God's heart toward the Ninevites. The people of Nineveh were living wickedly, and that greatly displeased God. However, God had compassion on the city and gave orders for Jonah to preach against the wickedness and warn the people of Nineveh (Jon. 1:2; 3:2). After the side trip that included time in the belly of a great fish, Jonah went to Nineveh and preached the coming destruction. The people repented and worshiped God, so God had compassion and relented in sending calamity to the people of Nineveh.

By the time of Jonah, God not only *goes* on mission; He *sends* others on mission. He sends us on mission. In this sense Isaiah, along with Micah, can be understood as proclaiming a universal appeal "and acceptance" among the nations (Isa. 11:10; 60:1–2; 2:1–5; Mic. 4–5). Amos 9:7 likewise emphasizes God's providential handling of the nations. Not only did He bring Arameans out of Kir; He also brought the Philistines out of Caphtor. God's love could not be confined to the chosen people of Israel.

From the beginning of time, God had a plan to get His message to all peoples. He created the Jewish people to be a channel of God's blessing, not simply a recipient of God's blessing. Jonah clearly understood this merciful aspect of God, and that is why he initially refused to do the will of God. He knew God was more than capable of forgiveness, He was also willing to forgive the evil Assyrians whom Jonah hated.

NEW TESTAMENT

Throughout the Old Testament we see God interacting with His people in various forms and in various ways. Yet the people needed Him to come into the world Himself so that they might better understand Him and choose to follow him.

God provided the ultimate demonstration of His passionate desire for His people to be reconciled to Him by leaving the throne of heaven to be born into a manger in Bethlehem to live as a flesh-and-blood man. God chose to move from unlimited power and glory to live in a state of humble status, few possessions, pervasive misunderstandings, continuous rejection, physical abuse, and then, finally, the ultimate societal shame—death on the cross. He bore the spiritual burden of the sin of the world on His shoulders.

Sometimes people have difficulty understanding why God chose to break into history in the form of flesh and blood. Sometimes stories best address such perplexing questions. The Christmas story escapes some of us, mostly because we seek complete answers to our questions, and this one is so utterly simple. For the cynics, the skeptics, and the unconvinced, I submit a modern parable. I am unaware of the origin of the story below, but it continues to touch my heart and speak truth.

This is about a modern man, one of us. He was not a Scrooge. He was a kind, decent, mostly good man. He was generous to his family, upright in his dealings with other men, but he did not believe in all that incarnation stuff which the churches proclaim at Christmas time. It just didn't make sense, and he was too honest to pretend otherwise. He just could not swallow the Jesus story and God's coming to earth as a man. "I am truly sorry to distress you," he told his wife, "but I am not going with you to church this Christmas Eve." He said he'd feel like a hypo-crite, so he would much rather stay home. He stayed. They went.

Shortly after the family drove away, snow began to fall. He went to the window to watch the flurries getting heavier and heavier and then went back to his fireside chair to read his newspaper. Minutes later he was startled by a thudding sound, then another, then another. At first he thought someone must be throwing snowballs against his living room window. When he went to the front door to investi-gate, he found a flock of birds huddled miserably in the snow. They had been caught in the storm and in a desper-ate search for shelter had tried to fly though his large land-scape window. He had compassion for them and wanted to help them. He couldn't let the poor creatures lie there and freeze.

He remembered the barn where his children stabled their pony that would provide a warm shelter if he could direct the birds into it. He quickly put on his coat and galoshes and tramped though the deepening snow to the barn. He opened the doors wide and turned on a light. But the birds did not come in. He figured food would entice them in. He hurried back to the house to fetch bread crumbs to sprinkle on the snow, in order to make a trail to the yellow-lighted wide-open doorway of the stable.

But to his dismay the birds ignored the bread crumbs and continued to flop around helplessly in the snow. He tried catching them. He tried shooing them into the barn by walking around them waving his arms. Instead they scattered in every direction—except into the warm, lighted barn. Then he realized they were afraid of him. "To them," he reasoned, "I am a strange and terrifying creature. If only

I could think of some way to let them know they can trust me, that I'm not trying to hurt them, but to help them." How? Any move he made tended to frighten them, confuse them. They just would not follow. They would not be led or shooed because they feared him.

He thought, *If I could mingle with them and speak their language and tell them not to be afraid and show them the way to the safe, warm barn. But I'd have to be one of them so they could see and hear and understand. If only I could be a bird myself.*

At that moment, the church bells began to ring. The sound reached his ears above the sounds of the wind. He stood there listening to the bells playing "Adeste Fidelis," pealing the glad tidings of Christmas. And he sank to his knees in the snow. At last, he understood God's heart towards mankind, and he fell on his knees in the snow. He had come to know the One who became one of us just to save us.[7]

Because of our need, God took action. Jesus entered into our sinful world in a physical body so that we would have the opportunity to join Him in His perfect world in an eternal body. While He was here on earth, Scripture tells us that Jesus interacted with many people in such a way as to express concern for them by providing them physical, emotional, social, and spiritual healing. He brought hope to the hopeless. He brought a means to deal with that which has plagued people from the beginning, their sin. He lived in obedience to the Father with the world on His mind and sacrificed His sinless life as payment for our debt of sin.

Jesus' coming was to be the ultimate inclusion. Even His birth line demonstrated God's love for all the peoples of the world. Jesus was born into a family line that included non-Jews: Ruth, a Moabite, and Boaz, a half-breed. From the beginning God had all the peoples of the world on His mind and in His plan (Acts 15:13–15).

Summary of God's Initiative

From the beginning of creation, God desired to have a relationship with mankind for His pleasure and for the benefit of His people. God stepped into the tabernacle to meet with His people. God stepped into the temple to meet with His people. God stepped into human history in the person of Jesus Christ to meet with His people. God steps into the hearts of individuals in the person of the Holy Spirit. We now are the temples of the Holy Spirit, God Himself. This demonstrates God's desire to interact with His people not out of obligation but out of His initiative and for His pleasure. The story does not end with God's desire; God took and continues to take action toward His creations.

Sacrifice on the Cross Provides the Way

The cross and the resurrection were and are the most important events in the history of mankind. Jesus' sacrifice provided a path to an eternal relationship with the Creator of the universe. Yet the work of Christ did not start with the cross. His interactions with people throughout His life demonstrated His love and compassion. From Genesis to Revelation we see God's desire to relate to His creations. God has been intimately involved with people. He created us and provided for our physical and relational needs, and then we blew it and broke the relationship with Him. He extended grace to us through Jesus Christ, and the ultimate sacrifice for the sins of the world was paid on the cross.

Jesus came to provide life. Jesus is able to give life because of His unique, once-and-for-all-time, substitutional death on the cross as payment for our sins. We have been "bought back" through the death and resurrection of Christ. The work Christ did on the cross is for all and payment for all who would receive Him.

Christ's work on the cross provides the way to salvation. There is no other name by which man must or can be saved. God's open invitation is to come to Him, the life giver, the purpose giver, the only one who can forgive sins and restore a broken spirit. John wrote, "The Spirit and the bride say, 'Come!' And let him who hears say, 'Come!' Whoever is thirsty, let him come; and whoever wishes, let him take the free gift of the water of life" (Rev. 22:17).

SALVATION IN THREE TENSES

Salvation is often described in three aspects or tenses: past, present, and future. These are often referred to as justification (past), sanctification (present), and glorification (future). We have been saved, are being saved, and will be saved from eternal separation from God. All three are essential yet distinct. Justification and glorification involve a single event. This is different from sanctification, which involves an ongoing process or series of events throughout one earthly lifetime. God is involved in the entire process of salvation, the saving conversion/regeneration event, and the sanctification process, and will be the Creator of the coming glorification moment.

God took the initiative in the salvation of man. We can see this clearly through the life and ministry of Christ. However, God's involvement in the salvation of mankind did not end there. The Holy Spirit is at work in the conversion of sinners into saints.

HOLY SPIRIT IN EVANGELISM

We are not alone in evangelism. Salvation began as a desire in the heart of God and resulted in God's taking the initiative on that desire. He acted on behalf of His people in the Old Testament, through the life of Christ as seen in the New Testament, and through the Holy Spirit when Christ left the earth.

Person of the Holy Spirit

The Holy Spirit is both divine and personal. The Holy Spirit is fully God and fully engaged in the works of God. He is not an abstraction or a thing. We should refer to the *person* of the Holy Spirit.

Humphries noted that "the most fundamental work of the Spirit is to testify to Jesus."[8] With regard to evangelism, the Holy Spirit is at work in the life of the witness, in the life of the lost person, at the point of regeneration, and after conversion.

Holy Spirit in Witness[9]

Precedes the Witness. We can mistakenly think that evangelism starts and stops with the words of the witness. As a witness you never share the gospel when the Holy Spirit has not preceded you. This should comfort you. The Lord opens the heart of the listener.

Lydia was a woman the Holy Spirit was drawing to Himself. "One of those listening was a woman named Lydia, a dealer in purple cloth from the city of Thyatira, who was a worshiper of God. *The Lord opened her heart to respond to Paul's message.* When she and the members of her household were baptized, she invited us to her home" (Acts 16:14–15a).

Leads and Enables the Witness. Have you ever found yourself with the right words to say and surprised yourself as you tried to communicate the gospel. You were not alone. In the Gospel of Luke, we find Jesus instructing the disciples: "When you are brought before synagogues, rulers and authorities, do not worry about how you will defend yourselves or what you will say, for the Holy Spirit will teach you at that time what you should say" (Luke 12:11–12). Our part is to be willing to speak.

A quote hangs in my mother-in-law's house. It reads, "A coincidence is when God performs a miracle and chooses to remain anonymous." We may assign Philip too much credit. Philip had a role to play in seeing the Ethiopian eunuch come to Christ, but the Holy Spirit led Philip to the eunuch (Acts 8:27–38). He was in the right place at the right time.

The Holy Spirit can lead a witness in where to go and what to say. We certainly have the option of not listening to the Holy Spirit, but God desires to lead us.

Empowers the Witness. The Holy Spirit empowers the witness with authority and wisdom as the gospel is shared. As the witness follows the direction of the Holy Spirit, the witness is guided and led by the Holy Spirit. This guidance brings assurance to the witness.

Anytime we respond in obedience to the leadership of the Holy Spirit, we can go and speak with authority and wisdom. If we respond in the flesh, disconnected from God, we will lack authority and the wisdom that comes from God alone.

Power. Personal evangelism is spiritual warfare and must be engaged on a spiritual level. The witness is to go in the power of the Holy Spirit. We have no ability to win souls on our own. Part of the power is unexplainable except the Lord moves as He sees fit. However, we can present ourselves as a clean vessel to be used by the Lord. It is important for us continually to submit to Jesus as Lord of our lives and to confess our sins for their forgiveness so that we do not quench the power of the Holy Spirit who is at work in the lost person and in us.

"But you will receive power when the Holy Spirit comes on you; and you will be my witnesses in Jerusalem, and in all Judea and Samaria, and to the ends of the earth" (Acts 1:8).

"Because our gospel came to you not simply with words, but also with power, with the Holy Spirit and with deep conviction" (1 Thess. 1:5).

Christians have power when they are following Christ's command to communicate the good news. Jesus gave the apostles the power to drive out demons. "He appointed twelve—designating them apostles—that they might be with him and that he might send them out to preach and to have authority to drive out demons" (Mark 3:14–15).[10]

Boldness. As a witness you need not muster up boldness on your own. As you connect with God through prayer, the Holy Spirit will empower you to speak the gospel with boldness. "After they prayed, the place where they were meeting was shaken. And they were all filled with the Holy Spirit and spoke the word of God boldly" (Acts 4:31).

When we are not filled with the Holy Spirit, we are less likely to speak with boldness.

To the yielded witness, the Holy Spirit precedes, leads, enables, and empowers the witness. It is our responsibility continually to be yielded to the Holy Spirit.

In Lost Persons

God is at work in us as we share the gospel with others (John 16:8–11), but that is not all God is doing. At the same time the Holy Spirit is also at work in the life of lost persons to draw them to Himself, reveal truth, and convict the world regarding the message.

Holy Spirit Draws. In the opening of chapter 3 in *Personal Disciple-Making,* Christopher Adsit provides an interesting story on his experience in personal evangelism while he was in college. He explains how he felt it was his responsibility to convert as many people as possible, yet he was ignorant about the role of the Holy Spirit. He was so zealous that he would even invent Scripture passages just to win an argument. Not until much later did he understand God's role and work in personal evangelism.[11]

We do well to remember that God alone saves people from eternal separation. Jesus said, "No one can come to me unless the Father who sent me draws him, and I will raise him up at the last day" (John 6:44). Without the drawing of the Holy Spirit, a broken relationship with God cannot be restored.

One implication of this truth is that people cannot just decide one day to surrender their life to Christ. You probably know someone who has experienced the drawing of the Holy Spirit and yet rejected that drawing, falsely believing that one day they would get around to making that decision. They may or may not get another day to live.[12] Additionally, they are unknowingly presuming upon the Holy Spirit that they will again be drawn to God, when in fact they may not.

Holy Spirit Reveals Truth. Christians do not introduce God to people for the first time. The Holy Spirit has been at work to reveal

God's divine existence and eternal power within them before we ever arrive on the scene to share our faith. God is at work in the lost person to create an awareness, or, as some have described it, a God consciousness. As witnesses we bring clarity to our lost friends about Christ and His redemptive work, but it is the Holy Spirit that reveals truth.

"The wrath of God is being revealed from heaven against all the godlessness and wickedness of men who suppress the truth by their wickedness, since what may be known about God is plain to them, because God has made it plain to them. For since the creation of the world God's invisible qualities—his eternal power and divine nature—have been clearly seen, being understood from what has been made, so that men are without excuse" (Rom. 1:18–20).

Holy Spirit Convinces/Convicts of Truth. It is easy for Christ followers to attempt to take on some of God's roles. One of those roles lies in the areas of conviction and convincing. The Holy Spirit is the one who convicts individuals of their guilt in the areas of sin, righteousness, and judgment. Therefore, we need not attempt to pressure people into a passive submission to parts of the gospel message. The Holy Spirit is the one who convicts in regard to sin in order to help them believe God, in light of His righteousness and the coming judgment. Without the Holy Spirit working, a person would remain spiritually blind to his spiritually depraved condition and the work of Christ.[13]

"When he comes, he will convict the world of guilt in regard to sin and righteousness and judgment: in regard to sin, because men do not believe in me; in regard to righteousness, because I am going to the Father, where you can see me no longer; and in regard to judgment, because the prince of this world now stands condemned" (John 16:8–11).

Holy Spirit in Conversion

The Holy Spirit is not only at work in our lives as we witness and at work in the lives of lost persons as they hear, but the Holy Spirit is also intimately involved at the point of saving conversion and the years following in the life of the new believer.

I mentioned earlier that evangelism involves a spiritual battle. This spiritual battle can manifest itself in physical ways. While teaching a personal evangelism practicum at my seminary, we sent out teams of three to share their faith in various parts of New Orleans and the surrounding cities. One particular team was out conducting evangelistic surveys in an apartment complex in Slidell, Louisiana, where one of our bilingual students, Steven, was serving as the pastor of a Spanish-speaking mission church.

The team came upon a Spanish-speaking person, so the bilingual student took the lead in talking with and sharing the gospel. Along with the other students in the class, I was enthralled to hear as one of the team members who did not understand a word of Spanish told the class of their experience. She said that as Steven began to share the gospel and as she began to pray silently, she could see the spiritual struggle taking place on the face of the lost person. She continued to notice the various forms of strain framing the person's face. And then she noticed a complete change. At this point she discovered from Steven that the person was accepting Christ. To the amazement of the student who could not listen with her ears, she saw the gospel's power through her eyes as she watched the physical transformation take place on the face on the new believer.

This happened because evangelism is a spiritual battle and because of the work of the Holy Spirit in conversion. When our lost friends trust Christ, the Holy Spirit brings about the conversion. Lost people cannot save themselves; it is a work of God (John 1:12–13; 1 John 2:29; Titus 3:3–7).

Brings from Death to Life. The Holy Spirit brings the spiritually dead person to life. From John's writings we read, "Flesh gives birth to flesh, but the Spirit gives birth to spirit. You should not be surprised at my saying, 'You must be born again'" (John 3:6–7). Paul also noted the role of the Holy Spirit in giving life to the new believer. "He saved us, not because of righteous things we had done, but because of his mercy. He saved us through the washing of rebirth and renewal by the Holy Spirit" (Titus 3:5).

Seals the Believer. Not only does the Holy Spirit give life; He also seals the believer at the point of conversion until the day of redemption. "And do not grieve the Holy Spirit of God, with whom you were sealed for the day of redemption" (Eph. 4:30). We are not sealed by the efforts or methods of evangelism or follow-up. Our salvation is protected and preserved until Christ's return solely by the work of the Holy Spirit.

Gifts the Believer. God is active in providing us as believers with what we need to live out our faith relationship with Him and those around us. The Holy Spirit not only gives life to that which was dead and seals the believer until Christ's return; He also imparts gifts to the believer to use in service to the Lord for the expansion and development of the church. In several parts of the New Testament, Paul wrote about the gifting of believers, but most specifically 1 Corinthians 12–14.

"Now to each one the manifestation of the Spirit is given for the common good" (1 Cor. 12:7). "All these are the work of one and the same Spirit, and he gives them to each one, just as he determines. The body is a unit, though it is made up of many parts; and though all its parts are many, they form one body. So it is with Christ" (1 Cor. 12:11–12).

Holy Spirit After Conversion

Confirms We Are Children of God. In America many people say they are Christians, but they have little idea what that means, much less actually acknowledge Christ as the forgiver and leader of their lives. I once had a baseball teammate tell me that he was a Christian. When I asked him to tell me about his relationship with Christ, I got an interesting answer. He said that when he was younger he went to his grandmother's funeral, cried, and then had peace about it.

Often people struggle after conversion with knowing whether they are actually saved. The temptation for believers is to offer reassurance. While some Scripture passages are helpful in terms of assurance, only the Holy Spirit can confirm that a person is a child of God. "The Spirit himself testifies with our spirit that we are God's children" (Rom. 8:16).

We would be wise not to try to convince persons that they are saved, especially if their lifestyle does not bear the fruit of walking with Christ. Paul exhorts the individual to test to see if he is in the faith. Paul said, "Examine yourselves to see whether you are in the faith; test yourselves. Do you not realize that Christ Jesus is in you—unless, of course, you fail the test?" (2 Cor. 13:5). If in doubt, you can also ask them to read Psalm 51 and 1 John, which specifically address this issue.

Lives in Children of God. The Holy Spirit is not only living and active in every phase of evangelism; He actually lives and works within the believer. "Do you not know that your body is a temple of the Holy Spirit, who is in you, whom you have received from God?" (1 Cor. 6:19).

It is not the purpose of this section to expound on all the ways the Holy Spirit impacts our lives, but professor Tom Steffen provided a quick summary list that I found helpful. He summarized various passages of the Bible when he wrote that the Holy Spirit "initiates, creates, enlightens, judges, persuades, enlivens, redeems, indwells, seals, energizes, empowers, disturbs, directs, comforts, teaches, transforms, informs, guides, preserves, leads and reveals."[14]

SUMMARY OF GOD'S INITIATIVE

Knowing that God is alive and active in the entire process of evangelism and solely is responsible for conversion, we should feel empowered to be active in sharing our faith. Many of the barriers we have constructed that prevent us from sharing our faith should begin to come down when we remember the faithfulness of God over time to reveal Himself, empower His witnesses, and draw lost people to Himself.

God is involved in evangelism at every point and level. Regeneration/conversion is 100 percent God. However, He chooses to use various instruments to draw people to Himself.

GOD'S TOOLS: NATURE, CIRCUMSTANCES, PEOPLE, AND TIME

God has and is revealing Himself and drawing people to Himself. In addition to the Holy Spirit's activities, God uses nature, people, circumstances, and time to draw people to Himself.

People respond to the call of God and efforts of people and circumstances in different ways. Some respond with receptive spirits, while others shut down their hearts and become closed to the gospel. People are wired differently and are at different distances from God. We will discuss this in detail in a later chapter. Here we will examine the various tools God uses to draw people to Himself.

NATURE

One of the ways God has chosen to reveal Himself is through nature. Nature declares and reflects something of the majesty, creativity, and glory of God. "The heavens declare the glory of God; the skies proclaim the work of his hands" (Ps. 19:1). "For since the creation of the world God's invisible qualities—his eternal power and divine nature—have been clearly seen, being understood from what has been made, so that men are without excuse" (Rom. 1:20).

The natural argument is that for every creation there must be a creator. There is now a small but swelling opinion that the physics around the creation of the universe with all of its intricacies points to divine intelligence. Whether skeptics want to accept the details of the creation account in Genesis, they are hard-pressed to deny divine intelligence and a creator.

Dreams are a natural part of sleeping. Some of us dream more than others. Researchers tell us that most dreams are actually forgotten before we awake. However, God throughout history has and still does use dreams to reveal His presence and His will.[15] It is imperative here that we not take as credible any dream that contains information that is divergent from the written Word of God. The Scriptures are the final court of appeal on all revelation and conduct.

One of the most quoted passages on this topic is Acts 2:17: "'In the last days, God says, I will pour out my Spirit on all people. Your sons and daughters will prophesy, your young men will see visions, your old men will dream dreams.'" People in the U.S., both Christians and non-Christians, are more open today to supernatural and spiritual things than they have been in recent decades. With the massive influence of Eastern religions and with the rejection of many parts of Christian church life in the West, people are more open.

This is not without danger because anything God has given has also been distorted, misused, and counterfeited by Satan. I believe that it will become increasingly important for mature followers of Christ to exercise discernment and good judgment as they learn to test the spirits. First John 4:1–4 is helpful in this area.

In addition to nature, God uses supernatural events to reveal His desires and will. We recognize that nothing God does is supernatural to Him. He speaks, and His desires happen. Every natural law and force in the universe is under His natural command. Although God does not ordinarily choose to use supernatural events as the norm, He did use them to speak to and reveal truth through Jesus, the disciples, Paul (Acts 9:1–19), Peter/Tabitha (Acts 9:36–42), and Cornelius/Peter (Acts 10:1–38) among many others in the New Testament.

God uses nature to help facilitate an awareness of His existence and something of His character and might. This can be a powerful aid in communicating the gospel message, especially to those who have lived with little influence from the Judeo-Christian parts of society. As Americans become more influenced by postmodern culture and less by the modern culture of the sciences and logic, we may just rediscover that God really does not have limits to how He can reveal Himself. God can choose to reveal Himself through natural and supernatural occurrences. God also chooses to use circumstances to draw people to Himself.

CIRCUMSTANCES

Recently a cut-through was built between a major road and my subdivision. We are excited to have this quicker way to get to and from our house. A new stop sign was placed on the cut-through by a local hospital. Traveling home with my wife from a trip to Wal-Mart one day, which happens not to be one of my favorite activities, my wife ran right through the stop sign. She hesitated just as she realized that she was blowing through it, but it was too late to stop. I wonder how many people are blowing through the stop signs God has given them through the circumstances of life. Often God desires to use various stop signs along the way to reveal himself.

Observation reveals that there are times when people are more receptive to the gospel than others. Receptive events are unique for different cultures, but in America people are more receptive during times of intense stress or change. However, as a reminder, God is not limited in any manner by our patterns of receptivity. Studies have been conducted to rate the level of certain stresses in one's life. One particular study, The Holmes & Rahe Social Readjustment Rating Scale, is probably the most popular life events stress test being used today.[16]

Critical Inflection Points

One of my mentors, Harold Bullock, talks about critical inflection points in the lives of people that indicate when they are most receptive to hearing and responding to the gospel. He refers to them as DDDIS: Divorce, Death, Divine Encounters, Illness, and Status Change. These seasons of life serve as critical inflection points in one's spiritual journey and receptivity.

These circumstances can lead to an open door for the gospel, and God often uses them to draw people into a relationship with Him. Divorce is traumatic for all involved, regardless of the circumstances surrounding the divorce. Having lost loved ones myself and having been a part of performing numerous funeral services, I know that the death of a loved one creates an openness to all kinds of things, including making some poor decisions during the grieving process. However, death does cause us to reflect upon the afterlife and the things that matter most in this life. Often at this point God uses a willing Christian to communicate the love of Christ to survivors.

God also uses illness to get our attention. Often during an illness we slow down long enough to think. During these times of reflection we can reevaluate what is important. Many people chose to follow Christ after a significant illness in their lives.

A status change is another critical inflection point that God often uses. A status change can relate to job, financial status, educational accomplishment, or any other significant change in status. These changes in status can be positive or negative, but either way receptivity to the gospel usually is heightened.

A Christian NFL head coach is reported to have discussed the most receptive periods for NFL football players. He said that there are two best junctures to reach out to lost players: (1) when the players are first coming into the league and trying to make the team or find their particular role on the team and (2) when the players are close to ending their football careers.

Divine Encounters

God is not limited to working within the circumstances such as critical inflection points or stresses in our lives. God also uses divine encounters with either Himself or with us, His people. For divine encounters we must be willing vessels of God's message and be in tune with the leading of the Holy Spirit.

Sometimes God just places us at the right spot at the right time with a person who needs Christ. Not typically easily moved toward strangers myself, I have found myself doing things to approach people that are much outside my comfort zone. I am amazed that each time I do so, God is faithful either to draw a person closer to Him or to teach me some important lesson for my life.

The student mission team I was leading had a long day conducting surveys in Waterville, Maine, before we drove to the northernmost part of the state late into the night. I was pleased to have arrived safely, and the students were settled in for a few hours of sleep. When checking into the hotel, I felt an unusual spiritual drawing to the hotel clerk. After making sure everyone was secure, I walked back downstairs to the lobby with a renewed sense of energy from a state of extreme fatigue as I followed the Spirit's leading. I listened to the clerk talk about her spiritual journey and her disillusionment with Christian churches. I was able to share the message of Christ, answer some of her questions, and pray for her. Not every divine encounter has a climactic ending. That night she did not trust Christ, but she did open her heart to hearing the gospel.

We must be obedient for divine encounters to work. When the Holy Spirit moves, we must continue to say yes. I heard a denominational executive communicate a story about a hotel encounter that was a little out of the ordinary. He had gone through the registration process and was eager to get to his hotel room. On his way through the lobby, he noticed a man sitting off to the side of the room. He walked on by the man in anticipation of going immediately to his room, when the Holy Spirit told him to go share the gospel with the man on the bench. He tried to argue with God, telling Him several reasons he should not.

However, after a quick debate with God, he submitted himself to God's leading and approached the man on the bench. He introduced himself and simply told the man that he felt compelled to come over to him. He engaged the man in a spiritual conversation centered on

Jesus and the gospel message. The man on the bench told the executive, "I prayed to God today out of desperation because I knew there must be more to life than what I had been experiencing. I told God that if He really did exist, He had twenty-four hours to reveal Himself or I would commit suicide." The man on the bench gave his life to Christ that night because God is faithful to reveal Himself to those who seek Him and because God was able to use a tired, reluctant, but obedient person to carry His love to a desperate man.

PEOPLE

The foundation and expansion of God's kingdom is centered in the Holy Spirit: "Played out through human agents (co-laborers)."[17] In spite of our weaknesses and imperfections, God still chooses to use people to communicate His message. In fact, Jesus took a most unlikely group of people to entrust the only message of hope to a desperate people through the history of time, all the time knowing that one of the Twelve would commit betrayal of the highest order.

God has no hands, feet, or mouthpieces except for ours. We are His agents to carry His message. Lee Roy Eims reminds us that regeneration is 100 percent God, and He chooses to use people—individuals and groups of people.

Individuals

God uses individuals to share His message. Ordinary people and extraordinary people alike are used in the hands of God. God uses the righteous and even the unrighteous to bring about His will and to deliver His message. When God uses individuals (coworkers, neighbors, hobby buddies, and strangers), he often uses several individuals working independently of one another to carry His message. This provides the credibility and power of accumulation of experiences.

His Body the Church

The testimony of one radically changed life is powerful. However, the testimony of a group of people who embody Christ and live out the message is even more powerful. The body of Christ can and should be the most powerful evidence of the truthfulness of our message. Jesus said, "A new command I give you: Love one another. As I have loved you, so you must love one another. By this all men will know that you are my disciples, if you love one another" (John 13:34–35).

As a person who is wired for math and science, I am drawn to the logic and sensibility of the message of God through Christ. However, the truthfulness and the reality of the message of Christ are not limited to appealing to the logic of people. Jesus clearly communicated that the reality of Christ rested to a large degree in how the disciples and other believers related to one another. It is hard to argue with a changed life. It is even harder to argue against a group of people who live differently as they follow the person and wisdom of God.

TIME WITH WEBS OF CIRCUMSTANCES AND PEOPLE

God uses time as a tool as well to draw people to Himself. Time allows for an accumulation of evidence from nature, circumstances, and people. Many times no to Christ will become a yes over time. Some people process the gospel message quickly, while others take months or even years.

Often God will use a web of influences to bring a person to Himself. It usually takes more than one tool and more than one exposure before a person surrenders his life to Christ.

With the Philippian jailer we see God using a combination of nature, circumstances, people, and time. God allowed Paul and Silas to be placed in a jail within earshot of the Philippian jailer. The seemingly negative circumstance of the imprisonment of Christians brought exactly what the jailer needed. God used the changed lives of the prisoners to create openness to the gospel. The Christians prayed, sang, and lived above their unjust imprisonment. This certainly must have caused the jailer to wonder how this could possibly occur. Then God caused a violent earthquake to shake the prison foundation, open the prison doors, and release the chains of the prisoners. When the prisoners did not leave under the cover of night, this must have been a shock to the jailer, who was about to take his own life.

God was not through. Paul and Silas certainly had already communicated the message to the jailer while they were imprisoned. God added to the mix the tool of time. Yet after viewing false imprisonment, a supernatural act of nature, and the living testimony and verbal witness of the Christians, the jailer was ready to surrender his life to Christ. And then, God used the jailer to influence his family. That night the jailer and his family were baptized (Acts 16:22–36).

Summary

God initiates conversion but uses humans. People have been and continue to be on the mind, heart, and agenda of God. Evangelism and conversion truly are spiritual activities. It is our privilege to be an active part of the process of evangelism leading toward conversion. In the next chapter we will examine our role in personal evangelism, knowing that apart from Christ we can do nothing (John 15:5).

CHAPTER 2

Understanding Your Role

W E HAVE SAID THAT THE SEED OF REDEMPTION of people began in the heart, mind, and actions of Christ. And there is no salvation apart from Christ and the drawing of the Holy Spirit. Yet God chooses to use flawed people like us to carry and share His message. This, then, begs the question, What is our role in evangelism? In this chapter we will examine various facts about our role and actions that are not our role.

UNDERSTANDING PERSONAL EVANGELISM

Personal evangelism has been defined in many ways. Perhaps the narrowest definition is reciting a few gospel facts in the presence of a nonbeliever. Others may give a broad definition that includes almost everything a Christian does. Neither of these definitions is adequate. The first approach allows us the excuse, "I told them." And the second allows the "I lived it in front of them" excuse. I am not suggesting that a positive response from the listeners determines whether we have been successful. However, I do believe that we should assume 100 percent responsibility for effective communication.

Many outstanding definitions exist, such as the simple one by Rebecca Pippert: "Evangelism in its simplest form is introducing our friends to Jesus."[1] J. I. Packer said that evangelism "is an act of communication with a view to conversion."[2] As you read through these pages, personal evangelism involves the effective communication of the essential gospel message with the view toward seeing people supernaturally become followers and imitators of Christ.

WHO IS EVANGELISM FOR?

In many ways the body of Christ is like an army. We have a purpose, a mission, a commander, soldiers, and an enemy to defeat. The soldiers are volunteers who have committed themselves to the battle at the direction of their leaders. The army of God functions best when each member carries out his or her unique role, contributing to the accomplishment of the given mission.

With America conducting a war against terrorism, we have been reminded of the unique and important role the special forces play in conducting the war. Yet an armed force only has a limited number of special force members such as the Green Berets. Green Berets play an important role in our military, but the entire army is needed to execute larger successful missions. The vast majority of the U.S. armed services are rank-and-file members, people who have volunteered for service.

Likewise, in the Christian life, when people yield their lives to Christ, they have volunteered for service. Often in the Christian life we separate salvation from lordship, decision from disciple. This separation is not taught in the New Testament. When we trust Christ, we become servants and ambassadors of the King, which implies that all of us are to share His message. He is Lord; we are followers.

Sharing the gospel is the privilege of every single believer. The norm should be that every Christian is actively sharing his faith.[3] Everything that has lived has reproduced, so too it should be with Christians. We are all to be the salt of the earth and the light of the world (Matt. 5:13–16). Evangelism is a command, not just a gift for a select few. Biblically the evangelist was given to the church as a position, role, office, or function, but evangelism is not just for a select few (Eph. 4:11–13).

Many of the evangelism programs have been geared for and attract the evangelistic Green Berets. However, personal evangelism is not just for the special forces in the Christian army. If the world is to be led to Christ, rank-and-file soldiers must show up for duty, become equipped, and take up their role in the army of God.

The nonnegotiable element is sharing our faith. Almost everything else about evangelism is related to form, and I am not sure that God has a preferred style. Choice of methods becomes a matter of effectiveness, assuming that we seek to honor and glorify God. We must learn to avoid methods that seem to distract or take away from the glory of God in preference to other types of methods.

HISTORICAL PERSPECTIVE

During most of the twentieth century, we left evangelism to the experts, primarily our church and parachurch staff members and those who displayed strength in the practice of evangelism. Experts were often relied upon, especially in carrying out evangelism with people who grew up under a modern philosophy steeped in logic, science, and arguments. Rick Richardson said, "In the past, being an expert and having the answers were what built credibility and a hearing. Today, having the same questions, struggles and hurts is what builds credibility and gains a hearing."[4]

Prior to the last two or three decades, most lost people fell into one of two major categories. First, there were those who had positive feelings and had some understanding about the church and about Christ yet had not personally yielded their lives to Christ. Our primary method for reaching these people was either to invite them to attend a special event at the church building or to share a few passages out of John or Romans in an effort to lead them to Jesus.

Second, there were those who were hard to reach. We often described them as cold or hard-hearted toward God. Many Christians were fearful of dealing with highly resistant people. We depended on the evangelism specialists to reach these people. Either we invited them to a revival or asked the pastor or the guest evangelist to visit them.

45

These categories have some limits, but hopefully they help you process approaches. Unlike the past, today people throughout the U.S. are much more diverse in their spiritual backgrounds and much more complex in how they process life. We will see that this impacts many facets of personal evangelism.

AGRICULTURAL UNDERSTANDING OF OUR ROLE

In the New Testament Paul indicated that God gives the increase in the harvest. He also said that we are to plant, to water, and to harvest. Paul is instructing us on the laws of the harvest. If we do not plant, then there will be no harvest. If we do not care for what we have planted, there will be no harvest.

Many times in witnessing encounters, our role is to plant seeds of the gospel. We cannot share the entire gospel message and expect a response every time we encounter a lost person. And we cannot harvest where no seeds have been planted. We plant seeds by loving people toward Jesus with small acts of kindness in the name of Jesus. We serve them, laugh with them, and cry with them in their times of grief. We speak positively about Christ and His church. These are some of the ways we plants seeds of the gospel.

My wife does most of our yard work because she likes to work with her hands and be outside for the exercise and fresh air. This past week she greeted me in the driveway through my car window with dirty hands and a sweet but sweaty kiss. This is not her favorite way to greet me, but it is the price she pays to keep a lovely yard.

Dealing with lost people will cause us to get our hands dirty and sweaty just like tending to yard work. Part of evangelism is to clear up misconceptions and misperceptions people have about the gospel. Dealing with people and evangelism is often messy.

There is no effective approach to personal evangelism that does not involve planting, watering, weeding, and then waiting for the harvest. Our role in working toward the harvest involves all these facets.

DEFINING SUCCESS

A worthy goal in preparation for most any task is to define success. Success sets forth the target, the mark, the goal. A clear understanding of success will affect how you approach a task. I have been coaching a developmental club volleyball team of fourteen-year-old girls. For most of these girls, this has been their first experience at competitive volleyball, while many of the teams we play have multiple years' experience at the club level. This means we will struggle at various points throughout our season, and winning regularly is not a realistic goal.

We have sought with the team to reach several different goals but not just in terms of winning matches. We try to play an entire match with a positive attitude and good effort and enjoy ourselves. We also try to improve various components and skills of volleyball, which will lead to more points and wins. Improving percentage of serves hit inbounds, making more accurate passes to the setter, and being in the proper position on the court will eventually help us win.

A clear understanding of success in personal evangelism will aid us as we carry out the Great Commission. What then is success in personal evangelism? To be honest, I do not exactly know. It will include both faithfulness and fruitfulness. Any definition of success will have to take into account God's role and our role. We have explored God's role but have yet to develop our role. However, I think we can move toward an understanding, starting with one often used by Campus Crusade for Christ founder Bill Bright: "Simply sharing Christ in the power of the Holy Spirit and leaving the results to God."

I am comfortable with this as a *starting* point. Often I tell my students Bright's definition. I then communicate that it is not enough for a seminary student or maturing Christian to stop there. My preference is to say that success involves simply sharing Christ *increasingly prepared* in the power of the Holy Spirit and leaving the results up to God.

What then is the role of the evangelist in relating to lost people? If we believe that evangelism will take place with or without us, our tendency is to be too passive. We are assuming little responsibility. In contrast, if we overemphasize the role of the evangelist, we put unwarranted pressure on the evangelist. The evangelist's primary responsibility is to be obedient to the leading of the Holy Spirit in preparing and sharing his faith. The activity of the witness will change according to his perception of the needs of the lost person.

Some believe and teach that Christians should just pray and leave everything else up to God. Reading Romans, we see Paul's answer to that question for the early Christians: "How, then, can they call on the one they have not believed in? And how can they believe in the one of whom they have not heard? And how can they hear without someone preaching to them? And how can they preach unless they are sent? As it is written, 'How beautiful are the feet of those who bring good news!'" (Rom. 10:14–15).

Skills are also needed for success. Although God can work around our lack of skills, it is much wiser to develop skills. Ecclesiastes 10:10 says, "If the ax is dull and its edge unsharpened, more strength is needed but skill will bring success." Success is not simply a matter of praying and leaving the results to God.

Going prepared is not going with all the answers to all the possible questions. However, we are to be prepared to share the hope that is within us (1 Pet. 3:15). We should do all things as unto the Lord (1 Cor. 10:31).

Just like coaching my girls' volleyball team, success depends on many factors, some of which I cannot control. People we meet have values, beliefs, experiences, and perceptions about religious matters. We cannot control these; we have to deal with them as we find them. Success will look different for each encounter. The church would benefit from focusing on the matters within its power to influence and giving less attention to matters outside the reach of our influence.

We would do well to reflect on the foundational principles for evangelism as given by D. Martyn Lloyd-Jones:

1. The supreme object of the work of evangelism is to glorify God, not to save souls.
2. The only power that can do this work is the Holy Spirit, not our own strength.
3. The one and only medium through which the Spirit works is the Scriptures; therefore, we "reason out of the Scriptures" as Paul did.
4. These preceding principles give us the true motivation for evangelism—a zeal for God and a love for others.
5. There is a constant danger of heresy through a false zeal and employment of unscriptural methods.[5]

Engel's Scale

James Engel's training is in the area of communication. He has written several books on the relationship between communication and evangelism. He developed the following scale that depicts the conversion process. His scale, The Complete Spiritual Decision Process, has been helpful in understanding that not all lost people are at the same point or have the same needs or are the same distance from God. It also reveals that as witnesses we have different roles at different points along the conversion process. Not all evangelistic encounters should be the same because people are at different points in their understanding and responsiveness to God.

Let me be clear. Regardless of how people live or how far they are from God, they are still lost until they have experienced regeneration. But this does not mean we should approach each lost person in the same manner.

DECISION-MAKING MODEL

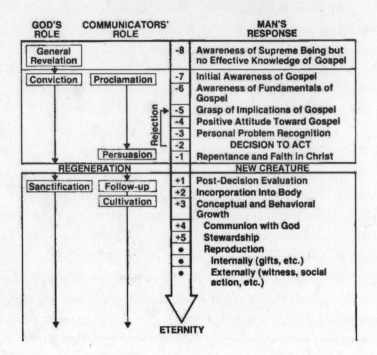

GOD'S ROLE	COMMUNICATORS' ROLE		MAN'S RESPONSE
General Revelation		-8	Awareness of Supreme Being but no Effective Knowledge of Gospel
Conviction	Proclamation	-7	Initial Awareness of Gospel
		-6	Awareness of Fundamentals of Gospel
		-5	Grasp of Implications of Gospel
		-4	Positive Attitude Toward Gospel
		-3	Personal Problem Recognition
	Persuasion	-2	DECISION TO ACT
		-1	Repentance and Faith in Christ
REGENERATION			NEW CREATURE
Sanctification	Follow-up	+1	Post-Decision Evaluation
	Cultivation	+2	Incorporation into Body
		+3	Conceptual and Behavioral Growth
		+4	Communion with God
		+5	Stewardship
		•	Reproduction
		•	Internally (gifts, etc.)
		•	Externally (witness, social action, etc.)

ETERNITY

Not all lost people are the same. Some are far from God, while others are closer to receiving Christ. Some people are receptive, while others are antagonistic. Some are fully informed about the claims of Christ, while others are ignorant of Christ.[6] Naturally, different people need different things from us.

Success in evangelism can involve seeing a person cross the line of faith. However, with people who are far from a monotheistic view of God, who possess little understanding of Christ, or who hold negative perceptions of the church, assistance in moving people a step closer to Christ could be seen as success in a single witnessing encounter. The Holy Spirit can help a person move from far from God to a complete surrender of life to Christ in one divine encounter. Our ultimate objective is larger than helping people take one small step forward, recognizing that people do not typically come to Christ in a linear fashion as reflected in Engel's graph.

Two Types of Evangelistic Encounters

Two basic types of evangelistic encounters exist. Both are legitimate and were used in the biblical accounts of the first century. Biblically, some evangelistic encounters involved ongoing contact with the lost person, while others were one-contact encounters. Our role will depend on the type of encounter we are having, whether it is a single encounter or a multiple-contact encounter.

Single Encounters

One type of evangelism involves single-time encounters with people. These encounters take place in a variety of settings such as a place of business, a recreational event, a retail store, or a variety of other situations where we come into contact with people just one time. W. Oscar Thompson Jr. referred to these as "People X" in his book *Concentric Circles of Concern*. These are the strangers we meet.

The New Testament contains multiple examples of single-encounter evangelism. We can have effective evangelism with strangers under the leadership of the Holy Spirit: the woman at the well (John 4:1–30), Ananias and Paul (Acts 9), Paul and Agrippa (Acts 25:22–26:29), Philip and the Ethiopian eunuch (Acts 8.26–39).

In dealing with single-encounter situations, we should seek to establish rapport with the person. A long-term relationship is not essential to share our faith, but we need to establish a positive point of contact.

As we share our faith in one-time encounters, success often will involve having an interaction with the person in a way that enhances his openness to receiving the gospel. This is not always easy, and even if we do interact in a wise manner, the spiritual battle within the person may lead to a negative reaction. However, this is not an excuse to offend people by cramming the gospel down their throats so that we can claim that we shared the gospel and feel better about ourselves. It is possible in our zeal to influence a person away from Christ with inappropriate methods.

In preparing for one-time encounters, we need to remember that while God can send someone to the lost person after us and may have sent several people before us, He is not limited to norms. We should remember that people typically do not go from being far from God to making an informed commitment to Christ in one sitting. We may in fact be the seventh or eighth encounter, so we need to anticipate seeing the person give his life to Christ.

It is possible for us to have an overly aggressive approach and leave a negative impression of Christians and even Christ. I recognize that we cannot get it right each time. Some people don't get it until we are direct, while others would be totally turned off by the same approach. For the postmodern person, we must demonstrate a concern for the person and not come across as just trying to get her to join our club or buy our version of the product.

Some people are gifted at single-encounter evangelism. They do this tactfully yet directly. However, the Christian has not completed his role if he just does a hit-and-run. Skilled single-encounter evangelists will want to make efforts to connect the new convert to a local church.

Single-encounter evangelism has a few advantages but significant disadvantages as well. An advantage of talking with a stranger about Christ is that our personal life before the encounter usually does not come into play. The gospel is not clouded with our past moral successes or failures. The person has no idea whether our life would validate or invalidate the message. Another advantage is that we meet people throughout our lives whom God loves and wants to touch, maybe even through us in a single encounter.

A disadvantage in single encounters is that we do not have credibility. We live in a society that places a high value on individual beliefs and is so skeptical of anything that people have not seen. "Agrippa said to Paul, 'Do you think that in such a short time you can persuade me to be a Christian?'" (Acts 26:28). Often it takes time to carry out our roles in the evangelistic process. We carry a message of great value and one that is highly personal and communal. If we are not careful in our approaches, we will present a God, who is personal and communal, in impersonal ways.

Regarding the goal of developing disciples, single-contact encounters present a challenge to follow-up and assimilation into a local church. People need friends to stick. The fewer relationships a new convert has in a particular church, the more difficult the task of seeing the person develop spiritually. Many precious saints today were led to Christ in one-time encounters, but the challenges are even greater today due to the decreasing influence of the church on the culture and mind-set of the people together with the many views of God that are presented in various media today.

Our role in the single encounter may involve leading the person to Christ; however, it may be in helping him or her become more receptive to the gospel by removing a barrier, building a bridge, or pointing the way. With each encounter we have, we do leave an impression. May God give us the wisdom to leave a genuine reflection of Christ in our single encounters.

MULTIPLE-CONTACT ENCOUNTERS

Most evangelism opportunities involve sharing the gospel through a series of encounters with people we know. These opportunities are all around us. These include interacting with relatives, friends, neighbors, work associates, and recreation buddies. We can also share Christ in places where we have repeated encounters with the same people as we develop patterns in shopping, conducting business, interacting with a sports team, or in other places. It is possible to fill up your car with gas with an eternal purpose!

There are numerous advantages in sharing Christ through our existing relationships. A new convert has a credible model lived out before him. The new believer has a potential network into the life of the local church, which greatly enhances the probability for assimilation and growth as she moves into unfamiliar territory, the church. The new Christian also has someone to go to with spiritual questions and difficulties. The thought of connecting with a local church can be scary for a person if church has not been a part of his or her life.

A danger lies in waiting to develop a relationship with someone until we are open to the Holy Spirit's leadership to share Christ. We cannot develop an ongoing relationship with everyone we have the opportunity to touch with the message of Christ.

The role the witness plays is influenced by the situation and the response of the listener. The issue becomes our faithfulness and being intentional with the opportunities God presents us to share our faith, whether in single- or multiple-contact encounters.

BIBLICAL EXAMPLES OF STYLES

Bill Hybels and Mark Mittelberg made a significant contribution to the field of evangelism by describing six different styles of evangelism in *Becoming a Contagious Christian*. These six styles are based on different evangelistic encounters in the Bible. A biblical example, a list of characteristics of people who have this style, and a caution for each style are summarized for your quick review.

Testimonial

Biblical Example: Blind man in John 9

Characteristics: Clear communicator, storyteller, good listener

Caution: Beware of talking about yourself but not relating your experience to the other person's life. You first need to listen to him to be able to connect your story to his situation.

Intellectual

Biblical Example: Paul in Acts 17

Characteristics: inquisitive, analytical, logical

Caution: Do not substitute giving answers for giving the gospel message, and be careful of becoming argumentative.

Confrontational

Biblical Example: Peter in Acts 2

Characteristics: Confident, assertive, direct

Caution: Be sure to use tact when confronting people with truth to keep them from becoming unnecessarily offended.

Interpersonal

Biblical Example: Matthew in Luke 5:29

Characteristics: Warm personality, conversational, friendship oriented

Caution: Avoid valuing friendship over truth-telling. Presenting the gospel often means challenging a person's whole direction in life, and that can mean causing friction in your relationship.

Invitation

Biblical Example: Woman at the well in John 4

Characteristics: Hospitable, relational, persuasive

Caution: Be careful not always to let others do your talking for you. You, too, need to "always be prepared to give an answer to everyone who asks you to give the reason for the hope that you have" (1 Pet. 3:15).

Service

Biblical Example: Dorcas in Acts 9

Characteristics: Others-centered, humble, patient

Caution: Just as words are no substitute for actions, actions are no substitute for words. Romans 10:14 makes clear that we must tell people about Christ.

All six of these styles are useful, and we have biblical examples to support the use of these different styles. As evangelists, we should play to our individual strengths. However, these authors rightly note the cautions that accompany each style if it is taken to extremes. I would suggest that evangelists, while playing to their strength in terms of style, must choose the evangelistic style that best fits the person they are trying to lead to Christ.

Having taken the test to determine style preference from their book, I confirmed that my preferred style of personal evangelism is the intellectual approach. However, situations arise that call for an approach that is outside my preferred style. In my first pastorate I had opportunity to share the gospel with the husband of one of my members. This man had a hard exterior and could only begin to process what I was saying when I spoke in a direct and confrontational manner. When I thought I was yelling (figuratively), he was just beginning to hear me. As a pratice, I have to choose the style that best communicates the message and fits the situation, not the style or method I am most comfortable with.

METHODS

In many ways our approach is a part of our message. It would be nice if we could remove the method from the message, but that is not possible. Regardless of the method—which includes tone, timing, inflections, and word choice—what the listener hears is indeed tied to the components of our methods. Too much of communication is non-verbal for this not to be true.

Jesus came to give us a message and a mandate, but I am not so sure He came to give us a method. He did give us guidelines for how we should relate to others and guard things that would damage His glory, but as for *the* biblical approach to evangelism, I just do not see it in the Scriptures.

It is easy to get caught up in trying to determine what is and is not biblical. Too often Christians tend to take a position and then to find a passage in the Bible to support it. Regarding biblical methods of evange-lism, Scriptures give guidance into which approaches are wise and right. Every Scripture that gives directives or insights into relationships can be applied when seeking to share our faith. Teachings such as gentleness, honesty, and respect toward those in authority provide us with insights.

Paul exhorted the early church to be flexible and adaptable in mat-ters of approach. "Though I am free and belong to no man, I make myself a slave to everyone, to win as many as possible. . . . I have become all things to all men so that by all possible means I might save some. I do all this for the sake of the gospel, that I may share in its blessings" (1 Cor. 9:19, 22–23).

Some will be open in their approaches, while others will be more guarded. I was taught a valuable lesson in my first pastorate by J. D. Lundy, a man who was in his early seventies and a member of my church. Brother Lundy was a former pastor and former director of missions. He was a godly man, a man who supported me as his pastor, and one to whom I could go to for advice. Several times during my years there, he and I knocked on doors together to share our faith and extend Christian love to the people who lived in the neighborhoods surrounding the church building.

He and his wife, Cara Lee, had several children. One of their teenage boys grew his hair long during a time when that was fashionable. He said it really irritated Mrs. Lundy, even though the son was a great kid and showed no signs of rebellion. After several discussions with Mrs. Lundy, he stumbled on a truth—not a biblical truth—but a truth of human nature. He said, "You know, some people are 'no' people until they know a lot of reasons for yes, while other people are 'yes' people unless they know a good reason for 'no.' I have found this to be true in many areas of life."

Regarding methods of personal evangelism, I fall into the "yes" category because I am open to using most approaches. I do recognize that some approaches reflect wisdom, while others are either out-of-bounds in God's sight or demonstrate poor or shortsighted judgment.

YOUR ROLE DOES NOT INCLUDE . . .

In seeking to determine what our evangelistic role includes, we might do well to discuss what our role does not include. The following section includes some reflection on matters that are inconsistent with our objective of communicating a God-centered message in a God-honoring way.

JUDGING

Our role is not to judge the world, a spiritually blind world that does not know Christ. That responsibility is left to the only One who is worthy and blameless to serve as judge. God knows and can rightly judge. Humans are too limited and without Christ stand guilty before God as well. We should extend the grace of God found in His message to the world. The message of Christ convicts an individual; we need not add our judgment.

I am not advocating that no one should judge anything as right or wrong. Where did common sense and good judgment go as a value? Christians are to develop sound judgment but not a judgmental spirit. The tendency of the Christian community is to invert the biblical pattern regarding judging. According to the Bible we are to judge other Christians out of love and for restoration, not judging those who are without Christ. Instead, we tend to judge non-Christians while turning a deaf ear to the harmful sins of fellow believers, maybe in hopes that our sins will be ignored as well. The result is that Christians are allowed to damage their relationship with God and others, while discrediting themselves as witnesses of the love of Christ.

SHAMING

Shame abounds in many circles today where people have been devalued and humiliated. Our role does not include shaming others. Sin is painful to God and in consequences to the sinner. When lost people adequately understand their broken relationship with God, they often feel a natural shame. But through Christ that shame can be lifted as people begin to understand their right standing before God through Christ's sacrifice on the cross. The Holy Spirit draws people to Himself; we need not shame people to Jesus.

Guilt is a lower level and potentially destructive form of motivation and a low level and nonsustaining method of motivating Christians to share their faith. G. William Schweer in *Personal Evangelism for Today*[7] has an excellent discussion on the potential danger of heaping guilt on people. Guilt often does bring temporary compliance, but the side effects can lead a person away from God and away from the witness. The Bible teaches us that Jesus did not come into the world to condemn the world but to save the world.

MANIPULATING

Our role is not to pressure someone into submitting to God. The Holy Spirit convinces people of the truth of Jesus Christ and their need for repentance, faith, and surrender. If we can talk someone into it, someone else (or a circumstance) can talk them out of it. In other words, it is not our responsibility or right to twist arms to get decisions to meet a personal agenda.

It is impossible to do God's will in evangelism in opposition to God's way. When we trick people or seek to bait and switch, we do not honor God. Manipulating will eventually hinder, not help, evangelism. A report from one of my students displayed an indictment against the Christians who seek to witness.

One young lady questioned me after the survey was completed. I thanked her for helping me and was about to leave her doorstep. In amazement she asked, "Is that all?" When I indicated that the survey was completed, she said, "Oh, I thought I was going to get a sermon or fussed at or something."

I responded that God doesn't ask any of us to "fuss" or "condemn" one another but instead to share good news and truth. I asked her if she wanted to talk further. She indicated that she had to pick up her children, but she would welcome such a time in the future. I gave her my card and informed her of my willingness to talk with her in the future and asked for permission to return and talk about spiritual things. She took my card and responded that she would look forward to such a visit.

My surprise was that she was surprised at the simplicity of the interview. She seemed amazed that what I introduced was exactly what happened. I believe this young lady was expecting some crafty plot to judge her. Through this experience, especially her response, I learned that my earlier hesitations about not presenting the gospel before the interviews might have been misplaced. The opportunity with this young lady may have actually opened the door in the future.[8]

We need to present the whole gospel, which includes a balance of the benefits and sacrifices necessary to follow Christ. Like Will Metzger covered in his book, *Tell the Truth: The Whole Gospel to the Whole Person by Whole People*, we need to use God-centered methods, not man-centered methods. Manipulation devalues people. It treats them as less than God created them.[9]

SAVING

We should communicate as effectively as possible, but the witness does not have the responsibility to save anyone. We do need to become emotionally engaged with the person with whom we are sharing, but we do not need to carry the burden to see people saved. We mistakenly think that we save people. God alone does this. Additionally, the Scriptures teach us that when people do not respond, they are rejecting the Holy Spirit, not us (1 Thess. 4:8).

GIVING SLICK PRESENTATIONS

In the past, flowing evangelistic presentations were written for witnesses to make. However, today, making a presentation to another person in a situation other than for business or educational purposes usually violates cultural norms. We have dialogues with people on an individual basis; we don't deliver slick presentations to individuals.

Some judge the quality of an evangelistic encounter by the quality of the presentation. People today are more media savvy and skeptical of slick presentations. The effective witness in America today is a person who can engage in Christ-centered dialogue rather than give a great speech.

Memorized presentations can be helpful to the witness but not because he will ever make a complete presentation. Learning a presentation or gospel outline will provide those who witness with additional confidence as they enter and provide direction to the evangelistic dialogue.

WINNING ARGUMENTS

Our role does not include winning arguments. We are to testify to what we have seen and heard. We can and should grow in our preparation to defend the faith, but that is not our primary role.

For a person whose primary evangelistic style is intellectual, there is room to help people answer some of the deep questions of their spirit and clarify their understanding of Christ. This will involve some level of apologetics. Classical apologetics still has a place in a postmodern context, but in most relationships we are not trying to win a debate.[10] The new apologetics will initially involve asking good questions, not winning arguments.

SELLING

If you struggle to sell, you are in good company with many effective evangelists around the world. I am intrigued and have a deep respect for people who can do things I cannot do or have not done. I would struggle financially if I had to work in direct sales, in spite of completing a college personal selling course with an A. We can improve our interpersonal skills and learn various communication skills from good salespersons. However, I am glad that personal evangelism is a matter of sharing, not a matter of selling.

We fall into a trap if we believe that witnessing is about selling a product to make people's lives better. When people surrender their lives to Christ, there are many benefits as a by-product. We are better served by inviting others into a vital relationship with the Creator of the universe, not by offering another self-help program.

BEING AN EXPERT ON THE WORLD'S RELIGIONS

The United States is highly pluralistic. Almost all the religions of the world are found here, as well as every possible mixture of religions. It is difficult to fathom the number of possible religious combinations. We can grow in our preparation to interact with people by becoming familiar with some facts about other religions, realizing that most Christians will never be experts on other religions.

As you find yourself facing similar sets of questions or religions, I encourage you to do some background study on the religion or life philosophy so that you will be more prepared to share your faith in that given context. Postmodernism is rapidly growing. Because we are and will continue to face this, I encourage you to explore it so that you might more effectively communicate the gospel in our modern world.

YOUR ROLE INCLUDES . . .

BIBLICALLY SPEAKING

We play various roles in personal evangelism. Biblically we are called to *testify* (John 1:7–8, 33; 3:11, 28; 15:27; 18:37; Acts 4:33; 10:42–43; 2 Tim. 1:8; 1 John 1:2; 4:14), to *witness* (Acts 22:15; 26:16), to be *ambassadors* (2 Cor. 5:20), to *proclaim* (Matt. 10:27; Luke 4:18; Acts 17:23; 20:27; 1 Cor. 11:26; Col. 1:28; 4:3–4; 1 John 1:2–3; Rev. 14:6), and to *persuade* (Acts 18:4; 26:28; 2 Cor. 5:11).

Multiple other passages have a bearing on how we testify, witness, and serve as ambassadors. We will examine them in light of several phases of our role.

PREPARATION PHASE FOR EVANGELISM

Before we ever engage a lost person, we can take actions to become prepared to share our lives and faith.

An Obedient and Tender Heart

It all begins with a willing spirit. God created us, and God can use us. Some people have been entrusted with five talents and others with one. Regardless of the number of talents we possess, we can sharpen the ones we have been given and present ourselves ready for service. Part of being ready involves making space in our hearts for lost people. Growing relationships with people is not easy, especially if we view them as burdens to our crowded schedules. However, if we are ready and show up for duty, God will use us to find people for Himself. As we show up for duty, we will want to reflect on what God has done in our own lives. This testimony is something God can use to share with others.

Filled with the Holy Spirit

The early church sought to carry out the Great Commission not out of obligation but as an overflow from following the Holy Spirit. In order to follow the Holy Spirit, we need to be continually filled (directed, controlled) by the Holy Spirit.[11] As we are directed by the Holy Spirit, we are in the only position where we are able to follow God's leadership. Believers need continually to demonstrate submission to God's leading.

Praying for the Lost and for Clear Communication

Evangelism at its core is a spiritual battle. This battle requires that we enter into it with spiritual weapons. Knowing and using the Word in an appropriate manner is a strong weapon in the spiritual battle. Prayer is another way to become involved in the spiritual battle. I have not actually seen an empirical study, but friends have indicated to me that in the areas where prayer walking has preceded door-to-door spiritual surveys, the number of decisions for Christ has been higher than those efforts where prayer walking did not precede the evangelistic effort.

Evangelism is a matter of spiritual conflict (Eph. 4:12). It is Satan and wicked spiritual beings that are seeking to deceive, to blind, and to confuse those who are struggling over the drawing of the Holy Spirit in their lives. The Christian can stand in the gap through intercession with the Father.

Part of seeking God's leadership involves asking God to open doors and to make the message clear. We can prepare for witnessing opportunities and for the gospel to be presented clearly. Paul wrote, "And pray for us, too, that God may open a door for our message, so that we may proclaim the mystery of Christ, for which I am in chains. Pray that I may proclaim it clearly, as I should" (Col. 4:3–4). Personal evangelism begins with making ourselves available, being filled with the Holy Spirit, and praying for the spreading of the gospel.

Several publications will assist you in praying for lost people. "Lighthouses of Prayer" and *Praying Your Friends to Christ* could be helpful to you.

Grasp the Gospel Essentials

Before we can share a witness, we need to understand the message and person of Christ. Without a clear understanding of the message, it will be almost impossible for us to encode a message that the lost person can receive. I am not suggesting that we all need to take a twenty-six-week personal evangelism training course. We can share what we know, but we need to grow in our understanding of the essentials of the message we are seeking to communicate. We can take a cue from several New Testament converts who upon receiving Christ went and invited others to meet Jesus.[12]

Becoming increasingly prepared with the essentials, we will be more prepared to answer about the hope that is within us and defend the faith when people ask questions and challenge the message. I am reminded, "That which is a mist in the pulpit, is a fog in the pew." The message that is a mist in the mind of the evangelist is a fog in the mind of the lost person. Spiritual and practical preparation will help to diminish this problem.

PREEVANGELISM PHASE FOR EVANGELISM: DEALING WITH PEOPLE

Some of what we do is preliminary to giving a verbal witness about Christ. There are several key facets of this important phase.

Build Credible Relationships

A significant part of evangelism in a postmodern context is building credible relationships with those to whom you are attempting to communicate the message of Christ. This involves building bridges, befriending lost people, and living a credible life.

Build Bridges. Our natural desires are to pursue selfish ambitions and personal comforts. We do not live in a society that places a high value on community concerns. We have elevated individualism to our own detriment. We no longer live in an environment where people walk many of the places they travel. People are on the move most all the time. Trying to connect with people is not an easy thing to do. Maintaining connections is even harder.

Donald McGavran, the father of the modern church growth movement, said that the gospel travels along networks of relationships.[13] Christians will intentionally have to engage those who are presently outside the family of God. We have to go to them, not wait for them to come to us. The Christian message has the church going into the world of lost people from which we also came.

Most of the people my students interview about spiritual matters see absolutely no reason to pursue a relationship with the church. Upon reflecting on his interviews, student Stephen DuVall reported, "Perhaps the lesson learned from this exercise is that the church needs somehow to break down the walls and go outside itself to reach the neighbor next door. None of those selected for this assignment seemed actively opposed to the church, but they did seem bewildered at the message the church is preaching. Perhaps one reason falls on the respondents because they are rarely inside the church proactively listening to the message, and as a result the message is either blurred or simply unheard. However, the more probable reason is the failure of the church to look beyond itself, and into the world, where Christ commanded it to go."[14]

If you are not presently engaged with lost people, you will want to find ways to intertwine your life with people for whom Jesus died. One way is to participate in your recreational activities in a way to engage lost people.

I have tried to capitalize on several of my interests—my girls, sports, and staying involved in the lives of lost people. I developed an affinity for competition through sports as I grew up in the home of a coach, which led to my playing two varsity sports at Mississippi State University. I have three girls, ages seven, ten, and thirteen, which has led to my coaching multiple seasons of their softball and volleyball. Teaching a full load at the seminary and leading a consulting ministry, I do not have time to coach teams, but I can ill afford not to be engaged with my girls and not to be engaged with lost people. If I am going to be faithful to expand the glory of God and teach evangelism to others, I have no choice but to maintain regular contact with people whose lives are often messy and in need of Jesus.

Be a Safe Person with a Dangerous Message. Jesus was a friend of sinners. "The Son of Man came eating and drinking, and they say, 'Here is a glutton and a drunkard, a friend of tax collectors and "sinners."' But wisdom is proved right by her actions" (Matt. 11:19). Andy Stanley of North Point Community Church in Alpharetta, Georgia, has said that "where there is no relationship, there is no influence."[15] Most highly active church members, including pastors, have few meaningful relationships with lost people.

It is easy to say we love the world; loving an individual is more difficult. For us to be effective in evangelism, we must learn to love people who do things that might offend us. For the sake of the gospel, find an unlovely person and love him anyway.

Part of our role as a witness is to be a safe person, in spite of the fact that our message has dangerous consequences. The consequence of salvation is that people must change loyalties. They must move from loyalty to themselves to loyalty to Christ. We model that by investing in others.

Jesus was clear that to love the lovely and love your friends is not enough. He exhorted His followers to love their enemies and even those who despised them (Matt. 5:43–47).

We have to invest in the lives of the lost. Evangelism does not happen without cost. Richardson reminds us, "As many of us have discovered, it takes a disproportionate commitment for evangelism to reach the level of intensity of other values and priorities."[16] "Evangelism is not the only thing or even necessarily the most important thing. But it takes a disproportionate investment of time, resources and energy to bring the value of evangelism to equal footing with other values."[17]

Being a friend of sinners will involve bearing some of the consequences that come from their baggage of failures. This is what friends do. It is what Jesus, Paul, and others modeled.

"We who are strong ought to bear with the failings of the weak and not to please ourselves. Each of us should please his neighbor for his good, to build him up. For even Christ did not please himself but, as it is written: 'The insults of those who insult you have fallen on me.' For everything that was written in the past was written to teach us, so that through endurance and the encouragement of the Scriptures we might have hope" (Rom. 15:1–4).

The movie *Pay It Forward* demonstrated an interesting twist to expressing gratitude for a kind deed received, which was to be thankful enough to pay it forward, not to pay back the giver. Instead of doing a good deed for the person who helped you, you were to help someone else. Typically we are taught to pay back, not to return thanks by helping others. As an expression of thanks to God and for the person or persons who brought us the message of hope in Christ, we too can express gratitude by carrying the message of Christ to others (Rom. 10:15–17).

Live a Credible Life. Part of our task is to gain a good hearing for the gospel. Living a credible life before others enhances this. With studies revealing that there are few differences in how Christians and non-Christians live, there is little curiosity about how we are living. How we handle difficulties and stresses, make decisions, rear our children, handle our financial matters and priorities, work, and live in a community of faith will either help us or hinder us in gaining a hearing for the gospel.

If we are living with Jesus and with lost people on our hearts, we will find ourselves validating our message through the small things we do. The other day someone approached my wife Sandy and said, "You are the lady who sings on the worship team." Sandy replied that she was, and the two of them struck up a conversation. People who know us are often watching even when we do not know they are watching.

As the world becomes more anti-Christian and looks more unlike Christ, it is imperative that Christ followers possess different values and behaviors from those without Christ. There is no room for cultural Christianity. In order to be credible, we must demonstrate that the Christian lifestyle works.

Look for Divine Appointments

As we build relationships and interact with people in single and multiple encounters, we need to be sensitive to the leading of the Holy Spirit. God can and does provide us with divine appointments to share His great love. We want constantly to be on the lookout for receptive people whom the Holy Spirit is drawing to Himself. This happens as we pursue lost people with our hearts and actions.

PRIMARY EVANGELISTIC PHASE: SHARING THE MESSAGE

Turn Conversations to Christ

There is a friendly debate among evangelists. Some believe that the most difficult phase of evangelism is starting a spiritual conversation. Others believe that knowing when to stop talking is the most difficult part of giving a verbal witness. Either way, a key role involves being able to steer conversations to spiritual matters and ultimately Christ. The more conversations you start, the more times you will communicate the full gospel message.

Communicate the Gospel Content

As we transition a conversation to spiritual matters, and ultimately to Christ, our role moves from preparation and preevangelism to the communication of the essentials of the gospel message. In order to communicate the message, we will want to refine our understanding of the essentials of the gospel message.

Verbal and Nonverbal Communication. We communicate the contents of the gospel verbally and nonverbally. At this stage in personal evangelism, we need to make sure that what we are saying and how we are saying it complement each other. A nonverbal message is always stronger when there is a conflict between the verbal and nonverbal messages. If we are violating cultural norms in our approach, the gospel message will probably get filtered out. This is not always true because the disconnect could actually create an interest, but as a general rule I would not violate cultural norms in an effort to communicate the gospel.

I had the pleasure of serving as the chapel speaker for several major league teams and now a triple-A team in New Orleans. I want to be available to communicate the gospel message to those who are spiritually receptive. However, in terms of sharing with players, if I violate locker room norms (such as seeking autographs in the locker room area), then the message of Christ will be associated with my insensitivities to their norms. The gospel message would not change, but it certainly would be distorted by such an approach.

As we communicate, we will continually want to evaluate whether the listener is decoding the message as it was intended. So our next role involves clarifying the gospel message.

Clarifying the Gospel Message

"Pray that I may proclaim it clearly, as I should" (Col. 4:4).

Everyone has a personal theology, whether it was intentionally formed or unknowingly shaped by surrounding influences. Part of the task of the witness is to clarify the mixed messages the lost person has received from various sources. Shaped by experiences, the media, and friends, most people are confused about spiritual matters.

Lost people's theology is usually jumbled as they have received conflicting and confusing messages. To clarify our message we need to become astute at asking heart- and mind-opening questions. The questions do not need to have a sharp edge, and they need to be questions that may require some thought and extensive answers. Good questions allow us to check for clarity.

As a former pastor, I have a high respect for the good intentions of many pastors. However, using yes/no evangelism questions at the end of a service in a highly pluralistic society is woefully lacking. At the end of services we often ask one or two yes/no questions and then present a person to the church with the intention of baptizing him at a later date. We then often leave this person to fend for himself spiritually. God forgive us when we treat people like prizes to be presented by hurriedly presenting decisions at the end of our worship services. A better approach is to affirm the person's responding to God's movement in his or her life and then to be deliberate in checking for clarity of the gospel message.

At a recent conference Harold Bullock reminded us that nothing about leading people toward Christ is efficient. Our goal is to be effective communicators and clarifiers because people matter to God. In our efforts to be efficient, we often unintentionally devalue the relationship we are asking people to establish.

Assess Readiness

Even if people understand the gospel message, they may not be ready to make a commitment of their lives to Christ. Jesus was a master at assessing readiness.

Our role includes checking for understanding and for commitment to the gospel. New Christians do not know everything they need to know and do not fully grasp all the ramifications of their commitment.

To avoid getting into trouble later, we need to be careful with the essentials. We must communicate the whole gospel. Otherwise, we are communicating half-truths which distort the truth we seek to share. For truthful communication to occur, the witness must become clear on the essentials.

Persuade

As people understand the gospel and as we assess their readiness, we then persuade them to surrender to Christ. We do not pressure them but give encouragement to surrender to Christ. Several passages deal with our responsibility to persuade people toward Christ.

"Every Sabbath he [Paul] reasoned in the synagogue, trying to persuade Jews and Greeks" (Acts 18:4).

"Then Agrippa said to Paul, 'Do you think that in such a short time you can persuade me to be a Christian?'" (Acts 26:28).

"Since, then, we know what it is to fear the Lord, we try to persuade men. What we are is plain to God, and I hope it is also plain to your conscience" (2 Cor. 5:11).

Mark McCloskey in *Tell It Often, Tell It Well* discussed two different roles of the communicator—proclamation and persuasion. Proclamation is used when the person needs information, and persuasion is used after a person has a grasp of the gospel and its implications on his or her life. Persuasion does not involve running over people.[18]

It is our privilege to compel people to come to Christ. We seek not to manipulate them but to encourage them to take the final step of surrender to God. For the postmodern, we need to be careful not to come across with arrogance, which violates one of their values. However, we can come across with quiet confidence in Christ.

Appropriate Aggressiveness. We need to be intentionally and appropriately aggressive in sharing the gospel (Col. 4:3). This does not involve kicking down resistant doors. We should be careful with our nonverbal communication and not seek to pressure people into a quick decision. Different cultures or subcultures have appropriate levels of directness in verbal communication. We will not always get it right, but we must continue to share while seeking God's wisdom in learning the cultural norms in which we are sharing.

Gentle. Jesus was gentle and humble in heart (Matt. 11:29). When we share the gospel, we are sharing with people who matter to God. If we value people and treat them appropriately, we will not see people only as potential customers to whom we are selling the gospel. We carry a dangerous message; we should seek to communicate it with gentleness (1 Pet. 3:15; 1 Cor. 4:21). Ironically that may include boldness. Boldness does not mean arrogance.

Closing the Conversation

Starting an evangelistic conversation is difficult, and learning how to close the conversation with grace is as well. As we close, the person has either accepted or rejected Christ's leadership. If the person has trusted Christ, we can pray, offer our support, and begin some follow-up. However, when people do not trust Christ for whatever reason, we need to allow them to exit with grace in an effort to keep the door open so that at a later date they may respond to the gospel message.

SUMMARY OF OUR ROLE

I am not keen on cute alliteration, but I will relent and use one to help you remember your role: We should prayerfully and persistently pursue the presence of lost people, then proclaim and persuade at the prompting and in the power of the Holy Spirit.

We are to seek to communicate clearly who Jesus is and what He expects, knowing that we are all flawed vessels but usable in God's hands. Metzger exhorted us to "tell the truth" and to do this by sharing the whole gospel with the whole person. This is our privilege and hope. Newbigin noted:

> If the gospel is to challenge the public life of our
> society, if Christians are to occupy the "high ground",
> which they vacated in the noontime of "modernity," it
> will not be by forming a Christian political party, or by
> aggressive propaganda campaigns. Once again it has to be
> said that there can be no going back to the "Constantinian"
> era. It will only be by movements that begin with the local
> congregation in which the reality of the new creation is
> present, known, and experienced, and from which men
> and women will go into every sector of public life to
> claim it for Christ, to unmask the illusions which have
> remained hidden and to expose all areas of public life to
> the illumination of the gospel. But that will only happen
> as and when local congregations renounce an introverted
> concern for their own life, and recognize that they exist
> for the sake of those who are not members, as sign,
> instrument, and foretaste of God's redeeming grace for the
> whole life of society.[19]

We have examined God's involvement and our role in evangelism. In the next chapter we will attempt to determine and describe the essentials of the gospel message we are seeking to communicate as we remember that God saves the lost and uses people to do so.[20]

CHAPTER 3

Understanding Content Essentials: Clarifying the Gospel Message

EVANGELISM IMPLIES THAT WE carry a message. It is important that we are clear in our understanding of the message we are communicating. The number of images we process each day is phenomenal. Only a limited number of messages actually stick. We want to make God's message clear in our efforts to help it stick.

Why take a fresh look at the message of the gospel? Should we not just pick up our favorite tract and tell people what it says? No. This task seems almost unnecessary, but I propose that it is essential.

The drift is away from the true message of the gospel, not toward it. Lesslie Newbigin reminded us that over time the gospel message gets clouded as it passes through cultural filters. These cultural filters need to be removed to see the gospel more clearly. Tom Steffen encouraged us to do as Peter did—experience some cultural conversions. He said, "This process is like peeling away layers of an onion; it can be a very tearful experience."[1]

People outside church often ask a question that is the title of a 1967 book by Fritz Ridenour, *So What's the Difference?* The Christian church must be ever aware that ours is a message among many religious messages. Therefore, we cannot afford to be unclear in our understanding or dissemination of our message. A close examination is necessary to understand our message as we seek to communicate it in a religiously pluralistic society.[2]

Along with the interviews I do with people I meet, my students interview lost people. A constant theme throughout the interviews by Stephen DuVall was that churches seem to be communicating many different messages. One of his interviewees said, "I think every church is saying something different."[3] This is another reason to review our message.

LIMITATIONS OF CLARIFYING THE MESSAGE

Communication of the gospel passes through the filters of perspectives and values of those sending and receiving the message. Senders encode the gospel from a given cultural perspective. Listeners decode what they receive, regardless of the source of the message, based on their own culture, perspective, experiences, and biases. Consequently, we should recognize our limitations in accurately communicating God's message as it is influenced by our own background.

Newbigin noted:

We must start with the basic fact that there is no such thing as a pure gospel if by that is meant something which is not embodied in a culture. The simplest verbal statement of the gospel, "Jesus is Lord," depends for its meaning on the content which that culture gives to the word "Lord." What kind of thing is "lordship" in the culture in question? The gospel always comes as the testimony of a community which, if it is faithful, is trying to live out the meaning of the gospel in a certain style of life, certain ways of holding property, of maintaining law and order, of carrying on production and consumption, and so on. Every interpretation of the gospel is embodied in some cultural form. The missionary does not come with the pure gospel and then adapt it to the culture where she serves: she comes with a gospel which is already embodied

in the culture by which the missionary was formed. And
this is so from the very beginning.[4]

This chapter considers two questions: What are the essential elements of the gospel? And what is necessary to receive Christ? I feel inadequate to answer them, yet I must attempt to do so. You too, each time you communicate God's message, must ask yourself these two questions.

A PROPOSAL

My former preaching professor used to say, "Words do not have meanings; they have usages." Writing a book has the limitation of using words that may or may not communicate well. I respond by thinking carefully about the message I want to communicate and the frames of reference of the readers.

My aim in this chapter is to assist you as you think through what God would have you communicate to lost people.

An encouraging reminder as we begin this journey together is this: the Holy Spirit draws people to Himself and helps to illuminate His truth in the hearts and minds of His people. It is not by our masterful communication that people surrender their wills to the will of the Father. God alone does this.

CHALLENGES OF CLARIFYING AND COMMUNICATING THE MESSAGE

Clarifying a precise gospel message brings significant challenges. One challenge is that flawed individuals have been entrusted with God's message. He even used a most unlikely group, the disciples.

Tom Steffen made the following strong claim and warning: "All evangelism-church planting is flawed. As human agents of the gospel, we present a flawed message. We tend to redefine the gospel, wrap it in cultural attire recognizable mostly to us, take shortcuts, lay little foundation, assume that our hearers understand much more than they probably do, forget our message's connection to the physical world or follow-up, and communicate it in ways that require mental gymnastics from the listeners. Fortunately, some understand the gospel."[5]

A second challenge is that the method is intertwined with the message. It is impossible to separate the message from the methods used to communicate it. Harold Bullock noted three factors related to this challenge.

1. Not only what we do but also the form in which we do it sends a signal about what we think to be reality.

2. The message we must communicate is the reality of God/Jesus Christ expressed in His Word, the Bible. Not only what we do and say but also the manner in which we do and say it must be consistent with the Word.

3. Thus, we think through not only what we are going to do but also the methods and personnel.[6]

A third challenge is that communication of the gospel is wrapped in culture, both the sender's and receiver's culture. Newbigin said:

Neither at the beginning, nor at any subsequent time, is there or can there be a gospel that is not embodied in a culturally conditioned form of words. The idea that one can or could at any time separate out by some process of distillation a pure gospel unadulterated by any cultural accretions is an illusion. It is, in fact, an abandonment of the gospel, for the gospel is about the word made flesh. Every statement of the gospel in words is conditioned by the culture of which those words are a part, and every style of life that claims to embody the truth of the gospel is a culturally conditioned style of life. There can never be a culture-free gospel. Yet the gospel, which is from the beginning to the end embodied in culturally conditioned forms, calls into question all cultures, including the one in which it was originally embodied.[7]

A fourth challenge is the use of words. We can attempt to communicate one message, and the listener receives another.

A final challenge is that our gospel message is multifaceted. It touches the hearts and minds of people at various points. McCloskey summarized six facets of the gospel.

1. The Gospel of Truth (Col. 1:5)
2. The Gospel of Hope (Col. 1:23)
3. The Gospel of Peace (Eph. 6:15)
4. The Gospel of Immortality (2 Tim. 1:10)
5. The Gospel of the Kingdom (Matt. 24:14)
6. The Gospel of Salvation (Rom. 1:16)

WHAT OUR MESSAGE IS NOT

As we begin to think specifically about our message, we might be aided by examining what our message is *not*. First, our message cannot be, "Come feel good about God." Tom Steffen called this "the Tylenol or therapy gospel that claims to address felt needs or life enhancement concerns."[8] If we are not careful, we will send the message that if you need a little boost in life, try Jesus because He will make you feel better. There are significant earthly and eternal benefits from following Christ, but that is not the entire story. If we are not careful, we will remake God in our image, based on our needs, rather than recognize the totality of who He is in the Scriptures and the revelation of Jesus Christ.

Second, our goal in evangelism is not only to register decisions. Our more complete objective is to make disciples. We cannot have disciples without decisions, but if our approaches are designed only to count decisions, we may hinder the expansion of the glory of God. We cannot find a hard line dividing Jesus as Savior and Jesus as Lord in the New Testament. Our message is not to come to Christ as Savior only.

Third, our message is not to surrender to Jesus and pull yourself up spiritually. Christianity is to be lived in community. Our goal is not to see people born into the kingdom without a spiritual family to support them. We cannot control all aspects of follow-up. However, as the norm, our desire is to see spiritual children born into a family, a church or community of faith, not to develop spiritual orphans. Part of the invitation is to become a member of a family of God.

Fourth, our message is not limited to a private Christian life. It extends into every area of life. Lesslie Newbigin said: "The gospel cannot be accommodated as one element in a society which has pluralism as its reigning ideology. The Church cannot accept as its role simply the winning of individuals to a kind of Christian discipleship that concerns only the private and domestic aspects of life. To be faithful to a message, which concerns the kingdom of God, his rule over all things and all people, the Church has to claim the high ground of public truth. Every human society is governed by assumptions, normally taken for granted without question, about what is real, what is important, what is worth aiming for. There is no such thing as an ideological vacuum."[9] Our message is that Jesus will impact every area of our lives.

Newbigin said, "I cannot doubt that the call to conversion is essential to any authentic understanding of the gospel. The ministry of Jesus began with such a call: 'Repent, for the kingdom of God is at hand.' The crucial question concerns the content of conversion."[10]

UNDERSTANDINGS OF GOD IN A PLURALISTIC CONTEXT: WHICH GOD?

We live in a world where people have radically different ideas of who God is and what He is doing in and around us. People believe what they want to believe. People want to feel good about themselves, and will believe whatever it takes to accomplish it. Many people believe that as long as they believe something or have good intentions, they are OK.

What must a lost person understand and commit to prior to or as a part of conversion? The answers to these questions are important in a pluralistic society. To hear people say that they believe in "God" means just one step above nothing. We had better check for understanding all along the way as we dialogue with people.

It is essential that students become experts on their message and on their target. In many of my classes I have students interview lost people in order to gain an understanding of the people they seek to reach. Almost without exception, students come back to class after completing eight to ten interviews with their eyes wide open about what people say they believe.

Two particular answers demonstrate the importance of being clear about our message and our view of God. I was sitting around a table with my students when one indicated that he had completed his interviews. With his perspective expanded, he said, "How do I respond to someone who says he is a Catholic atheist?" In a video-taped interview our students heard the person say, "God is everywhere and in everything." So the interviewer asked the person, who was smoking, "Is God in that cigarette?" To this the interviewee said, "Yes, God is in the cigarette." In this situation I would respond, "That's interesting. How did you come to that conclusion?" We must be clear on who God is and check for a biblical understanding when we hear someone say *God*.

SALVATION

The message of salvation is an essential part of the Christian message to a world without Christ. Salvation speaks to three of our most significant needs. Salvation speaks to our need for forgiveness of sins and the gift of the Spirit. People want to avoid the guilt they feel inside, even if they do not use the term *sin*. Salvation through Christ addresses this need. Salvation also speaks to the image of God in us longing for completion. Only God can fill this need. And finally, salvation speaks to our longing for wholeness and fulfillment in the midst of our fragmentation caused by sin. God knows our deepest needs, and He addresses them through salvation.[11]

Mark McCloskey in his outstanding book *Tell It Often—Tell It Well*, summarized seven pictures of salvation found in the Bible.

1. Regeneration: From Death to Life (2 Cor. 5:17)
2. Reconciliation: From Enemy to Friend (Rom. 5:10)
3. Propitiation: From Wrath to Mercy (1 John 4:10)
4. Sanctification: A Change in Ownership (Acts 26:18)
5. Redemption: From Slavery to Freedom (1 Pet. 1:18)
6. Justification: From Guilt to Acquittal (Rom. 3:24)
7. Adoption: A Change in Families (Gal. 4:4–7)[12]

The Bible reveals five descriptions of salvation.

1. *A Great Salvation*

   "How shall we escape if we ignore such a great salvation? This salvation, which was first announced by the Lord, was confirmed to us by those who heard him" (Heb. 2:3).

2. *A Present Salvation*

   "For he says, 'In the time of my favor I heard you, and in the day of salvation I helped you.' I tell you, now is the time of God's favor, now is the day of salvation" (2 Cor. 6:2).

3. *A Common Salvation*

   "Dear friends, although I was very eager to write to you about the salvation we share, I felt I had to write and urge you to contend for the faith that was once for all entrusted to the saints" (Jude 3).

4. *A Known Salvation*

   "To give his people the knowledge of salvation through the forgiveness of their sins" (Luke 1:77).

5. *An Eternal Salvation*

   "And, once made perfect, he became the source of eternal salvation for all who obey him" (Heb. 5:9).

ESSENTIALS FOR SALVATION

Salvation involves people moving from death to life by an act of the Holy Spirit based on the work of Christ on the cross. McCloskey defined *salvation* as "the divine act whereby a person is given a spiritual status change through his deliverance from the kingdom of darkness and his transferal into the safety and blessing of the kingdom of Jesus Christ."[13]

The "cigarette response" begs the question, What understanding of God is necessary for salvation? You will want to develop your own list of essentials, but here are some of mine. This does not comprise our entire message but reflects some essentials for salvation.

God—Be convinced that there is only one, eternal, holy, just, personal God who desires a relationship with them (Acts 17:24–31; 14:15–17).

Jesus Christ

- Jesus is God (John 1:1; Titus 2:13–14).
- Jesus Christ lived, died on the cross for our sins, rose from the dead and ascended into heaven (1 Cor. 15:1–5).
- Jesus' death on the cross paid the penalty for our separating sin against God (Rom. 5:8).
- Jesus is the only way to a relationship with God (John 14:6; Acts 4:12; 1 Tim. 2:5–6).
- Jesus will come back in glory to judge the living and the dead (2 Tim. 4:1; 1 Pet. 4:5).

Individuals and People

- People cannot pay the eternal debt of their sin by their efforts of righteous acts (Eph. 2:8–9).
- People must trust Jesus solely as Savior, the forgiver of their sins (Col. 1:20–22); the supreme and sole leader of their lives, as they choose to turn from self-leadership to yield to His direction as Lord (John 3:36; Matt. 7:20–21).

Michael Green noted four factors of Paul's conversion.

1. God touched his conscience.
2. God illumined his mind.
3. God touched his will.
4. God transformed the whole of the rest of his life.[14]

MAN'S PROBLEM AND NEED

A LOOK AT SIN[15]

You have heard it, and I have heard it. People say, "People are basically good inside." We continue to hear it, but that does not make it true. Francis Schaeffer said that man is capable of both nobility and cruelty. People who believe that humans are naturally good have not read a newspaper or watched the TV news lately. Man's sinfulness is natural, not his goodness. We are of value to God, but without Him we continue to self-destruct. Goodness and moral living are by-products of training and following God's standards, not living a certain number of days.

The late summer of 2001 brought a sports story that captured the attention of baseball fans and nonfans alike. It started with the underdog coming out on top. However, it ended with what we already know—that man is naturally not good but sinful and in need of a Savior.

The story involved the innocent, a youth. It surrounded a Little League team from the Bronx in New York. This team won the right to compete in the international Little League World Series. Their star pitcher became the pitcher of a perfect game with his blazing fastball and sharp-breaking curveball. He led his team to a third place in the overall World Series. This team went from heroism to shame when it was discovered that the pitcher's father and the founder of the league had falsified his birth certificate. He was playing as a fourteen-year-old in a league that had a twelve-year age limit.

For followers of Christ and those who do not follow Christ, our tendency is to underestimate how God views the sin in our lives and to overestimate our righteousness.

God's View

God is holy and will not have sin in His presence. It is easy to overlook the implications of serving a holy God. It is not as if God somehow is sleeping while we sin or that He winks when we sin. He knows and responds in perfect wisdom and timing.

All sin is sin against God, not just against insignificant people who will forget or get over it. Jesus said, "I tell you the truth, whatever you did not do for one of the least of these, you did not do for me" (Matt. 25:45). When we choose not to follow God's plan and ways with our actions, words, and attitudes, then we rebel against God Himself.

God takes sin seriously. He does not always respond to sin in the same manner. If He did, we might not be here today. By sending Christ to die in our place as punishment for our sins, He provided a way for us to escape the eternal consequences of our sin. He loves us passionately.

Our View

People tend to categorize and minimize sin. Shapers of media have so elevated tolerance as a value that many of us have lost the categories of right and wrong. We have moved into the age of preference and lifestyle, forsaking any notion that there is sin in our lives. It is much too easy to presume upon the grace of God.

The problem with such a view is that it is shallow and leads to incongruence. The deep longing of almost everyone's heart is to be free from guilt and shame. By elevating tolerance and removing *sin* from our vocabulary, we still cannot eliminate the consequences of sin or the need for removal of that sin. Incongruence occurs when what we appear to be and present on the outside does not match what is going on inside of us. In essence, we are two different people.

Through hundreds of interviews, I have discovered that people have many strange views of God and who He is or might be. In the series of five questions we ask, "To you, who is God?" We also ask, "What do you think it takes to be straightened out with God?" The answers to these questions have been interesting, especially since most people have an answer for this question even if they have previously stated they do not believe in God.

You never know what people might say. A student shared a funny story. "One young mother completed the interview while I stood just inside the door with her. Her husband was in a chair in the next room in plain sight watching television. When I asked the question about what it takes to be straightened out with God, her reply made me think that trouble was inevitable. She turned her head in the direction of her husband and said with an escalating tone from soft to loud and irritated as her attention turned to her husband, 'You got to do right and quit messing around with all them dopeheads!' Her husband never took his eyes off the television but snarled and replied, 'Shut up!' It was not pleasant at the moment but interesting in hindsight."[16]

Most people sense a need to be straightened out with the Creator of the universe. Christ alone through His atoning work on the cross can deal with our sin. He paid a debt He did not owe because we owed a debt we could not pay (Rom. 3:23; 5:8–10; 6:23). Some people try to rid themselves of consequences of sin by doing good deeds. When I hear this while giving a verbal witness, I often ask how many good deeds it takes to please God and soothe one's soul and what criteria do we use to determine whether something is a good deed.

Some cultures try to rid themselves of guilt by performing rituals or offering sacrifices to gods who cannot hear them. In America, if we are not careful, attending church a certain number of services per year or giving money to the church can become nothing more than a civilized ritual to rid ourselves of the guilt we feel inside.

Our Need

The sin of biblical unbelief separates us from God. This will surely bring about a day of judgment against all people. Our need is for a Savior to take away the guilt and shame that sin has brought into our lives. One of the deep desires of people is to be free from guilt. We can try to suppress it or ignore it, but the need remains.

MAN'S DESTINATION WITHOUT GOD

My preaching professor, Harold Bryson, wrote a book entitled *Yes Virginia, There Is a Hell*. Without Christ our eternal destiny is separation from God. People can rationalize and try to explain it away, but the Bible is clear. Luke 16:19–31 depicts the reality of an eternal separation between those who follow Christ and those who do not.

It is easy to get caught up in what hell might look like and whether Satan has horns. Several dramas have been written and performed in churches across America, especially around Halloween, in an effort to depict some of the possible realities of hell. *USA Today* published a poll in 1997 about people's view of hell. Fifty-two percent of adults are certain there's a hell, and 27 percent think there might be. Of those two groups, 48 percent believe hell is a real place where people suffer eternal fiery torment; 6 percent don't know; and 46 percent believe it is an anguished state of existence rather than an actual place.[17] However, the most severe punishment is the absence of God's presence and of His restraining hand over evil.

ROLE OF CHRIST ON CROSS AND EMPTY TOMB

The Christian message is embodied in Jesus Christ (John 3:16; 2·Cor. 5:21; 1 Pet. 2:24). Newbigin said, "That truth is not a doctrine or a worldview or even a religious experience; it is certainly not to be found by repeating abstract nouns like justice and love; it is the man Jesus Christ in whom God was reconciling the world. The truth is personal, concrete, historical."[18]

COSTLY GIFT

The Christian message centers on God's efforts to redeem mankind, not mankind's efforts toward God (Eph. 2:8–9). God Himself through Jesus Christ came from the holy places to live among us and to pay the ultimate price through His sacrificial gift to follow God to the cross. Christ gave the ultimate gift on the cross and through His resurrection. God did for mankind what we could not do for ourselves; He provided a perfect sacrificial substitute.

CROSS AS PAYMENT

There is no forgiveness of sin without the shedding of blood. This sounds a little strange if you listen through the ears of those who are listening to our message. But it is true and real nonetheless. There is a natural element of mystery in God. He is God and above us, so it is difficult to understand why God chose to redeem us through the shedding of blood.

Paul communicates the essential role of the blood in our salvation in Colossians 1:19–23. Other passages relate the importance of the cross.

"In fact, the law requires that nearly everything be cleansed with blood, and without the shedding of blood there is no forgiveness" (Heb. 9:22).

"This is my blood of the covenant, which is poured out for many for the forgiveness of sins" (Matt. 26:28).

"In him we have redemption through his blood, the forgiveness of sins, in accordance with the riches of God's grace" (Eph. 1:7).

RESURRECTION AS PROOF OF DEITY

On July 4, 1776, the thirteen United States of America declared independence from England. On April 12, 1861, the Confederate States, which began the Civil War, attacked the internal unity of America with the firing of the first shot on Fort Sumter. On December 7, 1941, Japanese warplanes bombed Pearl Harbor, marking a decisive day as the U.S. entered World War II. On September 11, 2001,

America experienced an attack by terrorists that changed not only the skyline in New York but also much about the American psyche. Many days are remembered throughout history as turning points.

The Christian story has such a turning point. What began as a black Friday with the death of Christ on a cross ended in a victorious resurrection Sunday. What a difference that day has made in the lives of so many from the first century to the twenty-first century. The evidence of the resurrection is seen in the lives of those who experienced Jesus after the resurrection. Let's look at the difference it made in the lives of some of the followers.

- Thomas—a doubting skeptic became a believer (John 20:26–29).
- Mary Magdalene and Mary—mourners became happy and celebrated (Matt. 28:1–10).
- A criminal became forgiven (Luke 23:39–43).
- Shy, scarred, timid, defeated men became brave and powerful (Acts 2).
- Peter preached at Pentecost and was later reported to be crucified upside down.
- Most of the disciples died as martyrs for their faith after the resurrection.

The resurrection is the single most important physical event and spiritual reality that has ever occurred in history. Without the resurrection Jesus would have been seen as nothing more than a good man who met a tragic death at the hands of overzealous religious leaders.

The tooth of Buddha is displayed around the world as a prized item. If Christians could display the tooth of Jesus, Christians would have no reason to claim a relationship with a living God. It is the resurrection, which left no physical body, that separates Jesus from all others who falsely claim to be god or a divine revelation of God.

EXCLUSIVE WAY WITH INCLUSIVE CALL

The gospel is for whosoever will; it is a completely inclusive call (John 14:6; Acts 4:8–12; 1 Tim. 2:5). The invitation is for all men, women, and children. Jesus did not show favoritism in who He died for. Like the old children's song says, "Red and yellow, black, and white, they are precious in His sight; Jesus loves the little children of the world."

I hear the question often. One such occasion was during a trip to Nashville. After working out in the gym, I headed for the best part, the hot tub. Once there I engaged the only other person there in a conversation. We introduced ourselves and then began to talk about spiritual things. After some discussions with this young man in his early twenties, he indicated that he was a Christian.

He was having a difficult time trying to communicate Christ with his Muslim friends. He asked me the big questions in his mind, "Do Baptists believe that Jesus is the only way to heaven, and are my Muslim friends going to hell?" He struggled with these questions in his own mind.

I responded by letting Jesus speak for Himself. The issue was not what Baptists believe, but what the Bible teaches. So I replied, "Jesus answered, 'I am the way and the truth and the life. No one comes to the Father except through me'" (John 14:6). I also quoted 1 John 5:11–13. "And this is the testimony: God has given us eternal life, and this life is in his Son. He who has the Son has life; he who does not have the Son of God does not have life. I write these things to you who believe in the name of the Son of God so that you may know that you have eternal life."

The exclusivity of the way to God will probably continue to be a significant area of questioning in the foreseeable future in America. As we communicate God's plan for salvation, may we extend the call to whosoever will.

UNDERSTANDING RECEIVING CHRIST
(ACTS 20:20–21; JOHN 3:15)

WHAT BIBLICAL BELIEF IS NOT

The problem with America is not that we do not believe but that we believe anything. I have not tested the accuracy of that statement, but I do know that we have different levels of belief. Some things we just kind of believe, while other things we hold with passionate conviction.

Using the word *belief* is similar to using the word *love*. In many respects the word *love* has come to mean very little. In my family we have a running, often-violated-without-penalty rule that says we do not say that we love anything but people and God. It means I cannot say that I love golf. My wife cannot say she loves chocolate. If we say that we love too many things, our children will struggle with the meaning of the word based on its varied and many uses.

Our courts of law recognize the various levels of belief. For some cases one side only has to have a probability of over 50 percent to win the case. The most serious of criminal cases require belief beyond a reasonable doubt. In becoming a follower of Christ, one must believe at a high level.

Belief is more than an intellectual consent to a given set of facts. Satan and the demons believe, with all assurance and without any reservation, that Jesus Christ is who He said He was and did what people said He did. James wrote, "You believe that there is one God. Good! Even the demons believe that—and shudder. You foolish man, do you want evidence that faith without deeds is useless?" (James 2:19–20). Biblical belief involves more than being convinced of the truthfulness of something. And belief is more than having an emotional response, as the demons have, while thinking about the reality of the power and person of Jesus Christ.

Biblical belief is not related to following religious rituals. In my denomination, a common practice is to have people walk an aisle to confess their faith in the front part of the building toward the pulpit. Other denominations have different cultural norms as a part of their religious experience. Some groups sprinkle children when they are small. This cultural religious form or any other form by other denominations is not an essential component of the gospel message.

In the James passage we come to understand that a saving faith that restores a broken relationship with God involves a commitment to act on that faith in a positive manner toward Christ.

RECEIVING CHRIST

What does it take to have the Son? John said that we must receive Jesus. "Yet to all who received him, to those who believed in his name, he gave the right to become children of God—children born not of natural descent, nor of human decision or a husband's will, but born of God" (John 1:12–13).

It is difficult to determine when another person receives Christ and experiences regeneration. Receiving Christ seems to have three facets. They are all sides of the same diamond but reflect the light in a little different manner. Properly understood, each one of the three encompasses the other two facets. Those three facets are (1) surrender, (2) repentance, and (3) faith.[19]

Surrender

The warning is haunting. The words of Jesus should grab our attention and hearts. Jesus said, "Not everyone who says to me, 'Lord, Lord,' will enter the kingdom of heaven, but only he who does the will of my Father who is in heaven" (Matt. 7:21).

Part of receiving Christ involves the surrender of our will to Christ's leadership (Rom. 10:9–10). It is like changing pilots on the plane. The pilot is in control. When we respond to the leading of the Holy Spirit to unite with Christ, we are giving over the controls of our lives. Surely we will continue to have to give over the controls day after day, but receiving Christ contains the foundational element of surrender.

Jesus as Lord demands that we surrender to Him. C. S. Lewis noted that ultimately there are two kinds of people: those who say to God "Thy will be done" and those to whom God says "Thy will be done." If we do not obey, is He truly Lord to us? A servant under a lord would follow the wishes and commands of the lord. So too, a facet of receiving Christ is to exchange our will for His will. Receiving Christ involves surrendering and acknowledging that Jesus is Lord, boss, controller of all. Lesslie Newbigin said, "An evangelism that invites men and women to accept the name of Christ but fails to call them to this real encounter must be rejected as false."[20]

An implication of surrender is the changing of loyalties, commanders. Our nature is to bow only to our own desires, not to those in authority over us. Following Jesus involves surrendering our will in deference to His will. As an example, Jesus called the rich young ruler to change loyalties from himself and his possessions to Christ (Matt. 19:16–30). (Also see Rom. 8:7, 10:3; Heb. 12:9; and James 4:7 for select passages on the importance of submission.)

Repentance

Another facet of receiving Christ is repentance. The Scripture is clear that there is no forgiveness of sin without repentance. This involves a turning from our own desires to follow Christ's desires. It also involves agreeing with Christ about our sinful condition. It is more than just feeling sorrow or guilt about an act.

Repentance also involves a changing of the mind that results in a change in life direction. Newbigin wrote,

> But—and this is equally important—the word spoken
> to his heart, while it accepts that language as its vehicle, uses
> it not to affirm and approve the life that Saul is living but to
> call it radically into question: "Why do you persecute me?"
> It is to show him that his most passionate and all-conquer-
> ing conviction is wrong, that what he thinks is the service of
> God is fighting against God, that he is required to stop in
> his tracks, turn around, and renounce the whole direction

of his life, to love what he had hated and to cherish what he had sought to destroy."[21]

The verses that call for us to repent are many. One verse is Acts 3:19–20: "Repent, then, and turn to God, so that your sins may be wiped out, that times of refreshing may come from the Lord, and that he may send the Christ, who has been appointed for you—even Jesus." These are a select few: Matthew 4:17; Mark 1:14–15; Luke 13:3; Acts 2:37–39; 3:19–20; 17:30.

Faith/Trust/Belief

Faith or trust is another facet of receiving Christ (Eph. 2:8). The faith required for salvation is not blind faith, but it does take faith in the unseen to become a child of God. Jesus told Thomas, "Because you have seen me, you have believed; blessed are those who have not seen and yet have believed" (John 20:29).

Several years ago my wife provided me with some insight on the subject of faith. She said that all people have faith, either in God or in themselves. She says that it takes more faith to believe that we can take care of our own physical, emotional, spiritual, and eternal needs than it does to trust those needs to God. Humans are a people of faith. The choice is the object of our faith.

A quick search of the NIV New Testament reveals that faith is used 231 times. The writer of Hebrews reminded us of the essential role of faith: "And without faith it is impossible to please God, because anyone who comes to him must believe that he exists and that he rewards those who earnestly seek him" (Heb. 11:6).

Faith, trust, and belief can be used interchangeably to describe more than an intellectual acknowledgment of facts about Christ. We must express intellectual belief to such a degree that it will cause us to take action, a step toward applying the faith.

Take action, a step toward applying the faith. It is belief that results in or displays itself in behavior that serves us, not the behaviors. "He who believes in the Son has eternal life; but he who does not obey the

Son shall not see life, but the wrath of God abides on him"(John 3:36 NASB).

James reminds us that faith without works is dead: "In the same way, faith by itself, if it is not accompanied by action, is dead. But someone will say, 'You have faith; I have deeds.' Show me your faith without deeds, and I will show you my faith by what I do. You believe that there is one God. Good! Even the demons believe that—and shudder. You foolish man, do you want evidence that faith without deeds is useless?" (James 2:17–20).

The works do not save us, however. "What then shall we say? That the Gentiles, who did not pursue righteousness, have obtained it, a righteousness that is by faith; but Israel, who pursued a law of righteousness, has not attained it. Why not? Because they pursued it not by faith but as if it were by works. They stumbled over the 'stumbling stone'" (Rom. 9:30–32).

Properly understood and applied, *surrender, repentance,* and *faith* describe how to establish a relationship with the living God. However, if any one of the three is emphasized to the neglect of the others, there is a problem and possibly a misleading interpretation of the gospel. If *faith* alone is emphasized, one can move to an "easy believism." If *surrender* is overly emphasized, one can move to legalism. And finally, emphasizing *repentance* alone can lead to a works salvation. In sharing our faith, we should listen carefully to hear these three facets, regardless of the words that are being used.

CHANGING COMMITMENTS AND LEADERS: FORGIVER AND LEADER

Part of entering into a saving relationship with Christ involves confessing Jesus as the forgiver and leader of your life. Jesus is the only means by which sins can be forgiven. Jesus took our sins and bore them in their full consequence on our behalf.

People have all types of loyalties, mostly to ourselves. We often submit to the desires of our heart and our affections. Some of us are loyal to the pursuit of financial independence. Others are loyal to a family as a chief value. Still others are loyal to various forms of idols or spirits. What has to change as we move toward conversion is the object of our loyalty. We have to be willing to acknowledge and follow Christ as the one who has the supreme, absolute authority to direct every area of our lives.

I recognize that over a lifetime we continually have to submit to Christ's leadership in new areas. However, we do an injustice to present a gospel that requires absolutely nothing on our part except to acknowledge a few facts about Jesus. In as much as we know, we must place our faith in Christ, repent of our sins, and surrender to the leadership of Christ.

CROSSING THE LINE

People often debate whether evangelism is a process or an event. Evangelism usually involves a process, but this is not to be confused with salvation/conversion, which happens at a given point in time. Conversion happens at a moment. People can often identify the exact moment at which they surrendered their life to Jesus through His work on the cross. Yet for others the moment at which they moved from darkness into light is more difficult to define. Whether dramatic or imperceptible, there is a point at which one moves from darkness into light, a decision is made, and a relationship with the living God is established.

While enrolled in seminary, I traveled regularly from Pascagoula, Mississippi to New Orleans to attend classes. My travel route included many miles, almost by autopilot, for those early morning drives down Interstate 10. The welcome center and the sign that read, "Louisiana State Line, Welcome to Louisiana," greeted me. I knew for sure that I was crossing from Mississippi into Louisiana. Other roads that lead into Louisiana do not indicate a change in state. If I left Pascagoula and then found myself in the French Quarter eating beignets, then I could be confident that at some point I had crossed the state line.

It is impossible to make a strong judgment about whether a person has crossed the line of faith. One reason is that it is possible to do religious things without crossing the line of salvation. Through a parable Jesus told His disciples how to respond to living in a world with true and false followers of Christ.

> "But while everyone was sleeping, his enemy came and sowed weeds among the wheat, and went away. When the wheat sprouted and formed heads, then the weeds also appeared. The owner's servants came to him and said, 'Sir, didn't you sow good seed in your field? Where then did the weeds come from?' 'An enemy did this,' he replied. The servants asked him, 'Do you want us to go and pull them up?' 'No,' he answered, 'because while you are pulling the weeds, you may root up the wheat with them. Let both grow together until the harvest. At that time I will tell the harvesters: First collect the weeds and tie them in bundles to be burned; then gather the wheat and bring it into my barn'" (Matt. 13:25–30).

MULTIFACETED END GOALS OF FOLLOWING CHRIST

On a corporate church level, a goal is to see the glory of God expanded throughout the earth. The aim of evangelism is to honor God by expanding His glory through the lives of His followers to every nation and tribe throughout the world.

On a local church level, a goal is to see a group of followers demonstrate the character and glory of God through how they relate to one another and those outside the family of God. By their love they validate not only the truthfulness of the message to bystanders but also the reality of the message for daily living. As local church members learn to walk with God, they will transform their sphere of influence into the image of Christ.

On a family level, one of the goals is to see family members relate to one another in ways that honor Christ and one another—to lead, correct, encourage, discover, and teach one another what it means to relate to God and to those outside the family unit and the family of God.

On an individual level, we are submitting ourselves with humility to the leadership of God, thereby demonstrating wisdom in choosing the less traveled but much preferred path of life. We are presenting our bodies as a living sacrifice.[22] Paul wrote, "Therefore, I urge you, brothers, in view of God's mercy, to offer your bodies as living sacrifices, holy and pleasing to God—this is your spiritual act of worship. Do not conform any longer to the pattern of this world, but be transformed by the renewing of your mind. Then you will be able to test and approve what God's will is—his good, pleasing and perfect will" (Rom. 12:1–2). In doing so, the fruit of the Spirit will be displayed in our lives (Gal. 5:22 25).

ADVANCING AS THE MESSAGE

Part of the message of Christ is the message of mission. It is impossible to separate the mission of the church from the message of Christ. The church is to advance to the ends of the earth the kingdom of God and His glory. The church is God's instrument to advance the gospel. A congregation over time can easily lose sight of its purpose. The church must press forward with its task if it is to be the church in today's world. Newbigin challenged us with his words.

> As a human race we are on a journey and we need to know the road. It is not true that all roads lead to the top of the same mountain. There are roads which lead over the precipice. In Christ we have been shown the road. We cannot treat that knowledge as a private matter for ourselves. It concerns the whole human family. We do not presume to limit the might and mercy of God for the ultimate salvation of all people, but the same costly act of revelation and reconciliation which gives us that assurance also requires us to share with our fellow pilgrims the vision that God has given us the route we must follow and the goal to which we must press forward.[23]

97

SUMMARY

We are wise to seek to uncover the essential components of the gospel message and to work toward eliminating cultural biases. This will allow us to move into and through various cultures without the message being wrapped in the distortions of American values.

My house has three external doors. All lead to the same house. As we present the gospel message, we can approach an individual or a group of people from a certain angle or perspective. Through the four Gospels we see God communicating His message with different emphases in order to establish credibility and connect the message to the frame of reference of the early readers of the Scriptures. However, the essential core of the gospel remains the same. So, too, today we must be true to the limited but essential core of the gospel message as we seek ways to connect the message to the experiences of the hearers.

Christ's message certainly contains hope that leads to celebration. However, the message also includes personal responsibility to walk the way of life with Jesus as He alone is the forgiver and leader of our lives. His message should cause us not only to rejoice but also to mourn over the impact our sin had on His life. Some will come to Christ rejoicing, while others will come out of a broken spirit because of the sin that separated us from Christ. Either way, to be the whole gospel, both sides need to be presented and lived out.

Christians do have a place in the spiritual conversations in this postmodern culture; however, we are not the only ones with something to say. The urgency is that we are not the only ones talking. We must choose to present the gospel message in a clear and compelling manner. The message is embodied in Christ. Kent Hunter reminds us, "Evangelism is not just presenting a body of knowledge to another person. It is introducing Jesus Christ Himself to another person. The Gospel is not only the Good News about Jesus Christ. Jesus Christ is the Gospel."[24] The church must once again get "on message."

CHAPTER 4

Communication in Evangelism: Making the Gospel Make Sense

G OD DESIRES ALL PEOPLE TO ENTER into a life-changing relationship with Him. He draws lost people to Himself and uses people as a primary tool to carry His message to lost people. As we become clearer on the essentials of the message, we can better know what to communicate. Our role is to help the gospel make sense to lost people through effective communication. In this chapter we will examine various facets of communication in order to become more effective in communicating God's life-giving message.

COMMUNICATION

Effective communication is *not* simple or easy. The gap between our intended message and the message that is actually received is often a canyon. Charles Kraft addressed this in his book *Communication Theory for Christian Witness.*

> When we attempt to communicate, we reach out to other people across whatever gap separates us from them. This may be a comparatively small gap, as between members of the same family, or a very large gap, as between members of widely different societies. At the very least, there will always be differences in the life experiences of those who participate in the communicational events.

Frequently, then, the participants will possess additional educational background, occupation, subculture, dialect, and the like. Often such differences affect less visible factors, such as trust and openness, that strongly influence communication at the deepest levels.

If effective communication is to take place, such gaps need to be bridged.[1]

We, as bearers of the good news do much more than tell the gospel. We are not dump trucks containing the gospel. We do not just back up to people and dump our load. We are to communicate as effectively as possible, checking for understanding and commitment along the way.[2]

MYTHS OF COMMUNICATION

Kraft noted several myths of communication. These are helpful as we seek to understand how most effectively to bridge the gaps between the message of Christ and lost people.

1. Hearing the gospel with one's ears is equivalent to "being reached" with the gospel.
2. The words of the Bible are so powerful that all people need to bring them to Christ is to be exposed to hearing or reading the Bible.
3. Preaching is God's ordained means of communicating the gospel.
4. The sermon is an effective vehicle for bringing about life change.
5. There is one best way to communicate the gospel.
6. The key to effective communication is the precise formulation of the message.
7. Words contain their meanings.
8. What people really need is more information.
9. The Holy Spirit will make up for all mistakes if we are sincere, spiritual, and prayerful enough.

·10. As Christians we should severely restrict our contacts with "evil" people and refrain from going to "evil" places lest we "lose our testimony" and ruin our witness.[3]

STYLES OF COMMUNICATION

People use at least three styles of communication. First, there is *self-centered* communication, where the focus is on the communicator. Fear and unease often accompany this style as users focus on how they are coming across to a fault. The self-awareness exists at exaggerated levels.

Second, there is *message-centered* communication. In this style communicators are less focused on themselves but highly focused on the message being communicated. The danger in this style is that monologue can become the mode of communication. People today are not likely to listen to a monologue. Even talk-show hosts who give monologues are more likely to involve the audience.

Third, there is *other-centered* communication. In this style, the communicator does consider self and the message but not to the neglect of the recipient. The speaker is committed to listening, sensitivity, dialogue, and understanding.[4] The sender demonstrates respect for the receiver, including language, frame of reference, life situation, social class, and values.

VERBAL AND NONVERBAL COMMUNICATION

Communication takes place in multiple forms, both verbal and nonverbal. Studies reveal that most communication is nonverbal. Nonverbal elements include such things as tone, timing, rate of speech, volume level, facial expressions, body posture, gestures, body motion, touching behavior, spatial relationships, and order of the presentation.

Personal evangelism involves verbal and nonverbal components as well. In addition to the elements above, our lifestyle is a form of nonverbal communication. Metzger reminds us, "The airplane of Christian witness always has two wings: our lives (conduct) and our lips (conversation)."[5]

COMMUNICATING GOD'S WAY

God does have a way of communicating with us. We see this best through the life of Christ, God incarnate. Jesus entered our world, our culture, a community, and even a family. Jesus learned the languages, customs, habits, hearts, and hurts of the people. He communicated up close and personal.

Kraft discussed God's strategy for communication in his chapter entitled "What Does God Want Communicationally?" These insights about God's strategy have significant implications for evangelism in any context and culture.

1. First, we recognize the loving nature of God in His communication activity. To love is to seek the best for the recipient at whatever the expense to the source. To love communicationally is to put oneself to whatever inconvenience necessary to assure that the receptors understand. So, the first thing we learn concerning God's strategy is that God is receptor-oriented, seeking to reach his receptors by entering their frame of reference and by participating in their life, in order to be maximally intelligible to them.[6]

2. A second characteristic of God crucial to his communicational strategy is *his personalness*. He does not, as we often do, seek either to love or communicate impersonally. Rather, God *identifies personally* with his receptors. As a person God *interacts* with and becomes vulnerable to his receptors. . . . Thus, communicators of Christianity are a more essential part

of the message they communicate than a communicator of nonrelational kinds of information.[7]

3. The God who is receptor-oriented and personal takes pains to see that his messages are presented with a high degree of impact. To do this he (a) develops high credibility with his receptors, (b) demonstrates, not just speaks, his messages, (c) deals with the specific people and issues, (d) leads his receptors to discover, and (e) trusts those who respond to do the right thing with his messages.[8]

COMMUNICATION IN EVANGELISM

COMMUNICATION AS PROCLAMATION

The biblical concept of proclamation is similar to the concept of communication today. Personal evangelism is much more than just telling. We are to strive to communicate the message effectively. Our role is not completed when we simply deliver the message. We are not the U.S. Post Office, just delivering the gospel package at the door and leaving the package for the spiritually searching to open on their own.

We can learn a lot of helpful information from the people we are trying to evangelize. During some interviews conducted at the University of South Florida, one of my students made a key observation while talking with two young female college students. One was currently a leader in the National Organization for Women who was reared in a prominent Baptist church in Florida, and the other also indicated that she had a Baptist background. One of the ladies surprised my student with the statement, "None of that makes much sense now."[9] Part of our role is to communicate the gospel so that following Jesus for a lifetime and for an eternity makes sense.

COMMUNICATION AS MESSAGE PACKAGING

Sandy Millar narrated the introduction to the evangelism video series Alpha course. In this introduction he touched on the importance of communication and the packages of our communication.

I think at the heart of the true Christian faith is a desire to communicate to the rest of the world. That is what set off the first-century church. It started with very few people. It had a mission given to them by Jesus Christ that was to go and make disciples of the whole world.

And any church that is concerned, I believe, with what God is concerned with, is concerned with those outside the faith. And therefore our function is to present the gospel in a package that today would be thought to be more acceptable and understandable by this generation. And I think our weakness in years past really is that we have retained the ancient packaging and in some respects actually altered the gospel rather than the packaging. I would want to see us retain the gospel . . . and try to find a package in which the gospel can be understood.[10]

COMMUNICATION AS CREDIBILITY BUILDING

Our communication in evangelism involves building credibility. Three facets of communicating with credibility involve being a credible person, with a credible message, using credible methods. Part of the credibility of the person and methods involves stereotyping. Kraft noted, "Assuming that a communicator is both a worthwhile person and has a worthy message to communicate, the major barrier to credibility is the human habit of *stereotyping*. . . . Our listeners have stereotyped expectations both of how we will relate to them and of how we will talk. Such stereotypes will be based on how others like us have performed. We can either conform to the stereotype and function with little, if any, credibility or imitate Jesus in being receptor-oriented and personal in seeking to earn the kind of credibility and respect that the stereotype could never give."[11]

HUMAN BEHAVIOR AND MAKING SENSE

PRINCIPLES

Methods are many; principles are few. Methods change; principles never do. Principles of ministry are prized. Harold Bullock summarized much theology and human behavior in two of his principles for ministry: (1) God does whatever He wants in the manner He thinks best, and (2) people do what makes sense to them.[12] The second principle acknowledges that all human behavior is purposeful, even if the purpose is unknown.

Bullock discussed an implication of the second principle. He said, "I need to grasp what makes sense to the people I want to influence. . . . Given the ministry of the Holy Spirit, people will come to Christ to the extent that it makes sense to them (they adequately grasp the ideas and come to the conclusion that their best lies in that direction)."[13] Consequently, our job is to communicate to them, in their context, based on an understanding of their use of language and perspective, so following Christ makes sense.

Christian witnesses sought to do this in various ways throughout the last half of the twentieth century. The problem is that we continue to communicate in ineffective ways and with answers to questions people are no longer asking. In an oversimplification, most of our evangelistic tracts and methods have been designed around two issues: (1) people want to avoid hell, and (2) people want to gain heaven. We approached lost people by appealing to their sense of wanting to avoid hell or wanting to get to heaven. We provide a scripted prayer that would help them do either.

From the story in chapter 1 about the father who came to understand the incarnation, we examine some of his words: "But he did not believe in all that incarnation stuff which the churches proclaim at

Christmas time. It just didn't make sense, and he was too honest to pretend otherwise. He just could not swallow the Jesus story." This well-intentioned dad became a follower of Christ when it finally made sense to him.

HUMAN BEHAVIOR AS PURPOSEFUL

In 1991 and 1992, I invested myself in completing my dissertation, "The Purpose-Driven Church: An Investigation into the Process of Developing and Implementing a Purpose Statement and Its Benefits to Church Growth." Through the study I came to believe that most churches have unknowingly substituted other purposes than God's for His church. My study toward the dissertation revealed that churches exist for a purpose and are purpose-driven. The question is, For what purpose?

Just as all human behavior is purpose-driven, an organization or a church is purpose-driven. The purpose can be to remain comfortable, feel good, portray an image, gain success or status, prevent pain, or a host of other purposes. Bullock developed a diagram to illustrate how people make decisions to show why they behave in a given manner.

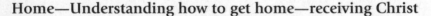

Home—Understanding how to get home—receiving Christ

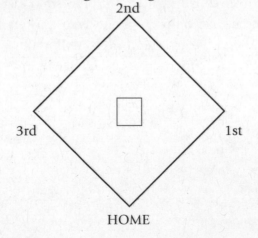

2nd

3rd   1st

HOME

Human behavior, both words and actions, flows out of the desires of the heart, which contains both God-honoring and evil desires. The heart is the seat of the will. Some desires are for selfish pleasures, while other desires are for the benefits of others. What is in the heart will ultimately come out in behaviors as it is filtered through (1) perspective and (2) values. The implications for evangelism are enormous, for both the witness and the lost person, as people will turn their hearts toward God as their perspectives and values are changed. In other words, when we, along with the Holy Spirit, help to shape their filters and it makes sense to follow Christ, they will do so.[14]

Notwithstanding the influence of the Holy Spirit, people will give their lives to Christ (behavior) as it fits into their perspective and values. Our role in evangelism includes the communication of the gospel in such a way as to shape the perspectives and values of lost people. Additionally, Christians will engage in personal evangelism to the degree that it fits their perspective and values. The Christian leader's role is to impact perspective and values to the point that behavior is affected. This sounds more difficult than giving people a tract and pushing them out to share it with a lost person, but the long-term evangelistic benefits are worth the effort. I invite you to examine the New Testament to discover how Jesus shaped perspective and challenged values.

FILTERS

How people hear and receive our messages, both verbal and non-verbal, has changed because postmodern filters are different. Words are no longer enough. It is no longer enough to speak the truth in Sunday school or proclaim the message from the pulpit; we must live and communicate our message effectively, remembering it is fruitless to blame the receivers if our message fails to get through. It has been said, "I can't hear you because your actions are speaking too loudly." In a postmodern culture Christians communicate with the sensitivities of a missionary in a foreign land. Jesus said people will know the truth by our love.

Communication of the gospel passes through the filters of perspectives and values of those sending and receiving the message. Listeners decode the message they are receiving, regardless of the source. Senders encode the gospel message from a given cultural perspective. Consequently, we should recognize the limitations of accurate communication of our message created by our cultural background.

PERSPECTIVES

When we share the gospel, we are not communicating in a vacuum. Part of communicating the gospel involves understanding others' perspectives, how people see things around them. It is a particular evaluation of a given situation or facts. According to Bullock, their upbringing, education, media exposure, personality type, self-concept, life stage, life experiences, spiritual gifting, and culture shape perspectives and values.[15]

As communicators we, too, have perspectives. If we see ourselves in a prophetic role, we are likely to confront. If we see ourselves as teachers, we are likely to inform. In dialogue, both our perspective and the perspective of the receptor are undergoing constant change.

When we share the gospel, people filter what we say through their personal point of view. For starters we should learn their significant life questions, religious backgrounds, values, world perspectives, interests, and perspective on Christ, Christians, and local Christian churches. People also have perspectives regarding God, us, their needs, their desires, their hurts, religion, and a host of other related matters. All of these impact how they decode the message we are attempting to send.

LANGUAGE FOR CLARITY (COL. 4:4; 1 COR. 1:17)

In addition to knowing the message and something of the filters of people's perspectives, we need to learn the language of the culture in which we will share the gospel.[16] We must start with language or vocabulary they understand so we might encode the message in a form that communicates to their culture. This is imperative. If we do not, then we cannot effectively communicate and clarify the message.

It would be unthinkable to go to China as a missionary from America without a background on the Chinese language, customs, and culture. Is it any more unthinkable that we prepackage a script and deliver it to all the peoples in the U.S. without understanding that a diverse group is receiving the message? I am reminded again that words have usages, not meanings apart from context.

Have you ever tried to share your faith without religious words? I encourage you to list all the spiritual words you know and then, using an interview format, ask people on the street to give you their understanding of the words. You get the point. We must take responsibility to understand how our message is being received by the culture in which we are speaking, starting with the terms we use.

The church's place in society has been called into question. Its message is not understood, and this involves almost every aspect of church life. Ron Hutchcraft said, "A lot of people are not rejecting our Christ, they are rejecting our vocabulary; they have no idea what we are talking about." As a group they do not understand our message, and it is our fault to large degree. All of our channels of communicating our message must be examined for clarity. This impacts our approaches to evangelism, preaching, and even our worship services.

A function of language is to allow us to check for clarity and for understanding. If we do not have understanding, we cannot move forward. Checking for clarity and for understanding involves more than asking yes/no questions or questions that can be answered with only a grunt. We check for understanding by listening with our ears and our eyes. We also need to ask good questions that allow people to explain their understanding.

TRUTH, VALUES, AND LIFE EXPERIENCES

Radical cultural change is not just a big city issue or a west coast issue. People everywhere are processing life in radically different ways. Cable TV, satellite dishes, and the Internet have not only brought America together but have also shaped the way we process truth and life. They have subtly influenced our values and thinking patterns. The media has been a primary source for the expanding influence of post-modernism, which has enhanced the speed of these changes.

Understanding how people process truth is important to effective communication. According to Yandall Woodfin, there are three channels of knowledge: (1) rational/reflective, (2) pragmatic, and (3) intuitive (affective domain).[17] These channels help people determine what is true and real. For modern man, the flow is from rational/reflective (logic) to pragmatic and intuitive. However, the order has been reversed for most postmodern men. They start with affective domain and move upward toward logic and reasoning. Those who have a postmodern paradigm place a higher value on experiences and relationships.

Truth/Reality Determination by Cultural Difference

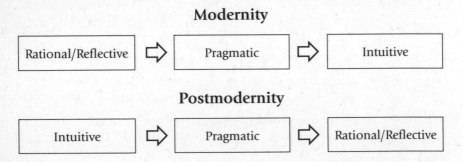

Modernity

| Rational/Reflective | ⇨ | Pragmatic | ⇨ | Intuitive |

Postmodernity

| Intuitive | ⇨ | Pragmatic | ⇨ | Rational/Reflective |

COMMUNICATING IN CULTURE

God is the creator of culture. By creating people, families, and communities of families, He created culture. By itself culture is neither positive nor negative. However, cultures are made up of sinful people who do act sinfully and who are in constant need of alignment to the will of God in how they relate to one another and to Him.

Christians cannot choose the context in which we carry out the Great Commission to make disciples of all nations. We cannot choose the worldviews of the people we seek to reach. However, Christians can choose how to respond to the various contexts in which we communicate God's message. America and the world are becoming more secular, urban, pluralistic, and postmodern. If this changing situation is examined through the eyes of the first century, we would see that the church can expand and thrive in the midst of a pluralistic society. The gospel spread through both the Jews and the Gentiles, the religious and the nonreligious. The early Christians found ways to communicate in their culture, and we can find ways to communicate in ours.[18]

Hugh Hewitt shared his insights on communicating in culture. He said, "Embarrassed believers have collectively lost their voice—their witness to the world in which they live—of a good news that transcends and transforms everyday life. Even if embarrassment at being thought slightly or greatly loony or out of touch can be overcome, then conviction to witness will have to be accompanied by new techniques of communicating the gospel. Luther needed German; Luthers of the twenty-first century will need all the techno-terms and immersion in the popular culture they can endure."[19]

COMMUNICATION AS BOTH SCIENCE AND ART

During the last half of the twentieth century, American evangelical Christians relied primarily on scientific facts, figures, and methods in our approaches to evangelism. This is not to say that there has been no creativity in our evangelistic approaches, but listen to the titles of some of the most popular gospel tracts: *4 Spiritual Laws, Steps to Peace with God, Do You Know for Sure?*

Science is part of what we get from modernity. There are many valuable contributions from scientific and logical thinking. However, not everything is scientific, and not everyone is wired for scientific methods of processing life and information. Some cultures of the world are more left-brain oriented, while other cultures seem to operate with a greater reliance and value on the activities of the right brain. America has been predominately left-brained in its approach to processing life, but a significant shift is taking place.

Postmodernism has its roots in artwork. Art has increased in value and use in postmodern culture. One way to sum up the modern mind-set is that it is an attempt to know empirically and rationally, to control and engineer reality. This is the work of the scientist. Another way to sum up the postmodern mind-set is that it is an insightful attempt to perceive, imagine, and create reality. This is the work of the artist.

Evangelism of the future will look more like an art form than a science formula. Learning to approach evangelism from this perspective is little known, even to our best modern evangelists. The unknown often leads to anxiety and fear, which contribute to our ineffectiveness in personal evangelism.

The goal of our evangelistic efforts will be the same, yet our approaches might have to be created on the fly. This is closer to the approaches in the early church, when they had to rely completely on the leading of the Holy Spirit and one another as they lived out their faith in front of their peers, the people they were trying to reach for Christ. In a highly scientific environment, the temptation has been for us to rely on slick, logical, precise presentations of the gospel.

There are components of the evangelistic encounter and training methods that we can teach with logic or reason and a set of methods. Yet the complexities of people's spiritual backgrounds will demand that we be more flexible. Personal evangelism of the past was described as making a "gospel presentation." This is scientific in its approach. Communicating the gospel message or sharing the gospel story is more artful in its nature.

COMMUNICATION AND CONTEXTUALIZATION: BILL BRIGHT'S INFLUENCE AND PASSION

Through Bill Bright's ministry, Campus Crusade for Christ, I learned to walk with Jesus and share my faith. I am forever indebted to his indirect but significant influence on my life and calling to vocational ministry. I cut my witnessing teeth sharing his tract, "The 4 Spiritual Laws."

This tract has been used to lead millions to Christ. However, this tract and CCC's primary evangelistic approach were developed within a given context. One of the aspects of that context was the emphasis on science and the laws of nature. There was a good match between cultural situation and the four laws. Today's context is different in most parts of the U.S. Modernism has lost much of its grip, especially on the younger generations.

While I believe that our evangelistic starting point has changed and the way lost people process information has changed, may we take the same passion Dr. Bright brought to evangelism! May we do in our generation what he did in his: develop contextually astute approaches for our culture and subcultures. Our role is to examine the culture not so we can bow to it but so we can communicate effectively in it. We must exegete not only the text but also the culture to which we are applying solid communication skills.

Postmodernism affects Americans individually and the church corporately at many different levels. David S. Dockery said, "Postmodernism is a new set of assumptions about reality, which goes far beyond mere relativism. It impacts our literature, our dress, our art, our architecture, our music, our sense of right and wrong, our self-identity, and our theology. Postmodernism tends to view human experience as incoherent, lacking absolutes in the area of truth and meaning. Goetz also noted that pastors are concerned at postmodernism's cavalier dismissal of absolute truth, given that Christianity rises or falls on the historicity of Jesus Christ. There's not much to cheer about in the claim that everything is relative, that nothing is secure. . . . And it certainly doesn't seem like much, an improvement on modernity."[20] However, in spite of the new challenges which postmodernism brings, it also brings rich opportunities for evangelistic witness.

TWO BIBLICAL EXAMPLES

The Bible reveals the importance of communication in your context. We have four different Gospels that were designed in the mind of God to communicate in contextually sensitive ways. Each Gospel was fashioned and arranged to speak to the peoples to which it was written.

Peter and Paul are two examples of effective contextualized communicators. They approached the communication of the gospel message in radically different ways. Acts 2:14–41 reveals the story of Peter preaching in a public forum, calling the Jewish people from every nation and residence of Jerusalem to accept Jesus as the Messiah and to repent. He referenced familiar Old Testament passages and used the promise of a coming Messiah in order to resonate with his particular audience.

Paul took the same message but communicated it in a thoroughly different form as revealed in Acts 17:16–34. In this passage we see Paul reasoning with the Jews, the God-fearing Greeks, and those in the marketplace. He did this not in one big preaching event, but day by day. With the philosophers who debated him, Paul engaged in reasoning in multiple encounters. Paul started by learning the religious beliefs and customs of his listeners. He affirmed their efforts and yet informed them that their unknown god was actually Jesus Christ. He started with the known and then moved to the unknown and the spiritual.[21]

Peter and Paul both adjusted their communication in many ways to fit their audience. One of the first rules of public speaking is to know your audience. In the next two chapters we will examine communication inside and outside of our most natural contexts.

CHAPTER 5

Communicating Inside Your Context

I N THIS CHAPTER WE WILL EXAMINE FACETS of communication with people who are inside our context. Our context contains people who are influenced by both modernity and postmodernity. Some primarily interact with people who process life through influences of the Enlightenment that aided in the development of modernity. Others of us have known little outside the deconstructive influence of postmodernity. The societal context of American adults contains both.

TODAY'S CULTURE AND CONTEXT

Today's culture is influenced by both modernity and postmodernity. We are a mixed bag.

MODERNISM OVERVIEW

Modernity started around the Renaissance and the Reformation. Modernity was built on scientific discovery, truth, individualism, and human progress. Modernists believed that man could perceive and know absolute truth simply through the rational mind.

Modernists believed that rational thought was the ultimate way to arrive at truth. We need to be logical, but modernists carried it to the extreme. They rejected faith (since it is "illogical") and ultimately declared that "God is dead." Modernism attempted to build a future on the progress of man while denying the existence of God, yet it failed to realize that people could not be satisfied with a spiritual void in their heart. Modernity left people spiritually bankrupt and searching.

Our world and people are changing rapidly. However, our message and task have not changed. We are called to communicate effectively the hope of Jesus Christ within us and to encourage people to follow Christ in a dynamic relationship with Him and others. So we should seek to understand the people in our context.

Marks of Modernity

Many authors have summarized the dominant influences of modernism. David J. Bosch describes seven cardinal convictions arising out of the Enlightenment:

1. Its emphasis on *reason* suggested that the human mind was the indubitable point of departure for all knowing.
2. It divided all of reality into thinking *subjects* and, over against these, *objects* that could be analyzed and exploited.
3. It dropped all reference to *purpose* and viewed every process only in terms of cause and effect.
4. It put a high premium on *progress*, expansion, advance, and modernization.
5. It proceeded from the assumption that all true knowledge was *factual, value-free,* and *neutral.* Over against *facts* there were *values,* which were not objectively true, the holding of which was, therefore, a matter of taste. Religion was, in the course of time, relegated to this category.
6. The Enlightenment proceeded from the assumption that *all problems were in principle solvable.*
7. It regarded people as *emancipated, autonomous individuals,* no longer under the tutelage of "superiors."[1]

For many, modernity did not deliver on its unstated promise. James Emory White said, "Rather than enhancing personal satisfaction and fulfillment, it has proven to be a barren wasteland. Moral relativism has led to a crisis in values; autonomous individualism has led to a lack of vision; narcissistic hedonism has created empty souls; and reductive naturalism has proven inadequate for human experience."[2] The conversion growth numbers of the churches in America indicate that Christians have not effectively presented a spiritual alternative worthy of the attention of those who were left searching from modernity or those who are embracing aspects of postmodernity.[3]

POSTMODERNISM OVERVIEW

Postmodernism

Postmodernity is a new approach to processing life, yet a clear understanding of this term is still lacking. J. I. Packer, theologian at Regent College, noted that postmodernism has never secured a dictionary definition and was quoted as saying, "Postmodernism is a throw-away word that means everything and nothing."[4] Postmodernism is a twentieth-century development that is impossible to describe precisely. The purpose of this section is to acknowledge that people use the term in different ways and to highlight a few common usages of this term.[5]

Postmodernity arises out of the recognition that something was terribly wrong with the living out of modernity.[6] Therefore, it is a rejection of many components of modernity. Much that was thought to be absolute is now being debated and reexamined. Postmodernity highlights experience, subjective knowledge, community, and preference.

Postmodernism is a moving and multifaceted target, not a rigidly designed package of thought. Some have described it as an attitude. Others describe it in terms of a negation of various aspects of modernism. Still others such as Thomas C. Oden discuss postmodernity in terms of a time span, an ideological spell, and a moral spinout.[7]

Many authors have attempted to summarize the dominant themes of postmodernism. David L. Goetz noted that postmodernism has at least two distinctives: "First, postmodernism doesn't put much stock in the progress of humankind, that things will be getting better anytime soon. Modernity believed science would save the world. Today, science by no means is dead; it still rules in the universities. But the postmodern outlook has nicked it."[8] "Another distinctive that gets a lot of press is the postmodern notion that all truth, even to some extent scientific knowledge, is biased and socially constructed. That is, truths are relative and depend on what one's culture regards as truth."[9]

Postmodernity influences a range of people, from those with little exposure to it to those who are completely immersed in it. There are both positive and negative implications for evangelism.

SHIFT FROM MODERN TO POSTMODERN

Modernity and postmodernity mean different things. An illustration might help us grasp the difference. I was a former Mississippi State University baseball pitcher in the mid-1980s, so Walter Anderson's story communicates to me.

Three umpires were sitting around before a game talking about their job. The first umpire [thoroughly modern] said, "There are balls and there are strikes and *I call them.*" The second umpire [a bit of both] said, "There are balls and there are strikes and *I call them as I see* them." The last umpire [thoroughly postmodern] said, "There are balls and there are strikes, and *they aren't anything till I call them.*"

Modernism involved *construction*, which means to give things meaning. It is the building of new things. Postmodernism is based on *deconstruction* or questioning meaning. It breaks ideas and once-held truths into small parts (fragmentation). A commonly held belief that postmodernists emphatically reject the idea of absolute truth or universal morals is not accurate. They reject any one individual's ability and right to determine absolute truth for another person.

THE ART OF PERSONAL EVANGELISM

Almost everything is now being debated and reexamined because postmodernity challenges everything that was thought to be true. The problem is, postmodernism also leaves people spiritually bankrupt. Foolishly, people are trying to *reconstruct* their broken lives with experience as the final arbiter of truth.

A danger always exists when one tries to generalize, but in an effort to give his readers some useful handles, Jimmy Long summarized the differences or the changes from modernism to postmodernism.

Modernism	Postmodernism
From Truth	to Preference
From Autonomous Self	to Community
From Scientific Discovery	to Virtual Reality
From Human Progress	to Human Misery[10]

One of my assumptions (perspectives) in dealing with the typical lost person is that they are farther from God and the church than in recent decades. I have a presentation entitled, "This Cannot Be Your Father's Evangelism and Why." In it I demonstrate that in several respects the typical lost American is farther away from a true understanding and commitment to Christ because of pluralism and lack of biblical knowledge and influence. Therefore, our personal evangelism approaches must now include an acknowledgement of the increased role of the process of evangelism.

RESPONSES TO POSTMODERNISM

William Grassie noted:

On the one hand, postmodernism and deconstruction are celebrated as the end of philosophical self-delusion, a critical attack on all oppressive metanarratives, and the final dissolution of foundational thought. On the other hand, postmodernism and deconstruction are denounced as relativistic, nihilistic, irrational, and hyperrational. The inaccessible philosophic language of most post-modern thinkers and the heated confusion about what postmodernism represents make it difficult for the average professor teaching a science-and-religion class to acquire a working overview. And yet, at least a cursory understanding of these debates is essential to any discussion of science and religion in the late twentieth century.[11]

How has the church responded, and how should the church respond to these changes? The church has not been effective in the last several decades in evangelizing an America that has been dominated by modern thinking. Now that America is becoming more postmodern, the church must respond. The church can over or under respond to postmodernism.

Five Possible Responses

Christians are to be neither modern nor postmodern in our thinking patterns or lifestyles. Our goal is not to hold tightly to the philosophy of the past or wholeheartedly embrace the latest worldview but to become biblical in how we see the world. Like Paul in Athens (Acts 17), we live in a culture that has the potential to pull us away from God's desired purpose. So how should the Christian church respond to the challenges posed by postmodernism? There are no easy answers, no easy solutions.

There are at least five possible responses to postmodernity, which were the same options the church had when modernity came on the scene.

1. *Deny, ignore it.* To ignore the emerging postmodern culture seems to deny the reality of its existence and therefore forfeit our impact on the people who reside in the culture.

2. *Build up fortress—sectarianism.* To shore up a fortress does not take seriously the command to go into the world to evangelize and disciple the nations.

3. *Fight against it.* At times resistance is needed, but as a primary strategy, it seems to sidetrack us from the focus on Christ and the gospel.

4. *Adopt it, embrace the cultural changes.* To embrace all aspects of the postmodern culture seems to ignore the dangers.

5. *Adapt to it.* Be missional in our approach. This is the response that is most consistent with the heart of God and the mission of the church.

Three Primary Dangers

Three major dangers appear when reflecting on how the church can respond to postmodernism: the first two are syncretism and sectarianism. Syncretism is absorbing all the values of the culture. It is dangerous for the church simply to adopt the new culture that is developing. Sectarianism is rejecting everything in society. It is also dangerous to retreat and disengage from the people we are called to reach. John exhorted us to "be in the world" and yet "not of this world." Both parts of this passage apply.

A third danger is holding to our forms of ministry so tightly that we forget the real function of the church. Forms should always follow functions. Forms can become comfortable and therefore ineffective substitutes for the real thing. The danger occurs when we begin to be more passionate about forms (styles, rituals, practices, times, methods, etc.) than we are about being the church to the people who need Christ.[12]

The call is to embrace the biblical mandate to make more and better disciples, regardless of the form it takes. Christ gave His life for people and the church. Should Christians not be willing to sacrifice personal cultural preferences and comforts like missionaries around the world do every day to reach those who do not know Him?

ASSUMPTIONS: MOVING THE STARTING LINE

Every gospel proclamation and tract makes certain assumptions, often so subtle that we do not even detect them. The gospel message is then constructed in light of these assumptions. Let me illustrate this through the four spiritual laws. Law 1 says that God loves you and has a wonderful plan for your life. Certainly Christians all agree with this statement. What assumptions are being made here? Did you see them? The assumptions are that the listener believes God exists; there is one God and a certain type of God. This assumption is not bad or wrong; it just needs to be checked against the interpretive framework of the lost person.

ASSUMPTIONS ABOUT GOD

Many of our evangelistic approaches and materials were built on assumptions that were more valid in the 1950s, at least in the Bible Belt. We can no longer use those assumptions. Before we propose some reasonable assumptions for today, let's think about the past.

When people generalize, they generally get it wrong. So I encourage you to work through your thoughts regarding assumptions, but here are some I think we could reasonably make in the 1950s. I would like to think of these in three categories because there have been significant shifts in these areas: (1) how people view Christ/God, (2) how people view the church, and (3) how people view their spiritual searches and options.

In the 1950s, as compared to the early part of the twenty-first century, there was (1) a higher level of trust in the reliability of the Bible itself and its ability to speak to life issues, (2) a higher percentage of people who owned and read the Bible, (3) some understanding of the deity of Christ, (4) a higher level of respect and trust in religious leaders and religious people, (5) a higher regard for the local church and its members, (6) for most people a positive background or experience with the local church, (7) a belief that if you were spiritually searching, it was toward the local Christian church, and (8) a belief that if you were spiritually searching, it was toward a monotheistic view of God.

People were lost, but in terms of Engel's scale, they were closer to the line of conversion. Methodologically, our approaches and tracts and training were designed primarily to help people cross the line of conversion. Therefore, process was not as important in evangelism as it is today. In essence, the people had been in process through the various systems that were communicating and upholding some of the messages Christians were attempting to communicate.

PRESENT ASSUMPTIONS

The assumptions from the 1950s are not valid today. People know less about God the Father, Christ, the local church, and the teachings of the Bible than ever before in American history. Pluralism has made people more aware of and has given people more options in every area of life, including spiritual choices. People today can consider themselves spiritual completely apart from the local church, especially the Christian church. This great divorce between being spiritual and having a connection with a local church presents new challenges. People have many different views of "god," often even conflicting views within their own minds, and yet they do not see a problem with their view. Therefore, process in evangelism is increasingly important for lost people and for us as we share the gospel.

Is it possible that our assumptions about our listeners' backgrounds should change based on these changes? Absolutely. When several generations are ignorant of basic Christian beliefs, have almost no Christian memory, know little about Jesus, have lost a sense of guilt, and have many contradictory spiritual views, we should carefully examine the communication of our message.

I am reminded of political pundits on TV talking about whether candidates were "on message." Through the course of campaigns, candidates have to talk about a great number of different issues. However, they usually have a central message that they want to communicate. If the candidate is not careful, he or she will get sidetracked from the central, on-point message. Because we live in spiritually turbulent times like today, it is essential that we get back on point with our message.

CHANGING PERSPECTIVES: HOW PEOPLE SEE THEMSELVES

Typically individuals see themselves as the final arbiter of truth and reality. They process life through their own experiences and logical faculties. Extreme individualism is not a healthy perspective and presents some challenges as we attempt to introduce people to God through a relationship with Jesus Christ. Newbigin said, "The old patterns of belief and behavior that ruled because they were not questioned have largely dissolved. Each person makes his or her own decisions about what to believe and how to behave."[13] This is especially true if you are a member of the dominant culture group.

If you are a part of a small subculture, however, you begin to think more in terms of the group.[14] An individual's processes for making decisions, determining facts, and setting values flows through the filters of how it affects the group and how the group is responding. As Christians seek to communicate the gospel to people who value community, current postmodern people among others, we will have to consider the negative ramifications of sharing our message from an extremely individualistic perspective.

People today want to live guilt free. American pop culture has skyrocketed the value of tolerance. This has led to the almost complete elimination of the concept of sin. The value of tolerance has moved through several phases to the point where not only are we expected to tolerate the views and practices of others, but we are also expected to celebrate the fact that they have them. To offer a different view of reality or practice is now seen as a moral and social taboo.

The problem with wanting to live guilt free is that we do not use good judgment and that we evaluate others in hopes that they will overlook our faults as well. Another problem with this is that God sees everything. Also, something inside most of us knows that if we just ignore our guilt, it will not go away. Consequently, we seek spiritual outlets in various forms. Today when that happens, the Christian church is seen as a less than desirable place in which to search for spiritual answers.

People usually move within and among at least three views of themselves. Some people are happy and healthy, so they see little need for God. Others are in crisis and hurting, so they look for almost any solution to ease their pain. Still others view themselves as searching and longing for something more. This can include a search for spiritual wholeness or something more in life. People are more receptive to spiritual matters when they are either hurting or searching.

Most people today, especially those under forty, consider themselves spiritual as opposed to religious. This does not mean they are following Christ. While modernity challenged the existence of God, that aspect of being lost has changed. People reared in a postmodern culture usually believe in some form of "god." Instead of questioning the existence of God, they are more likely to ask which god and how they become one than for proof about the existence of God.

MISSIONARIES

The task before God's church in America is not one that is foreign to missionaries who have served abroad among people of various political, social, economic, and religious cultures. Our missionaries have been seeking ways to interpret and contextualize the message for people who have different lenses from which to perceive reality.[15]

Lesslie Newbigin shared from his missionary experience: "On the other hand, we have had a plethora of studies by missionaries on the theological issues raised by cross-cultural missions. As Western missionaries have shared in the general weakening of confidence in our modern Western culture, they have become more aware of the fact that in their presentation of the gospel they have often confused culturally conditioned perceptions with the substance of the gospel, and thus wrongfully claimed divine authority for the relativities of one culture."[16]

What I am suggesting—that we help people make sense of the gospel in order to lead them to a saving, dynamic relationship with Jesus Christ—has been the practice of missionaries throughout the ages. Missionaries translate within human limitations, but in the power of the Holy Spirit, the life-giving message of Christ to people just as they are and based on a growing understanding of the lost person or group.

EVANGELISTIC COMPARISON IN OUR TWO CULTURES

Brian McLaren, in his book *Church on the Other Side,* made the statement, "If you have a new world, you need a new church. You have a new world."[17] Recognizing the limits of the statement, if you have different kinds of lost people, you need different approaches to personal evangelism—not a different objective of evangelism but a different approach.

POSSIBLE STARTING POINTS

The starting point for spiritual conversations is changing. Most lost people are not ready to work from a Judeo-Christian understanding of God and a common Christian understanding of Jesus Christ or the Bible. Therefore, the evangelistic conversation must start closer to Genesis than Romans.

Modernity	Postmodernity
Heaven or hell	Significance, meaning, purpose
The Bible	Life issues
Our agenda	Their situation
Universal truths (death, taxes)	Personal examples
"Nice to meet you"	"Because we are friends, I . . ."
Confrontational	Relational
Church or religious topics/experiences	Spiritual topics and experiences
"How do you stand with God?"	"Describe your spiritual journey."
Jesus	God

Giving information	Asking inquiring questions
Having the right words	Living the right way
John 3:16; Romans 3:23	Genesis 1:1; Jeremiah 28:11
Gospel facts	Gospel's impact and testimony

QUESTIONS/ISSUES FOR LOST PEOPLE

The questions and issues for lost people have changed. I am not sure that we are listening to the questions any longer. Is it possible that in our effort to communicate we are simply shouting our answers at a higher pitch?

Modernity	Postmodernity
Is Christianity rational?	Do you care about me?
How do I know there is a God?	What is my purpose in life?
Are miracles possible?	Is there ultimate meaning?
Do science and Scripture conflict?	How can I experience God?
Are Christianity's claims valid?	How can I become God/ get right with God?
Why does God allow suffering and evil?[18]	Is Jesus the only way to God?
What are the essentials of the gospel?	Do Christian claims match my experience?
Are the gospel essentials true?	Are gospel essentials real? (Do they make a difference)
Is it worth the sacrifice to follow Christ?	Integrity—does it work?
Has no one told them about Jesus?	Which god?
Is the Bible trustworthy?	What can God do for me?
Evolution—(Bible versus science)	Which religion is right for me?
Gospel facts	Which holy book is right?

Not enough answers to questions	No one has shown them Jesus
Existence of God	Poor image of the church
Can't explain God	Lack of credibility of Christians
Suffering in the world	Not enough mystery of God[19]
Bible versus science	Make sense of life, TV, virtual reality
Darwinism	Make order/meaning out of chaos
	Exclusivity of Christ in the midst of pluralism
	Terminology/understanding a message
	Looking for hope
	Bible versus Experience
	Connecting with God

I believe the ultimate, deep questions of life do not change, but the initial questions are radically different as the starting point is further away from a biblical understanding of God and in the twentieth century. Only after the initial questions are addressed do lost people begin to consider and to ask about the answers to their deeper questions.

EXPLORATORY QUESTIONS

I learned to share my faith by asking the Evangelism Explosion diagnostic (those with an asterisk in the following list) questions and a couple of other similar questions. These questions can still be used today. However, I believe there are other questions that will get to the same end more effectively and with greater receptivity.

It is possible to shut down a person's openness to hear the gospel by the way we approach them. Lest we blame them for causing us to rethink our starting of spiritual conversations, who are we to tell lost people how to receive our benevolent efforts? We should seek, knowing we will fail at times, to communicate in ways that give us the best opportunity to share the gospel.

Modernity	Postmodernity
Are you saved?	Do you think much about spiritual things?
Are you born again?	Where are you on your spiritual journey?
*On a scale of one to one hundred, how sure are you that if you died you would spend eternity in heaven?	Has your spiritual journey answered your deepest questions and life issues?
*Have you come to a place in your spiritual life where you know for certain you have eternal life, or is that something you're still working on?	Have you found the meaning and purpose of life?
*Suppose you were to die tonight and stand before God, and He were to ask you, "Why should I let you into My heaven?" What would you say?	Tell me your spiritual story.
Are you a Christian?	Do you consider yourself a religious person?
Do you love/know Jesus?	To you, who is Jesus?
Do you want to go to heaven?	What is your understanding about God?
You don't want to go to hell, do you?	What is your religious background?
Where do you go to church?	Why are we here?

Do you believe in Jesus?

What happens to us when we die?

What is your favorite part of (their holy book)?

Tell me more about

_____.

What do you think is wrong with the world?

What shape do you see the world in?

Is there absolute truth?

Who am I? (and) What am I doing here?

HOW TO DETERMINE TRUTH

Truth is certainly determined differently than before. For many people, even the concept of truth is relative. One twenty-two-year-old female, when asked about absolute truth, replied, "I believe in an individual absolute truth." However, for most postmodern, what is *real* is more important than what is *true*. The shift in how people determine truth has produced a significant challenge to our evangelism. We can no longer easily present a message of Christ with credibility and believability to this audience without living out the message in front of them.

In the past, Christians could say, "Thus saith the Lord" and "It is true, so you must believe it." Jesus said, "By this all men will know that you are my disciples, if you love one another" (John 13:35). Could it also be true that if we do not love one another, people will struggle to know that we are His disciples, and even worse, whether Jesus is the one real God?

Bill Easum stated that "the early settlers of North America established European systems all of which were based on a Germanic education based on intellect, authoritarian posture, and distrust of the laity. Reality was processed through the *head to the heart*. Today, indigenous ministry requires church leaders to reach unchurched people through the heart not the head, develop teams and collaboration, credentials aren't as important as holiness, and to mobilize the laity. The three primary traits of successful local church ministries are emotive, immediate, and trust. Reality is processed today more through the heart and through the head. In the industrial world the best way to reach people was through the head to the heart. Today, the best way to reach people is through the *heart to the head*."[20]

Modernity	Postmodernity
Facts	Relationships
Science	Community
Linear thinking	Friends
History	Does it work?
Archaeology	Experience
What see	Pragmatism
Natural	Supernatural
Logic	Conflicting views
Absolute truth	Unclarified views
Human progress	TV in some respects
Does it help me achieve my individual goals?	Preferences
	Groupthink
	Fractured thinking patterns
	Virtual reality

KEY PASSAGES

Using the Bible with good judgment is always helpful in sharing the gospel. For moderns who have some familiarity with the Bible and the story of Christ, it was appropriate to start with Scriptures from John or Romans. It is not wrong to share these verses with those who have grown up outside the shadow of the Christian church, but we need to clarify that we share a common understanding about any religious terms or biblical concepts. In terms of Scripture memorization, we need to beef up the number of verses from which we can share God's story so that people might see themselves in God's redemptive plan.

Modernity	Postmodernity
John 3:16	Those used in modernity plus
Romans 3:23	Jeremiah 29:11–13
Romans 6:23	Genesis 1:1–2:3
Romans 5:8–10	Genesis 2:3f
Romans 10:9–10	Deuteronomy 29:29
Ephesians 2:8–9	Luke 19:10
John 10:10	2 Corinthians 5:16–20
1 John 5:11–13	Luke 15
1 John 1:9	John 1:1
John 14:6	John 4
See old tracts	Psalm 139
	Acts 17
	Overview of biblical story

STRATEGY CHOICES FOR OUR CONTEXT

George Barna conducted the largest marketing research project on the Southern Baptist Convention that has ever been done. His findings substantiate the fact that Christians, the church, and the SBC in America are suffering from a public image problem. The fact that no county in America is more churched than it was in the mid 1980s supports this fact. The church is even seen by many as being on the wrong side of moral issues. This has greatly affected the church's ability to use one of the three major categories of evangelism, *attraction strategies.*

Attraction strategies involve getting lost people to come to our buildings to hear about Christ. Some churches are using this strategy with some effectiveness, but most pastors and churches are not capable of attracting large numbers of people based on what they are offering in their services.

This leaves most churches with two other options for evangelism. They can use either *media strategies* or *projection strategies.* Most churches are not in a financial position or do not have the media expertise to do quality media evangelism. So most churches are left with trying to make projection strategies work for them. Projection approaches involve resourcing the church laity to carry the gospel to the world of lost people instead of waiting for the lost world to come to it (attraction). The church must find a way to penetrate the lost world or to project the message outside the walls of the church.

Christians and the church in America are suffering from a public image problem. I am not placing my hopes in the media, our government, or other institutions like public schools to solve this problem for us. So what is the church to do? Is all lost? Can we recover? Do we or should we even care?

Tip O'Neill was the former Democratic speaker of the House of Representatives. He made a statement about politics that has great application for the church today. O'Neil said, "All politics is local." When the public image is poor or our big services and events are not attracting lost people, the church can go straight to the heart of lost people. All Christian influence can be local and personal.

WINNING FRIENDS, RELATIVES, COWORKERS, AND STRANGERS

For some of us, sharing Jesus with those who know us best is difficult. Others find witnessing to strangers to be among their greatest fears. Let's examine the issues involved in both of these witnessing environments.

SHARING WITH THOSE WHO KNOW YOU BEST

Family and Close Friends

There is some truth in the saying, "You can fool some of the people some of the time, but you can't fool all the people all the time." Fooling family members and close friends is especially difficult. People determine credibility on several levels. They examine the messenger, the message, and the method used. If the messenger of Christ is not credible in the eyes of their lost family members and friends, seeing them come to Christ will be difficult.

Personal Credibility. A friend grew up in a Catholic family with a mom who was particularly faithful to the church. However, in his late teens he received Christ in a personal way. His mother's heart was bruised because, as she watched him leave the Catholic Church, she interpreted his excitement as her failure in his religious training. One Saturday he was in his bedroom reading his Bible when his mother walked in and said, "If you believed what is in that book, you would be outside helping your father cut the grass."

Broken Relationship. A prerequisite to evangelism with family and friends is relational credibility. Where relationships are broken and strained, there is little chance for us to reach those closest to us unless we first address the relationship issues. We can do this by assuming responsibility for the broken relationship and seeking forgiveness. This can be done even if we are not at fault, because fault is really not the primary issue; the broken relationship should move us toward reconciliation.

Long-Term Silence. What are we to do when we have remained silent about Christ for the entire relationship but then become concerned about a lost person close to us? A direct and honest approach is helpful in this situation. We can say something like, "I need to ask you for your forgiveness. We have known each other for a long time, and I value our relationship, yet I have remained silent about the most important aspect of my life." If you sense the time is right, you can add, "I have committed my love and life to Jesus Christ, and this has radically impacted my life." If the Spirit is not leading you to share at that moment, you can say, "I would love to schedule some time with you to talk about it in the near future."

Coworkers

In order to evangelize coworkers, employers, or employees, we must have developed credibility with them. The items discussed in the previous section are still important, but there are work-related considerations to build credibility. Professional integrity needs to match our verbal witness.

Think about what others have to do and be for you to listen to them on such important matters as their spiritual life and destiny. This is an important matter. Lost people are wise to use good judgment in choosing who they listen to for spiritual insights.

People around us at work observe us in many different settings. They watch how we handle relationships, conflict, stress, success, and how we respond to those who work above and below us. They also look to see how we handle our work responsibilities. If we are late, leave early, cheat on expense reports, give less than a full effort, or do lousy work, we will have limited credibility as we share Christ. If we are harsh to employees, show unjustified favoritism, or serve as the water fountain gossip, we have erected an unnecessary barrier to our sharing the gospel as we represent Christ before them in such a poor fashion.

SHARING WITH THOSE WHOM YOU DO NOT KNOW WELL

Most of our efforts in personal evangelism have been targeted toward people we do not know. As a primary strategy, this dramatically limits the number of Christians willing to be involved in evangelism. Using this as a primary strategy makes difficult our task of making disciples. The ability to assimilate and disciple converts from efforts with strangers is dramatically reduced because the new convert does not have a web of relationships with people connected with the church or even the person who led them to Christ.

However, we cannot establish a long-term relationship with everyone who needs Christ. As the Holy Spirit leads, we can develop a rapport with strangers and capitalize on interactions with casual acquaintances to communicate the hope that is within us, at least parts of it. We can establish rapport by talking about common experiences. The acrostic FIST may be helpful to remember: family, interests, spiritual experience, and tell the story of Christ.

Many of our neighbors are casual acquaintances. We can take intentional steps to express interest by being a good neighbor, doing small acts of kindness, and demonstrating interest and concern for them. Kindness is so rare that it is usually noticed and is attractive. Maybe you will develop a several-month plan to enter the world of your neighbors to touch them with the love of Christ. We can reach out to them individually, as a family, or in conjunction with other Christian neighbors.[21]

People have realistic and unrealistic expectations of Christians and how they should behave in given situations. It is impossible for us to meet everyone's expectations, especially the ones that are unknown. We never know when someone is watching us.

A pastor went to a store to make a purchase. He got to his car, checked his purchase and receipt. He noticed that the clerk had not charged him for one of the items. He returned inside to pay for the item. When he returned to the store, the clerk said, "I know the item was left off. I did it on purpose to see if you practice what you preach." Granted, the pastor may not have checked his receipts, and the clerk would have made an unfair negative assessment but an assessment regardless.

Most people are unwilling to listen to a stranger talk about such a serious topic in a presentation form. However, if we demonstrate interest in those we meet, they are likely to be open to hearing our story, including the parts about the transforming power of Jesus. If there is limited time, you may not get the chance to share your testimony. In this situation, look for an appropriate opportunity to say a positive word about Jesus or pass along a point of contact if you can serve them in some way.

If a newly met person surrenders to Christ, the challenge in this situation is in the area of follow-up. This is also true if the person is open to further dialogue about Christ. The witness will have to be intentional about either connecting with the new believer in the future or helping the person to make a connection with a church in his or her area.

CONCLUSIONS

From interviewing college students, one of my students, who serves as a campus minister, came to the following conclusions.

One conclusion is that people are all spiritual in some form. There is within us the spiritual quest that drives us to search for answers that originate outside of ourselves.

A second conclusion is that many people are searching in the wrong places because they have a mistrust of the church and the teachings about God. Hollywood and TV have shaped most of our students' beliefs about the nature of God more than the teachings of the Bible or any other religious literature.

A third conclusion is that students have a positive idea about the nature of Christ that must be used to lead to a personal conviction about the true meaning of His life and death as more than just a good example to follow. To accomplish this we must meet the students where they are and begin a relationship with them that will allow us to earn the right by our convictions to share the real truth about Jesus with them.

My final conclusion from this assignment is that people do not mind sharing their ideas about spiritual matters, but they do not want to get into a debate with a stranger about this deeply personal area in their life.[22]

Opportunities and challenges are before the church of America. We should face the opportunities before us with anticipation. James Hampton noted, "Postmoderns want something bigger than themselves in their lives. They're starving for encounters with the living Christ—and try Buddha, the New Age movement, and countless other belief systems. It's an all-out, unashamed effort to fill the spiritual voids they know exist inside themselves."[23] And we have what they are looking for!

I think the churches of America can benefit from the jolt postmodernism has brought. The potential freshness and the discovery of some lost biblical emphases will probably occur with the arrival of converted postmoderns to our churches.

Postmodern people generally start further away from Christ than their predecessors and therefore will usually take longer in surrendering their life to Christ.[24] So Christians will have to be intentional about developing relationships and planting seeds through servant and ministry evangelism projects. I hope that their slower process will lead to more contemplative decisions and stronger commitments when they do trust Christ and become disciples.

The gospel message will center on the person and uniqueness of Christ. The three primary delivery systems will be (1) narratives, parables, and testimonies, (2) creative worship appealing to all the senses, and (3) authentic community in the forms of meaningful, safe small-group experiences for discovery and development of relationships with one another and God and conducting acts of community service.[25]

What an opportunity! In a postmodern world Christianity has a seat at the table. It is up to the church to determine what it does with this offer from the spiritually searching.[26]

CHAPTER 6

Communicating Christ Outside Your Context

NOT ALL THE EVANGELISTIC CONVERSATIONS we have are with modern or postmodern adults like ourselves. Evangelism also occurs with people who do not share a similar stage of life, philosophical perspective, or cultural background.

A report by George Barna indicates that if we do not reach a person for Christ by the age of fourteen, the chance of reaching the person for Christ dramatically decreases. Less than a decade ago, the age was seventeen before the chance of reaching them was dramatically reduced, but we are now struggling to reach youth in addition to adults. This trend toward the necessity of reaching people at younger and younger ages is frightening in light of the New Testament pattern of significant adult evangelization.

Are we in danger of being accused of possessing a message that can only be used to fool the young, but with adults the Christian message and lifestyle do not work? Teens are dropping out of church at staggering rates. Younger adults can scarcely be found in a majority of churches. As my younger students say, "What's up with that?"

In spite of the need to be effective in evangelizing adults, our children and youth are God-created gems who need Christ. God has entrusted their care to us, and we as adults should honor that trust by effectively communicating Christ with them. Also, people outside our culture and subculture need Christ. In this chapter we will overview communicating across age groups and cultural barriers.

COMMUNICATING ACROSS AGE GROUPS

CHILDREN

As a pastor I felt somewhat inadequate in skillfully dealing with the unique needs of children, partly because of the mistakes and abuses I had observed. I have seen excessive pressure placed on children. I have talked with children who claimed to have received Christ but had no clue about what they were doing. Another pastor in the region negatively impacted my church's Backyard Bible Clubs because he baptized a child after a VBS without the permission of the parents.

As the father of three young girls, I have a strong desire to see children and youth come to faith in Christ. There are many benefits in coming to know and grow in Christ at an early age. Children are more easily reached and taught than adults. When children trust Christ, not only is their eternal destiny changed, but also almost every aspect of their life on earth will be positively impacted.

Spiritual Condition of Children

There are unique issues in making disciples of children. However, children are in the same spiritual condition as adults. They have the same sin problem and need for salvation. Children will receive the same consequences if they die without Christ and the same reward if they die with Christ. Children are completely saved by grace through the working and gifting of the Holy Spirit just like adults.

The gospel essentials are the same for children. They receive Christ like adults, but the difference lies in how the gospel is presented to them. Children need us to paint a picture, as they process what is true, because they process differently from adults.

Select Considerations in Evangelism with Children

Counseling children about Christ brings several potential problems. First, there is little information from the Bible on the conversion of children. Second, parents and churches can pressure children to make a profession prior to their being ready to make such a commitment. Children can be more easily manipulated than adults, so we need to be careful how we use their psychological needs in order to share the gospel. Third, other parents are overly guarded and do not discuss or allow anyone else to discuss Christ with their child. Fourth, in some denominations there is a trend toward baptizing children at younger ages.[1]

Developmental Makeup of Children

Each child is unique and learns at a different pace, but there are common developmental factors in how children process and perceive. Children are concrete, literal, and simplistic in their thinking processes. Until around age twelve, it is difficult for a child to handle abstract thoughts such as those involved with salvation. Therefore, children need us to draw a picture to see, not just expound on, theological concepts. Children have basic psychological needs: to belong, to achieve, freedom from fear, love and affection, freedom from guilt, and ability to contribute.[2] Each need can be an effective tool for evangelism, but a witness can easily abuse each one during an evangelistic encounter.

Keep in mind that each child is an individual. We should be sensitive to the particular developmental stage of the child to whom we are witnessing, and continue to check for understanding at each major aspect of the gospel message.

Assessing Readiness

My own seven-year-old Macy is asking her mother and me about baptism. We share her anticipation about this, but she is not ready to surrender to Christ. Her mother and I continually monitor her readiness. It has been interesting to listen to her two older sisters trying to explain the gospel to her.

There is no single way to assess readiness, but there are some good questions you can ask and some signs to look for in your child. Ask children open-ended questions, not yes-no questions. Rather than ask questions such as, "Do you believe Jesus died and rose again to pay for your sins?" ask questions such as, "Who is Jesus? Why did He have to die? What happened to Jesus after He died? What do you want Jesus to do for you today?"[3]

Here is a list of other questions that you may find helpful.

- What would you like to talk to me about?
- What do you think it means to be a Christian?
- What made you think about this? When do you think about this? How long have you been thinking about this?
- What else do you know about being a Christian?
- How would you describe God?
- How do you think God feels about you?
- Who do you think God is?
- Why do you think a person needs to become a Christian?
- Let's pretend that a friend of yours at school asks you to tell him what it means to become a Christian. What would you tell him?
- What other things are you wondering about?[4]

There are several signs that may indicate a growing readiness to receive Christ.

1. *A change in disposition*. Serious meditation, sober thoughts, or expressions of worry could evidence a conviction of the Holy Spirit.

2. *An inquiring mind.* Questions concerning church membership, baptism, forgiveness, the resurrection of Jesus, or death could indicate an interest in salvation. Be aware that such questions may only indicate a growing interest and not an immediate readiness.

3. *The development of concepts.* An ability to explain adequately the person and work of God, Christ, or the

Holy Spirit, or a clear understanding of the nature of sin may indicate readiness.[5]

What They Must Understand

Because many children are eager to accept Christ in order to please an adult or to copy the actions of a sibling or friend, they must clearly understand their own personal need for Christ. They must understand that Jesus is the only way of salvation. They need to know what it means to trust Christ.[6]

A witness should explain the gospel clearly to a child, being careful and flexible with terminology. Concepts such as *faith* and *belief* should be thoroughly explained, perhaps even terms such as *trust* or *receive.* Some basic discussion necessities in witnessing to children include:

1. The nature of sin and the need of the individual
2. The person and work of Christ
3. God's requirement for salvation
4. Results (what God does through salvation)

Guidelines for Child Evangelism

The following is a list of guidelines and tips for sharing Christ with children.[7]

- Never assume anything; always start at the beginning.
- Use words and concepts the child can understand.
- Children think in concrete, literal terms. (For example, "invite Jesus into your heart.")
- Ask open-ended questions and listen to the answers they give and do not give.
- We do not want to give answers they have heard from church leaders or parents if they don't understand what the words mean.
- Children may not answer with standard Christian terms, but may in fact be receiving Christ.

- Stick to the basics when explaining the gospel, because understanding is gained through previously explained concepts and truths.
- Assist children as they ask questions and the Holy Spirit moves, but do not pressure a child.

Using a traffic light as a visual reminder, Paula Stringer encourages us to: STOP—Listen to the child's answer; CAUTION—Think about what the child is saying or not saying; GO—go ahead and answer, but use the child's words in your answer.[8]

Christian Terms Made More Understandable. We should make every effort to clarify terms that are not understood, but ideally we should use terms that make sense to the children hearing the message. Below are a few terms that children often struggle to understand. Look for understanding and commitment to the concept, not the term.

Sin—Sin is when you choose your way instead of God's way. Sin is when you know what you are supposed to do, but you choose to do something else. Sin separates you from God.

Repent—Repent means that you decide to do things God's way instead of your way. You are sorry for the wrong choices you have made.

Obeying God—Obeying God means choosing to live God's way.

Christian—You are a Christian if you have asked God to forgive you for the wrong choices you have made and asked Him to be in charge of your life.

Savior—Jesus is my Savior because He does for me what I cannot do for myself. He saved me from being separated from God forever because of my sin.

Righteousness—Always doing and saying what God would do and say.

Holy Spirit—"God is the Boss and the Holy Spirit is the One who tells you what the Boss wants you to do."[9]

There are other terms you will want to reexamine in light of communicating with children and even lost adults without a church background: lost, saved, blood of Jesus, give Jesus your heart, Jesus in your heart, baptism, and Lord's Supper.

Do's. Each situation is different. In some situations we have ongoing relationships with the child, while at other times we interact with a child in a single encounter. This variable and others will affect how to do evangelism with children.

1. Do be available to talk with children and be a safe person to them.
2. Do clarify incorrect or inadequate understanding.
3. Do stick to the basic issues.
4. Do use the Bible (the child's if possible) within the intellectual limits of the child.
5. Do teach the need, concept, and urgency of faith without pressure.
6. Do encourage the child to communicate with the Lord Jesus.
7. Do verbally affirm desires for baptism and the taking of the Lord's Supper, even if the child is not ready to receive Christ.
8. Do distinguish between receiving Christ and subsequent baptism and church membership.
9. As they demonstrate readiness, allow children to receive Christ.
10. Do inquire about and review what the child did and said in receiving Christ.
11. Do communicate with the parents as soon as reasonably possible.
12. Do beginning follow-up whenever possible.
13. Do provide resources for Christian parents of new children who are Christ followers.
14. Do share the gospel with lost parents of the child.

Don'ts. 1. Don't lead a child into a decision he or she is not ready to make.

2. Don't just use a memorized presentation. Children are unique.

3. Don't ask questions with the answer in or implied in the question.

4. Don't confuse the child with too many illustrations, Scripture verses, or concepts.

5. Don't expect adult Christian terminology from the child.

6. Don't assume the child is unsaved. Some children who respond to a personal invitation may already be saved and are seeking assurance.

7. Don't overemphasize fear and the threat of hell.

8. Don't tell the child everything you know about the Bible or sanctification.

9. Don't insist the child get saved now.

10. Don't tell the child he or she is saved. Let the Word of God and the Holy Spirit do that in due time.

11. Don't think your responsibility is over when a profession of faith has been made.

12. Don't baptize a child or allow a child to join a church without the permission of parents.

Baptism and Follow-up Issues

There are some unique concerns and possibilities in baptizing and following up with children. Do not baptize a child or allow a child to join a church without the permission of the parents. My preference is to wait to baptize children until they are at least nine years old. This is not a salvation issue but it helps to enhance the child's ability to remember the experience.

Make the experience meaningful by doing things such as clearly explaining the role and procedure of baptism, providing a baptism certificate, videotaping the baptism, interviewing the child about his experience in trusting Christ, inviting family and friends of the child (both saved and lost), and planning a baptism party after the service for the guests of the child. The responsibility does not end with baptism; children need immediate and ongoing training in how to walk with Jesus.

CHILDREN AS MESSAGE CARRIERS

Without fanfare children naturally pick up values from their parents. From the time my children were born, they have been involved with their mother and me in various aspects of ministry. Whether meeting new neighbors, doing surveys door-to-door in church plants, or conducting servant evangelism projects, our children have accompanied us. Children help to create a safe climate and one of immediate trust when they are with us just being kids during ministry activities. They also pick up on the value of lost people.

While we should not pressure children to share their faith, we should encourage it as a natural part of what they do as followers of Christ. My eldest daughter led a neighborhood boy to Christ when she was only ten years old. My wife provided almost no assistance except to confirm and affirm the commitment to Christ after the fact.

Resources for Additional Study

For additional materials, see *MEGnet.org*, the Web site for my ministry. Also see:

- Sara Covin Juengst, *Sharing Faith with Children: Rethinking the Children's Sermon*, Louisville, Ky.: John Knox Press, 1994.
- "Thank You Jesus," Billy Graham Evangelistic Association (Lots of words need to be explained.)
- Kidsbible.com
- New Century Translation, third-grade reading level
- New International Version, eighth-grade level

- www.street.ns.ca/adventr1.html, stories and lesson plans for work with children (lesson, goals, opening, rules, prayer, singing, games, memory verse, story, leader's conclusion, dismissal)

Teens

I have added a teenager to my home; my firstborn has turned thirteen. Teenage boys are increasingly on my radar screen, hopefully not hers for a few more years. I have begun to think more and more about the type of world that her future boyfriends and possible husband are growing up in today. I am concerned about the spiritual climate that exists for our teens.

There are many similarities to reaching youth and adults for Christ, especially the factors related to postmodernity. This section highlights a few of the particular issues related to doing personal evangelism with youth.

Developmental Makeup of Youth

Youth have similarities with both children and adults. Like children, youth are still developing their identity, but they are increasingly able to process information with a wider perspective and in abstract terms like adults. The following are a few developmental facets of teenagers.

- Able to process concepts rather than just tangible facts.
- Able to be introspective, analyze their own thought process, and see themselves in the third person.
- Can think ahead and face hypothetical problems.
- Tend to be self-conscious, self-centered, and self-reliant.
- Have the ability to be disillusioned, dishonest, and deceptive.
- Focused on the present, not on the future.

- Lack a moral compass based on a critically developed value system.
- Are media savvy and therefore skeptical of the inauthentic.
- Greatly influenced by negative experiences and perceptions.

Portrait of American Teens

Teens are not all alike, but there are some significant generalities we can make that are helpful as we seek to understand them. First, teenagers are generally open to spirituality, but most are not searching for answers at local churches. According to Barna Research Group, only 4 percent of teenagers fit the evangelical criteria, but they are searching for spiritual realities among many and often conflicting spiritual sources and information.[10] Pause and think about the future consequences of this for our churches!

Second, teenagers are oriented to relationships. This makes them susceptible to peer pressure, both positive and negative. This is a stage-of-life truth, but it is even more true with the number of broken families and the number of avenues to develop relationships. The Internet is a place where many teens are finding relationships.

Teens are spending blocks of time in chat rooms, exchanging E-mails and instant messages. These sources allow teens to speak freely and be heard, without interruption and condemnation, on a wide variety of subjects that interest them. My own daughter regularly checks her E-mail as soon as she arrives home from school where she saw many of the people who would be E-mailing her. She has a long list of people who are on her Instant Message Buddies list.

Third, teens think inclusively. Everything in their world screams tolerance and promotes the value of inclusivity. A mark of postmodernity is fragmentation. This fragmentation has created a greater desire for putting the pieces back together and for including everything and everybody. This is the postmodern world of American teens.

Fourth, teens validate what is true and real through the filters of their experiences. Reality is determined as they hear information and then check that information against the grid of their experiences. If it does not ring true to them, then it is discarded as unreliable. This applies to hearing from authority figures, spiritual or otherwise. Tim McLaughlin said, "If American adolescents accept authority, they tend to do it because the authority connects to their experience—not because of an appeal to ultimate truth."[11]

Fifth, teenagers are receptive to stories. This generation is accustomed to watching their music told in story form. Movies are a significant factor in shaping their perspective on reality. A mark of postmodernity is the rejection of a common story in favor of "their" individual story. This is referred to as anti-metanarrative. The lack of a common story only creates a desire for one among our teens.

Implications for Evangelism

Teens are open to talking about spiritual things, even Christ, under the appropriate circumstances. Teens who have found something spiritual that has made a difference in their lives will be attractive to youth who are spiritually searching. Today's youth have more options for spiritual teachings than ever before in the history of the U.S. It is no longer the Christian church or nothing. The local Christian church is in serious competition with other groups vying for the attention of our teens.

Christian adults and youth can talk with teens about God and the implications for their lives if they have a relationship with them. Without a relationship it will be difficult to communicate Christ because people are more willing to talk about spiritual matters with those with whom they have a relationship. Impersonal methods will have limited success with teens. Christian teens sharing with lost teens will be the most effective method.

Christians should focus on the inclusive nature of the call to all peoples through Christ. Jesus as a person with His inclusive lifestyle is attractive to teens. Because of the uniqueness of Christ, the resurrection, and His inclusive call, lost teens will have to struggle with the exclusive claim of Christ. However, Jesus' credentials are impeccable to make such a demand.

Spiritual experiences are important to youth. What is lived is what is real to teens. They are not interested in factual information about God that is not supported by their experiences with those who claim to know Christ. Christians living the Word before them will have greater initial impact than the written Word. This will help to establish the necessary credibility from which to give verbal witness of Christ. Also, the ability to draw spiritual truths out of normal experiences of life can be helpful in leading youth toward Christ.

Because they have not grown up under the influence of a local Christian church, most teens are biblically illiterate. They are unfamiliar with the biblical stories of God's activities with His people in both the Old and the New Testaments. Sharing the stories of Christ and His followers is a powerful communication tool with teens. Many youth are trying to find their place in the world, so connecting their experiences and life story to God's overall story is helpful. Finally, the use of testimonies, especially those of fellow teenagers, will be an important vehicle to carry God's message to them.

Tim McLaughlin noted: "As uncompromising as Bible truth may be, the parts that today's teens will respond to—especially unchurched teens—are the stories. Thank goodness, much of the Bible is largely story after story, from Genesis to Revelation: patriarchal escapades, royal schemes, prophets' predicaments . . . and then there is The Story, the gospel, the Good News. In the most remarkable true story that ever was, it's all there: God in human flesh, miracles galore, jealousy, intrigue among His followers, an innocent death by execution, an inexplicable resurrection, and ordinary converts who follow Him in life and death."[12]

Guidelines for Youth Evangelism

Helpful Do's

- Do build a base of loving acts and time from which to share Christ (preevangelism).
- Do build relational bridges to youth.
- Do become a safe person for them.
- Do accept them and be approachable.
- Do create safe environments for teens to ask questions and explore the Christian faith.
- Do use words they can understand.
- Do share your spiritual testimony.
- Do train youth to share their faith with other youth.
- Do communicate the full message of Christ to them, including the costs involved in following Christ.
- Do validate facets of the gospel by sharing personal experiences.
- Do answer their questions with honesty, even if your answer is "I don't know."
- Do provide assistance and let them choose, in their timing, under the leadership of the Holy Spirit.
- Do follow up on spiritual conversations and conversions.
- Do lead teens to explore and discover spiritual truths.
- Do be sensitive to teachable moments.
- Do make sure teens know they must make their own decision for Christ.
- Do provide appropriate outlets for them to respond to Christ.
- Do connect new teen converts into a group as soon as possible.

Don'ts

- Don't be judgmental.
- Don't cram the gospel down their throats.

- Don't provide overly simplistic answers to complex issues.
- Don't tell teens the benefits and ease of following Christ to the neglect of the costs.
- Don't claim to follow Christ and yet live an inauthentic life in front of them.
- Don't baptize a youth without parental approval, as the parents are the primary God-given authority for the teenagers.

Group Settings Tips

- Make the Christian home a fun gathering place for youth.
- Offer exploratory Bible groups.
- Christian families "adopt" a neighborhood teen. Express love and concern through involvement with a hobby or special interest.
- If your church has a climate that appeals to lost people, invite teens to attend an appropriate event of the church.

Conclusions on Evangelism with Youth

The youth of America are open to authentic spiritual life found in Christ as it is lived before them by loving, trustworthy people, especially other teens. They are looking for direction and are more likely to follow a person or group that seems to be heading in the right direction. As with adults and children, youth will surrender their lives to Christ to the degree to which it makes sense to do so. Christians' responsibility is to get to know them so that we might make sense of following Christ from the lenses of their perspectives and values.

Some say that teens are a different breed. Teens can come to Christ and learn to impact the world around them. I trust that they will become different as they come to Christ, and many of those will selflessly and boldly serve as missionaries to the lost around them.

SENIORS

Despite increasing physical limitations, we do not retire from service to His kingdom. The senior adult population in America is exploding in size. This presents the Christian church with opportunities for ministry, if seen and seized by seniors and their leaders.

Some senior groups have caught a vision for ministry. They take trips to prayer walk, work with underprivileged children, and reach out to youth. However, after reviewing one of the many church brochures I receive in the mail, I was reminded how many senior groups seem to exist only to take pleasure trips.

Seniors play a vital role in personal evangelism. Seniors are best positioned with relationships to evangelize other seniors. If seniors don't, who will? There are few barriers between seniors and teenagers and those in their twenties. Younger generations long for relationships with senior adults. Seniors can also invest their time and wisdom to reach out to hurting young adults who need them.

There are a few unique considerations when seeking to evangelize senior adults. Lost senior adults are at a stage in life where they are reflecting on the past and are more open to considering what will happen to them after death. If we talk with them in their homes without a prior relationship with them, they may be concerned about security issues. Seniors may also be overly sensitive to scams and thus be resistant to visits by strangers. Most will not, but some seniors may not be responsive because of hearing problems. Therefore, the delivery methods we use need to take into consideration these and other concerns of seniors.

There are also a few unique considerations when seeking to involve senior adults in personal evangelism. Seniors often have large blocks of time, and some have financial resources to invest in ministry. They may have physical limitations, but most seniors still want their lives to count by helping others.

COMMUNICATING CROSS-CULTURALLY

Through the Internet, voice phones, video phones, affordable international travel, and world trade, the exchange of ideas among different cultures has never been higher. As the world becomes more global and pluralistic, the demand for quality cross-cultural communication has never been higher. Cross-cultural communication is impacting war and peace, prosperity and poverty. Relationships between countries, families, and friends are at stake, as well as evangelistic effectiveness.

Cross-cultural communicating is no longer just a foreign missionary task. If we are to communicate the gospel to all the peoples of the world, it will also involve cross-cultural communication evangelism inside the U.S. In the past, missionaries were the only ones on the front lines of this type of communication. This is no longer true. Most of us live or operate within more than one culture.

Several settings require cross-cultural communications. In several respects moderns and postmoderns are using cross-cultural skills when communicating with one another. When adults share the gospel with children, they are applying cross-cultural communication principles. When the rich share with the poor, or the uneducated share the gospel with the educated, they are crossing cultural barriers.

PERIOD OF THE MISSIONARY

Intrinsic to the gospel message is missions. Intrinsic to the church's existence is missions. Bosch warned us, "Unless the church of the West begins to understand this, and unless we develop a missionary theology, not just a theology of mission, we will not achieve more than merely patch up the church."[13]

Most Americans are serving in a cross-cultural mission field. We live in multicultural environments and no longer have a home field advantage in the U.S. Additionally, Christian churches are a subculture with their own worldviews, language, rituals, and social patterns. In order for us to evangelize others, we have to move outside of our comfortable subculture and enter into the cultures of other groups. We have to go to the world of the lost, not sit around expecting them to come to ours. We are all missionaries to those around us.

TASK OF THE MISSIONARY

As Christ followers serve as missionaries to the world outside their Christian circles, we need to see our task as containing at least three parts. We need to (1) understand their position correctly, (2) encode our message appropriately, and (3) speak relevantly to their concerns.

Early missionaries saw their role as reaching beyond their local church and simply telling the message. Hesselgrave noted that "the early missionaries understood that their commission to make disciples of all nations involved the ultimate in communication—not only reinforcing the Christian message behaviorally, nor simply delivering it verbally in writing or speech, but also persuading men and women to be converted and become faithful and fruitful followers of the Master."[14]

Our task is not to make them like us. We want them to be like Jesus in their culture.

UNDERSTANDING CULTURE

The word *culture* is used in various ways with varying degrees of emotions, some positive and others negative. For Hesselgrave, culture includes "all the ways in which people perceive and organize material goods, ideas, and values; it embraces the ways in which people interact in society as well as a person's substitutes for God and his revelation."[15] Louis J. Luzbetak said, "Culture is a design for living. It is a plan according to which society adapts itself to its physical, social, and ideational environment."[16] Clyde Kluckhohn said, "Culture is a way of thinking, feeling, believing. It is the group's knowledge stored up for future use."[17] An essential element of effective communication is to understand something of the lost person's culture in order to make sense of the gospel from the lost person's perspective.

KEY CROSS-CULTURAL DIMENSIONS

Communicating cross-culturally has been divided into manageable parts. David Hesselgrave identified seven dimensions of cross-cultural communications. These are: (1) worldviews—ways of perceiving the world, (2) cognitive processes—ways of thinking, (3) linguistic forms—ways of expressing ideas, (4) behavior patterns—ways of acting, (5) social structures—ways of interacting, (6) media influence—ways of channeling the message, and (7) motivational resources—ways of deciding. All of these impact how we carry out personal evangelism.[18]

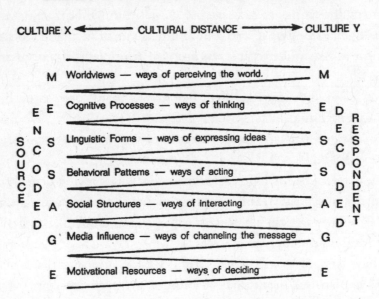

DIMENSIONS OF CROSS-CULTURAL COMMUNICATION

Regarding worldview, missionaries have several options. We can (1) invite our non-Christian respondents to lay aside their own worldviews and temporarily adopt the Christian worldview in order to understand the message (an impossibility), (2) temporarily adopt the worldview of the non-Christian respondents, or (3) invite the respondents to meet us halfway. Regardless of the culture and the means by which the gospel is communicated, the missionary as a source, the content of his message, and the style by which it is delivered remain suspect to the lost.

Communication has been consumed with *what* people think instead of *how* people think. Effective missionary communication cannot consist of heaping information about God upon people. We need to learn how people come to know in the cognitive process. As examples which are changing, for the Western (Occidental) person, the thought process has typically been scientific, intellectual, and aggressive. For the Oriental or tribal person, the thought process is primarily mythological, emotional, and artistic, giving rise to feelings. How people come to determine what is real and true is of utmost importance in evangelism.

Not only do Christians need to learn the language of the recipient's culture; we also need to understand the culture's behavioral patterns. These patterns communicate nonverbally. Christians must pay particular attention to those practices which are inherently objectionable. Hesselgrave stated, "It is the moral, ethical, and spiritual life of the missionary that makes his message credible and persuasive."[19] Therefore, the missionary has a responsibility in regard to behavioral norms.

The more the Christ follower understands the social structures, media sources, and motivational resources, the better the opportunity for effective communication of the gospel. Each of these dimensions impacts the hearing of the gospel and the decision-making process.

CREDIBILITY IN CULTURE

Credibility is a major factor in developing receptivity to the gospel. How we interact in various settings either aids or detracts from our credibility. When operating in cross-cultural settings, developing an understanding of and sensitivity to the significant cultural differences is a key to establishing credibility for the message. It is difficult if not impossible for the lost person to separate the message from the messenger and the method of evangelism.

If our habits and approaches to evangelism violate cultural norms, this can hinder our credibility as witnesses to Christ. This does not mean that we have to adopt cultural norms that violate God's commands, but most cultural norms are amoral. Our responsibility is to build as many bridges as possible to the gospel and intentionally limit the number of barriers we erect, save the gospel itself.[20]

A pastor friend told a story of two women who had invested decades serving as foreign missionaries among tribal peoples but they had little fruit to show for their faithful service. As they were leaving the country for the final time, they were shocked to find out that the juice they had been drinking regularly was thought to be a pregnancy preventing juice. The members of the tribe where they lived thought the two women had been having sexual relations with the men in the neighboring tribe. This meant the women had no credibility because of their practice of drinking the juice. Fair, no, but reality, yes.

EFFECTIVE CROSS-CULTURAL COMMUNICATION

Communication involves encoding information (putting together), transmitting (sending through means of communication), and decoding (understanding by the receiver). In order to be effective in communicating cross-culturally, followers of Christ need to immerse themselves in the respondents' culture. Jesus said, "Go into all the world" (Mark 16:15) and "while I am in the world, I am the light of the world" (John 9:5). This is easily overlooked in an effort to limit the influences of the ungodly aspects of a given culture.

While learning the language is important, this is only part of our understanding of another culture. Christians have to move beyond knowledge of the simplistic of such things as observable behavior and institutions to the complex issues of culture. These include learning about values, ideology, cosmology, and worldview, while divesting ourselves from our own culture. Hesselgrave believes missionaries must "study the rhetorical process implicit and explicit in any culture, not just in terms of *what* people think but in terms of *how* they think and formulate their ideas."[21]

Eugene Nida developed a three-culture model of communication to aid missionaries in their task.[22] In order for missionaries to communicate effectively, they must take several key steps. Hesselgrave stated, "The missionary must divest himself as much as possible from his own . . . culture, interpret the gospel in terms of the . . . culture in which it was revealed, and deliver the gospel in a way that will be meaningful to people in the target . . . culture."[23]

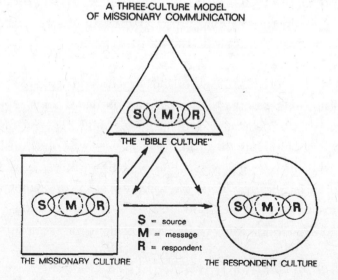

A THREE-CULTURE MODEL
OF MISSIONARY COMMUNICATION

THE "BIBLE CULTURE"

S = source
M = message
R = respondent

THE MISSIONARY CULTURE   THE RESPONDENT CULTURE

All people are a certain distance from God and from the witness. The further a person is from God, the longer it generally takes for a person to come to Christ. Distance can be relational (the unknown person), or the distance can be cultural. The greater the number of cultural barriers, the more difficult the task of effectively communicating the gospel. The correlation is also true as it relates to cultural distance.

CROSS-CULTURAL ASSUMPTIONS: WORKS

When faced with a cross-cultural witnessing encounter, you can make few assumptions. You will need to ask questions and listen carefully to assess the situation. However, you can assume that most of the religions of the world are based on the efforts of people to reach God. The typical response of what it takes to enter into eternal life of religious people is to work for their salvation.

Some religions teach adherents to recite prayers. Others emphasize attendance at various worship services throughout the year. Still others teach service to others through good deeds. And the American favorite is to do just enough good in your own mind so that you feel like God will be appeased. However, no one can earn salvation by works (Eph. 2:8–9).

In the aftermath of the terrorist destruction on September 11, 2001, Americans were exposed to the teachings of the Muslims. One of their teachings is that if you perform a jihad, by giving your life for the destruction of infidels, then your reward is heaven. Other Muslims earn favor with Allah by giving one-half of their wealth as a payment for their place in eternity.[24] These are extreme acts of working for salvation, but most religions of the world are based on human efforts to appease their god by whatever means necessary.

CONTEXTUALIZATION DANGERS

Contextualizing the gospel into other cultures is not without dangers, but there are even more dangers if we do not contextualize. As a matter of unnoticed fact but extreme importance, the gospel in any culture has been contextualized. There is a danger of changing the essential gospel message with subtraction or addition to the essentials. Another danger as we contextualize is that the receiving cultures syncretize the message into their existing religious beliefs. They may add Jesus to their present objects of worship, yet not see the exclusivity of Christ's demands on their allegiance.

CROSS-CULTURAL COMMUNICATION MODELS

We all look for models to use to shorten the learning curve or development process. Newbigin offers a model of what is involved in communicating the gospel across cultural barriers.

1. The communication has to be in the language of the receptor culture. It has to be such that it accepts, at least provisionally, the way of understanding things that is embodied in that language; if it does not do so, it will simply be an unmeaning sound that cannot change anything.

2. However, if it is truly the communication of the gospel, it will call radically into question that way of understanding embodied in the language it uses. If it is truly revelation, it will involve contradiction, and it will call for conversion, for a radical *metanoia*, a U-turn of the mind.

3. Finally, this radical conversion can never be the achievement of any human persuasion, however eloquent. It can only be the work of God. True conversion, therefore, which is the proper end toward which the communication of the gospel looks, can only be a work of God, a kind of miracle—not natural but supernatural.[25]

SUMMARY

The adage, "Seek first to understand before seeking to be understood," is helpful to remember when evangelizing within or outside of your context. As you reflect on God's role, your role, and the gospel message, you can apply principles and skills in cross-cultural communication to connect the gospel with those who desperately need Jesus, whether separated by age, culture, or other factors.

CHAPTER 7

Conversation Tips— Conversation Aids in Personal Evangelism

PEOPLE ARE SEARCHING. According to a 1997 *USA Today* poll, 46 percent of the men and 40 percent of the women in the U.S. are "searching for the meaning and purpose of life." However, that search has long since moved beyond the local Christian church. Self-help books, community groups, and false religions have replaced the Bible, Christian small groups, and the church as places to discover God and community. Followers of Christ have the answers to the search of a large portion of the U.S. population. Christians have the privilege of taking the message of Christ to a nation of spiritual searchers.

MODERN VERSUS POSTMODERN IMPLICATIONS FOR EVANGELISM

CONVERSATION CHARACTERISTICS IN POSTMODERN CONTEXTS

Evangelism in a postmodern context has some distinct characteristics. Examining the characteristics of spiritual and evangelistic conversations will provide you with insights into evangelizing people increasingly influenced by postmodern thought. The following chart is designed to give some insights into the changes that accompany postmodernism. This list is not exhaustive, but the list should provide you with insights into sharing your faith.

Postmodern		Modern
• Multiple encounters	less	Single encounters
• Listener-centered	less	Witness-centered
• Dialogical	less	Monological
• Gospel story	less	Gospel presentation
• Story, then proposition	not	Proposition, then story
• Asking good questions	not	Giving lots of information
• Community integration	not	Individual isolation
• Soft	not	Loud
• Consideration[1]	not	Argumentation
• Guided tours	not	Ticket sales
• More supernatural	less	Supersales (natural)
• More earthly benefits	less	Eternal benefits
• More relational validation	less	Evidentiary validation
• More % of time planting	less	% of time harvesting[2]

Multiple Encounters; Less Single Encounters

Much of the personal evangelism in the past generation centered on single or one-time encounters. With people being further from God and further from Christians in terms of their knowledge and acceptance of Jesus Christ and His church, evangelism is more a process than an event. Therefore, it usually takes more than one encounter with the gospel message to trust Christ. Marketing experts expect that it takes six to seven contacts with information about their product before the person will actually buy the product. In evangelism, most people will have to move through a process to deal adequately with the message and implications of the gospel on their lives. The witness can expect multiple encounters to be the norm.

As a word of caution, when you are dealing with a stranger, you may in fact have only one encounter, but you may be the fourth or tenth person whom God has woven into his life to communicate the love of Christ. Do not assume that because you only can interact with a person one time that a person will not surrender to Christ.

Listener-Centered; Less Witness-Centered

Much of the evangelism training in the last half of the twentieth century centered on preparing the witness to talk. In order to be clear, witnesses would focus on what they were trying to say and the words they were using. An evaluation of a witnessing encounter of the past would probably focus on how organized and how well the witness presented the message. This is in contrast to evaluating how well we respond to the lost listener.

Today we need to give more attention to training the witness to listen.[3] We should ask ourselves questions such as, "How is the listener responding to the message and to me? Is the listener connecting with the message?" Watching the body language and listening attentively to the lost person can help us do this. Remember the team of three students who led a Spanish-speaking person to Christ. The English-speaking female student team member noted in class that in spite of her not speaking a word of Spanish, she watched the listener's body language go through several changes as the gospel was presented, implications were considered, and the listener surrendered to Christ.

Dialogical; Less Monological

Evangelism training in the second half of the twentieth century often centered on preparing the witness to make a quality presentation. However, most evangelistic conversations with people who process life through a postmodern grid will not sit still and listen to a monologue. Your personal evangelism needs to be more dialogical in nature. A norm of American communication is that after you listen in a conversation, you are then asked or expected to respond in a give-and-take fashion.

Gospel Story; Less Gospel Presentation

Christians need to communicate the gospel story to postmoderners, not tell gospel facts. When people do not grow up in a Judeo-Christian environment, they do not know the Christian story, symbols, doctrines, or ethics. They need to hear God and man's story throughout history. The testimony is an effective method of communicating the truth of the message. Postmoderners are much less likely to listen to a presentation where one person is doing the vast majority of the talking, but they are open to hearing and discussing a story.

Story, Then Proposition; Not Proposition, Then Story

In most sermons and in the sharing of our faith, propositional statements usually preceded illustration. The witness would communicate spiritual facts and then illustrate or explain the spiritual reality. However, in a postmodern context, the witness should communicate the gospel story and then draw out the appropriate spiritual truth. When people do not know or understand God's story as told in the Bible, they need to get a framework of the story so that individual truths can be seen in the backdrop of the story.

Jesus often used natural situations or common experiences to communicate spiritual truth. With the woman at the well (John 4), Jesus started by discussing water but moved from talking about physical water to talking about spiritual water. In a modernity context the witness would typically have begun talking about spiritual cleansing and then illustrated with a discussion on the use of water.

Asking Good Questions; Not Giving Lots of Information

In modernity, the weight of factual evidence really mattered. Evangelism focused on giving lots of information, the gospel basics, and answers to the questions the listener might have in response to the information. Postmoderns will need information, but until the witness asks questions and listens well, the witness will not know what information to give. Nick Pollard in *Evangelism Made Slightly Less Difficult* discussed the concept of what he calls "positive deconstruction."

In a context where people have little background with the true gospel and also consider themselves spiritual, a key is for the witness to ask a series of good questions. These questions need to be presented in an appropriate tone, not judgmental but inquiring. The goal is not biblical superiority but to encourage thinking and dialogue. Questions also demonstrate genuine interest.

Community Integration; Not Individual Isolation

In a modern worldview the value of the individual is raised to extreme heights. This norm has affected overall evangelism approaches. The Christian would reach out to individual non-Christians with the message of Christ in hopes of their surrendering to Jesus Christ. The new convert would then be invited to become a part of a Christian subculture or church family. Often our evangelism has been marked by a focus on the individual response and then the integration into a church family.

In a postmodern context, the value of community is being rediscovered and more highly valued. Postmoderns process truth through the context of their relationships. Evangelism efforts will often involve integrating the listener into a Christian circle of people prior to the person surrendering his life to Christ. Non Christians will want to test-drive the Christian faith as they seek to determine its truthfulness as judged through watching the lives of those who claim to know Christ before they surrender to Christ.

There are several implications regarding community integration. The up side of this is that assimilation often will take place prior to people giving their lives to Christ. Conversion may be slower but should result in more solid decisions and produce them in bunches. As people determine truth in the context of their relationships, the wise evangelist will seek not only to reach one individual person but also reach into and probably step into that person's circle of relationships.

Several ministers who are leading ministries to reach postmoderners have validated this point through their experiences. Often one person of a group is won to Christ, and then that person serves as the catalyst for reaching a group of similar people.

Soft; Not Loud

As the father of three young girls, I find it easier to parent with volume than with quiet, wise words. However, children are not taught through volume. They learn from consistent instruction with a visible model. Passion is important in evangelism and can enhance our believability. However, among highly trained skeptics and pluralistic thinking people, the volume of evangelism needs to be lowered. Soft, calm, thoughtful words will resonate more clearly than high decibels. A life lived in calm confidence in God is more likely to be noticed than words shouted from a red-faced, Bible-waving stranger.

Consideration; Not Argumentation

With moderns, reason is supreme. Argumentation is a key to skillful witnessing. Evangelism in a pluralist society will use less argumentation and more consideration. Christians are wise to ask lost people to consider our beliefs, especially the implications of the resurrection and Jesus' claim to be God.

Tolerance has been taken to new heights as a societal value. We can stand firmly on our positions and beliefs and come across with confidence, but in order to get a full hearing, we cannot be seen as trying to force our beliefs on others. We can, however, skillfully ask others to consider our position in light of their positions. We attempt to surface inconsistencies in their beliefs through asking questions and asking them to consider our beliefs in light of our credible lifestyle and the Word of God. We can inform their considerations with apologetic supports such as archeological and historical evidence.

Asking others to consider our position can put our faith in God to the test. I am reminded of the story of Elijah and the false prophets of

Baal. Questions for us to answer are: How big is our God? Is He capable of making Himself known? I believe that He can and does reveal Himself to those who seek Him.

Linda Bergquist was a college student of Fred Jappe, a professor who was a member of Pastor Sam Williams's congregation. She was postmodern in much of her thinking and was a passionate atheist. Sam gave his class the assignment of attending three different religious services. One of those worship services had to be held by an evangelical Christian church. After class she noted to her professor that she did not know of a service in this category to attend. So Fred gave her the name of the church he attended in San Diego. Linda attended and then eagerly awaited a pastoral visit from Pastor Sam. She always wanted to interrogate a pastor in hopes of showing him how weak and ridiculous Christian positions were.

When Sam made a pastoral call, he was greeted at the door with warm but cautious hospitality. They exchanged views with neither making progress into changing the other person's beliefs. Linda had taken the position that there was no God. As Sam started to leave, he asked Linda to do two things: (1) pray that God would reveal Himself if He really existed and (2) read a chapter from the Book of John every day and consider the implications of what the chapter says about Jesus. Linda was hesitant, but to prove her confidence in her position, she agreed. Several days later she called Sam and simply said, "Pray for me. I'm losing the battle." A few hours later that day, she called back to tell Sam that she had placed her faith in Jesus Christ. People like Linda test us about how big we believe our God really is.

Guided Tours; Not Ticket Sales

Because personal evangelism usually involves a process, the witness needs to provide a guided tour of what it means to be a Christian while presenting the claims of Christ. Christians can be appropriately aggressive but must not let excessive zeal determine their methods without knowledge (Rom. 10:2). No informed Christian would make such an approach, but I am referring to the perception of the lost person. Seekers desire to see Christians themselves on a spiritual journey. The lost want us to walk beside them and provide answers to questions along the journey.

I do not remember a great deal from the book on transactional analysis, *I'm OK, You're OK*, but I do remember two types of conversations. One type is parent to child. This involves talking down to people. A second type is child to child, where both parties get on the same immature, childlike level in talking with each other. A third and more positive type is adult to adult, where we talk to each other in mutual respect. Christians can ill afford to take the posture of talking down to the spiritually searching as if we are superior and they are inferior. The witness in a postmodern context will have to use language and a communication style that demonstrates an adult-to-adult conversation. We need to talk *with* people, not *to* them, especially not *down* to them. Doing this violates a cultural norm and gives us little chance to reach a person for Christ.[4]

More Supernatural; Less Supersales

Missionaries told radical stories but not during their public presentation. After they finished and in a side conversation, they would tell about the supernatural things they had experienced when taking the gospel to remote parts of the world. The story often goes something like this: "We arrived in a village, and the people greeted us, expecting to hear how they could find God. They had dreams that a specific group or a specifically attired person would arrive to bring them news about Jesus. We were the people in their dreams."

God desires to draw people to Himself. Evangelism is a frontal attack on the gates of hell. Therefore, we can expect to engage in battles that involve spiritual beings, whether from God or representing Satan. People will be drawn more out of the supernatural movement of God than the natural abilities of the witness.

Remember Linda. Her conversion story highlights a couple of key principles in personal evangelism. Sam demonstrated a belief that his God was able to reveal Himself to Linda. There are many times when the witness will need to demonstrate a great faith in God to reveal Himself when no other method gets through to the unbelieving heart. Another key is found in Sam's wisdom in asking Linda to consider the claims of Christ on her life. He did not simply argue by using logic but asked her to consider his position in light of her own background and experiences. Stay tuned for the rest of her story.

Maybe it is the influence of Eastern religions and other counterfeit efforts, but I will be surprised if we do not see an increase in the number of recognizable spiritual encounters. Christians will need to develop discernment as it relates to spirits because not everything that is supernatural is from God. Satan is a masterful counterfeiter. John tells us to test the spirits. I encourage you to read 1 John for additional insights on this subject.

More Earthly Benefits; Less Eternal Benefits

In today's culture the wise witness will invest more time discussing earthly benefits and costs, while investing s smaller population of witness time discussing the eternal benefits of following God. The eternal benefits dramatically outweigh any earthly benefits from following Christ. However, we need to demonstrate with our lives and support by our words that Jesus makes a difference in every aspect of life.

I have required my students to develop a list of twenty-five reasons why people would want to give their lives to Christ. The students usually do OK coming up with the first fifteen or so but then begin to struggle to crystallize how Christ impacts their lives. My contention is that if Christians are not experiencing Jesus in the everyday concerns and problems of life, then we will miss most of the potential transition points to talk about the impact of Christ in our lives. For what is on the heart and mind will also be on the tongue. If we are not experiencing Christ in the ordinary affairs of life, then we do not have

Christ on our hearts. As we listen to people talk about their marriages, finances, or disappointments, we need to hear opportunities to talk about how our relationship with Jesus has made a difference in those areas of our lives.

More Relational Validation; Less Evidentiary Validation

People today determine truth differently than they did in previous generations. Postmoderns place a greater weight on relational validation than evidentiary validation. Evidence is important and can be found, but there are still mysteries about God. Postmoderns are more likely to seek to determine how their friends are responding or feeling about the message of Christ.

We may see an increasing number of people making decisions in groups. This is not without biblical precedent. Throughout the New Testament we see examples of entire households coming to faith in Christ (John 4:53; Acts 11:14; 16:15, 31; 18:8; 1 Cor. 1:16; 16:15). This does not mean that each individual does not have to respond to Christ, but it does demonstrate the power of relationships in validating what is true and real. Jesus said, "By this all men will know that you are my disciples, if you love one another" (John 13:35).

More Time Planting Seeds; Less Percentage of Time Harvesting

Much can be learned from the laws of the harvest, such as you reap what you sow, reap more than you sow, and reap later than you sow. With postmoderns, we will need to invest significant time and resources in sowing seeds for the harvest. If we do not sow seeds, we will not harvest. Dr. Chuck Kelley stated, "Southern Baptists are a harvest-oriented denomination living oriented in an unseeded generation." This does not mean that we can no longer harvest, because without the goal of harvesting there would be no reason to plant. However, we must think of evangelism in terms and methods beyond that of just harvesting.

Most approaches and even the common understanding of evangelism have been built almost exclusively on harvesting. Because evangelism is a process, we need to increase others' interest through various forms of planting seeds. A higher percentage of our time will be invested in planting, all the while being ready to harvest.

GENERAL TIPS

Most of the principles of interpersonal relationships are applicable in sharing our faith.

- Use common language, not religious terms that can be understood by the lost person.
- Avoid being argumentative.
- Listen without interruption when the other person is talking.
- Avoid trying to shame others with what they do not know.
- Respect the time and schedule commitments of others.
- Recognize that *no* means *no*, at least for the time being.
- Respect the right of the listener to end the conversation at any point.
- In explaining new concepts, start with something the person understands and move toward new ideas or truths.
- Try to maintain goodwill so that you can engage in future conversations.
- Avoid talking down other religious groups or individuals.
- Remember that people have intellectual limits, so do not overwhelm them with too many Scriptures.
- Avoid embarrassing the lost person.
- Talk with people, not down to them.

- Try to leave with a win/win approach, not create winner and loser.
- Maintain control, even if you are attacked or questioned.
- Remember that many people are not avid readers so other forms of material will be needed—videos, DVDs, CDs, etc.

COMMON SENSE PRINCIPLES: PRACTICAL POSTMODERN EMPHASES

Develop Rapport

In single-encounter witnessing, it is not possible to develop a relationship, but we can develop a connection. You may develop a conversation with an adult by discussing family, hobby, hometown, work, successes, spiritual and/or religious background. We can create opportunities to develop rapport by serving others through small acts of kindness. Times of crisis or need, such as death, job loss, or physical illness, also drive people to seek connections with other people.

Demonstrate Personal Intrigue

One of my classes conducted an interview with Pastor Ron Johnson of Pathways Church in Denver. Ron told the students that his top piece of advice for reaching postmoderns with mixed-up views was to demonstrate intrigue with them. People are responsive and receptive to us when we consistently display interest in them.

Part of showing intrigue is to ask people questions about themselves. As you get to know them, the questions can become more personal and specific to their hurts, desires, dreams, hopes, failures, and struggles. The wisest people are the ones who ask questions. Most people respond positively to those who ask their opinion, insight, or assistance.

In the American culture in particular, there is an unwritten rule that if someone asks us questions about various areas of our lives, we are to reciprocate by asking them questions of a similar nature. People who violate this norm are viewed negatively. So as we ask questions and listen, we often will get the opportunity to share the gospel when they ask us questions.

Listen Actively

In reflecting on the experience of the assignment of interviewing lost people, student Tom Higginbotham wrote: "The approach recommended in the syllabus of honestly seeking answers to a religious survey helped tremendously. When asked the questions, each person honestly seemed to be reflecting on his or her own personal answer and not on an answer just to please me. The fact that these people had never been asked questions like these was obvious and almost overwhelming."[5] This highlights the importance of listening. Christians have a reputation of doing more talking and little listening. We can possibly break down that stereotype and thereby create some interest in our message.

You understand by talking with people. In keeping with my professor's role, let me suggest an assignment. Interview seven to ten unchurched adults under the age of thirty-five. Use the interview guide in the appendix. Focus on listening rather than on trying to convince or debate. Posture yourself as someone who is seeking to understand what people are thinking and feeling. You might be pleasantly surprised how open people are to talking with you about spiritual matters.

Doctoral student Dale Funderburg drew a significant conclusion from completing the assignment to interview some lost adults. In a summary paper he wrote: "It became apparent that most people have a willingness to talk about spiritual matters as a matter of opinion. The rejection comes when those people think they will be judged. Most people think of Christians as judgmental and argumentative. If we can show a genuine interest in them as persons and value their thoughts, they may be more open when we introduce the gospel."[6]

Share Authentically

Media-savvy adults are naturally skeptical, especially of Christians. In order to gain a hearing, we must present ourselves as authentic in our concern for people and credible by our lifestyles and witnessing approach. Peter Berger captured the style of witness that is dead for most people today: "A peculiar mixture of arrogance ('I know the truth') and benevolence ('I want to save you') has always been the chief psychological hallmark of missionary activity." "People can smell this combination of arrogance and benevolence a mile away. At the first whiff they will fly away—miles away."[7]

Capture Imagination

A stereotypical Christian is one who has turned off his brain. This need not be true. The story of Jesus is captivating. One of our roles is to tell it over and over again. Rick Richardson said, "The uses of media and movies for communicating and exploring truth have exploded. Our evangelism must take this revolution into account. How does this affect the ways we respond to people's questions today? We must become great storytellers, verbally and through media. We want not only to respond to the questions logically but to capture people's spiritual and moral imagination."[8]

Conduct Positive Deconstruction

Most people do not have well-defined spiritual beliefs. We can discover and help lost persons discover the inadequacies of their personal beliefs. I use the term *belief system,* but most people do not have a thoughtfully defined system. They have flexible beliefs from which they review new religious ideas.

Most people have a thrown-together hodgepodge of beliefs. By asking them questions that allow them to think through and explain their spiritual perspectives, values, and beliefs, people will discover the inadequacies of their views. This allows them to deconstruct their own religious beliefs. In this way the Christian witness is conducting positive deconstruction. During the guided reflection and self-discovery, people often become more receptive to the Christian worldview and message.[9]

ASSESS THE WITNESSING SITUATION

Some situations provide green-light witnessing opportunities, while others are yellow or even red. Part of our role is to use good judgment under the leadership of the Holy Spirit to assess the situation. Charles Kraft gave us five questions to ask ourselves about any particular imaginary or actual evangelistic witnessing situation.

1. How would I introduce the subject in that setting?
2. What kinds of perceptions will be in the receptors' minds concerning me, my message, and the appropriateness of the message to that place and time?
3. What kind of vocabulary should I use?
4. What may I assume concerning the receptors, given the fact that they have come to that place at that time?
5. What are the advantages and disadvantages of that setting for presenting this message, and how may they be utilized or overcome?[10]

TRANSITIONING TO A SPIRITUAL CONVERSATION

Last summer my family traveled with me to Arizona for some personal time and to lead a conference in New Mexico. Just outside the beautiful red rock city of Sedona, Arizona, was a state park with a natural spring-fed swimming hole. After swimming across to the other side, my girls and I climbed up the rocks to an area that was about twenty feet high. Blakeney, then twelve, was a little timid about jumping off into the cold springwater, in spite of the prodding from her younger sister, Hadley, who had already made the leap. In an effort to calm Blakeney's fears, I said, "Only the first step is tough; after that it is a snap!"

For many in personal evangelism, the first step is tough; after that it's a snap. Transitioning a conversation to the topic of spiritual matters and Christ is often the most feared and difficult part of sharing our faith. How do we begin a witnessing conversation? If we do not start conversations, we cannot close conversations. The battle is more than half won once the ice is broken on the topic of Jesus Christ.

In America today, talking about spiritual things is a common experience. Television shows discuss every spiritual topic. Oprah talks a great deal about discovering your spirit. *Seventh Heaven* is a show that highlights the life of a pastor's family. *Touched by an Angel* is another positive drama about angels teaching humans lessons about life and faith. Evil, Satan, and the demonic are not without their share of airtime—*Buffy the Vampire Slayer*, *X-Files*, *Charmed*, and *Sabrina the Teenage Witch*. Movies also have picked up on the spiritual theme: *The Sixth Sense*, *The Truman Show*, *The Matrix*, and *Star Wars*.

JESUS EXAMPLES

Jesus can be found turning conversations to spiritual matters time and time again in the Scripture. He was a master at transitioning a conversation from everyday topics and events to spiritual values.

- The woman at the well sought water. Jesus offered her living water.
- The blind wanted physical sight. Jesus offered spiritual sight.
- The men with leprosy wanted physical healing for their sores. Jesus offered spiritual healing for their sin.

EXAMPLES OF TRANSITIONAL ISSUES AND STATEMENTS

- When someone presents a major statement about a significant life issue, you can say, "That's interesting. How did you come to that conclusion?"

- Who has had the greatest impact on your life?
- What do you think is our purpose here on earth?
- Do you think much about spiritual things?
- Has your spiritual journey helped you answer the deepest questions you are asking?
- To you, who is Jesus Christ?
- What do you think happens to people when they die?

Use transitions that fit you, but by all means, use them. People want to talk about spiritual things.

Twenty-five Areas of Life to Use for Transitions

In the past, the church was an influential part of most aspects of society. This is no longer the case. This fact reduces the opportunity for us to share common experiences with people. Therefore, we cannot rely on transitioning to Christ from a conversation about the local church experience of the lost person. There are, however, many topics that present us with opportunities to talk about Jesus.

- financial stress
- financial pursuits
- job promotion
- job loss
- economy
- stress
- family
- work/job
- children
- divorce
- conflict in a relationship
- death of a public figure
- public tragedy or news
- illness
- looking for purpose/meaning
- church

- hobbies
- religious background
- beliefs of a public figure in the news
- hope
- hell
- death
- heaven

DEALING WITH OBJECTIONS

Understanding objections will help you learn to respond to them appropriately.

FORMS OF OBJECTIONS

Objections take several forms. They usually come in the form of a question but can also come in the form of a harsh or negative statement. People will also seek to divert the conversation to another topic or to a scapegoat person or issue (smoke-screen tactic).

Objections can be both verbal and nonverbal. We need to listen with both our ears and our eyes. Sometimes people are finished talking about a subject, and we can run right through the nonverbal stop signs. When this happens, we come across as insensitive, and we may make God look bad at the same time. We are Christ's ambassadors by representing Him to people.

COMMON REASONS FOR OBJECTIONS

- A deflection from dealing with the spiritual issue at hand
  - Spiritual discomfort or resistance due to the working of the Holy Spirit
  - Defense mechanism
  - Anger or hang-ups from past bad experiences
  - Need time to process

- A legitimate question or concern about the implications of the gospel
- A way to communicate that they are not ready to deal with the topic in that setting or at that time
- A method of maintaining some control in the conversation (the one asking the questions is always in control of the conversation)
- Lack of understanding the gospel
- A disconnect between our message and their grid of religious teachings or beliefs

CATEGORIES OF OBJECTIONS

- Credibility or believability of the messenger
- Lack of understanding the message
- Struggling with the implications of the message
- Gospel message particulars
  - God
  - Their sinful condition
  - Work of Christ
- Timing or setting
- Our approach
- Misconceptions about Christianity
- Negative experience with a church or a Christian

RESPONDING TO OBJECTIONS

We can make several mistakes when people present objections. First, we can become defensive and come across as unsure of our God or our ability to respond to the questions. Second, we attack the person directly or negatively respond to the question/issue raised. Third, we can avoid or ignore the objection. All of these responses are likely to hurt, not enhance, the receptivity of the lost person.

We should embrace positive attitudes concerning objections. We should remember that questions and objections are legitimate. They are a necessary and welcomed part of the process toward regeneration. If we expect and welcome objections and questions, we are more likely to respond in a positive manner. We should respond with confidence, humility, and gentleness as we treat people in ways that reflect the value God has bestowed upon them.

ASSESSING READINESS

You must care enough to encourage the lost person to respond when the time is appropriate. But how do you know when the time is appropriate? The easiest answer is to follow the leadership of the Holy Spirit. For this to happen, we must continue to position ourselves to hear the voice of God. A by-product of witnessing on a regular basis is that the witness develops greater sensitivity and skill in knowing when to move forward and when to stop.

Two different types of assessments need to be used. One type involves getting permission to take the conversation to the next level in communicating the gospel. This may be done indirectly and will happen several times in the conversation. We are assessing questions, understanding, feelings, obstacles, clarity, and commitment. A second type involves assessing for the saving commitment to Christ. Both are important in personal evangelism.[11]

Not all lost people are at the same point, nor do they need the same thing from us.[12] The following chart describes people's levels of spiritual development, the characteristic they are displaying, and the appropriate witnessing tactic that should be taken.

Matching Spiritual Development with Witnessing Tactic

Level of Spiritual Development	Characteristic	Witnessing Tactic
Ignorance	Uninformed	Pray, instruct, nurture
Indifference	Unconcerned	Share, confront with Christ

Hostility	Bitter, angry	Love, listen, and share Jesus; be patient
Interest	Concerned	Explain the gospel, ask for a commitment
Conviction	Heavy Hearted	Show work of Holy Spirit; steps to coming to Christ; ask for commitment
Conversion	Ready	Guide through conversion; show how to follow Christ
Growth	Christian	Share in fellowship; encourage to witness; pray for lost
Spiritual Decline	Overcome by sin	Show patience, love, listen, encourage, bridge gap

ASSESSMENTS OF JESUS

Like me, you might be surprised to learn how Jesus assessed people's readiness to surrender their lives to Christ's control. Some people indicate an interest in following Christ, but there is a huge difference between inquiring and surrendering the controls. Jesus asked the rich young ruler to sell his possessions and give the resources to the poor before following Jesus. Several times Jesus warned that following Him would have costs. Following Jesus would involve suffering, cross bearing, and even death for many.

ASSESSMENT CONCERNS

It is possible to use the same words as a lost person and think that we are talking about the same thing, but in fact we may have different understandings of the terms. Words that had common usages in the past no longer have common usages and understandings. Witnesses must use discernment and inquiry to make sure they are communicating clearly, whether they are listening or talking.

When people say "God," you need to ask questions to ascertain exactly how they are using that term. They may in fact be referring to a single God who is all knowing, personal, above us and with us, omnipotent, omnipresent, and capable of doing anything He desires. However, they may be using *god* to mean anything and everything except the understanding of orthodox Christians. Even the term *Christian* cannot be taken to have a common, universal usage, especially among twelve-step people.

Another deep concern is that we may be tempted to communicate only part of the gospel by telling lost people the potential benefits of following Christ and neglect communicating the demands that come with following Christ. I do not believe we do this intentionally, but I believe that we do it too often in an effort to hear someone say yes to Jesus.

The altar call presents a potential challenge to effective gospel communication. Southern Baptists often use an altar call at the end of the service, similar in nature to the invitation extended at Billy Graham's crusades. A typical altar call in the South would include a call for (1) rededicating one's life to Christ, (2) joining the church by letter or statement, (3) seeking salvation, baptism, and church membership.

There is a danger persons will come forward in response to the spiritual moving of God in their lives for clarification or information but not to make a first-time decision for Christ. They may be confused and need assistance. However, if we limit their response choices or ask them if they want to give their lives to Christ, they may have no idea what we are talking about but say yes because they think that is the right answer. This leads to all kinds of problems down the road, including the possibility they may actually think they are saved while they are lost. Practicing this approach can produce voting, unregenerate church members who are setting poor examples as they try to live the Christian life without the Holy Spirit in their lives.

I am not opposed to the altar call. However, I believe we do searching people a disservice by treating them efficiently in order to close the service quickly. Everyone benefits if the church provides the opportunity for clarification through dialogue with a trained decision counselor. The seriousness of the call to follow Christ demands that we take time with people who respond to God's moving in their lives.

EXAMPLES OF READINESS QUESTIONS

I grew up watching police shows. Often in the interrogation process, one police officer would befriend the criminal while the other officer asked the hard, pushy questions. This technique was referred to as "good cop, bad cop." When learning to share my faith in my college athletic dorm with my spiritual mentor, we used a mild form of good cop and bad cop to assist us in checking for understanding and commitment. It was a form of advocate and devil's advocate. We did this to assess readiness, not to be cute or to trick people.

There is no one best way to assess readiness. Skill and sensitivity need to be developed with practice, not in theory only. You will have to find questions and methods that fit who you are and help you to assess readiness within the limits of being human.

Several people have developed lists of questions they use to assess readiness. Bill Faye included a helpful list in *Share Jesus Without Fear*. These questions are limited because they have yes and no characteristics, but you can adapt them to fit the situation.[13]

- Do you have any kind of spiritual belief?
- To you, who is Jesus Christ?
- Do you think there is a heaven or a hell?
- If you died tonight, where would you go? If heaven, why?
- If what you are believing is not true, would you want to know?

Poor Questions

Work to stay away from yes/no questions. The answers do not tell you much.

- Does what we have been discussing make sense to you?
- Do you understand?

The questions above can be used, but not by themselves, to determine readiness to receive Christ. Assessing readiness occurs not in a single question but in several questions and observations throughout the dialogue. As we check for understanding and clarity, we are also checking for commitment to go to the next level. Agreement does not necessarily equal commitment to change life direction.

Better Questions

- Where are you with what you are hearing?
- How would you like to proceed?
- If you do not mind, would you please tell me the implications of what we just talked about?
- What are you thinking?
- What are you feeling?
- Are you ready to surrender your life to Christ?
- Are you ready to ask God for His forgiveness and leadership in your life?

THE INVITATION

JESUS EXTENDING THE CALL

Jesus extended the call to follow Him. The following are just a few of the passages that reflect Jesus' call to follow Him (Matt. 4:19; 8:22; 9:9; 10:38; 16:24). By following Him, we establish a relationship with God and learn from Him.

INVITING TO CHRIST AND HIS FAMILY

Prayer of Invitation

People respond to the drawing of the Holy Spirit in several different ways. Do not be surprised if people respond differently than you expected. Some who are typically not emotional will respond with great passion; others who are often emotional will respond with calmness. Some will be overwhelmed with tears for their utter dependence on Christ's work on the cross to bear their sin. Still others will respond with great joy.

There are several ways to lead persons when they indicate a desire to commit their lives to Christ. You can ask them if they would prefer to (1) pray themselves, (2) repeat a prayer after you, or (3) pray after you finish praying for them. My preference is to pray along with them. This allows them to speak from their heart and also allows me to lead them in several specific areas. If you lead them, prompt them to (1) ask for God's forgiveness, (2) ask for God's leadership, and (3) give thanks for the work of Christ.

Celebrate Their Commitment

Not everyone will react the same, but everyone will have a story to celebrate, one of moving from death to life. I encourage new followers of Christ to tell several people who they think will be happy to hear about their response to Christ. This gives new converts a good start by involving supportive people in their lives and by seeing the value of a Christian family. This will also get them sharing their story with believers, which should make it easier to share with lost people as well.

CHAPTER 8

Removing Barriers

BARRIERS SERVE MANY PURPOSES. They obstruct, protect, limit access, and prevent injury. They keep things from coming in or going out. Some barriers are physical, while others are emotional or relational. Barriers can be both real and imaginary, and either kind can be effective.

In evangelism, barriers hinder the spreading of the gospel and are often not easy to remove. In this chapter we will examine both internal and external barriers to evangelism. The internal barriers are those which we erect that prevent us or hinder us from sharing our faith. The external barriers are those that lost people erect; we must find ways around those barriers in order to reach them for Christ.

IDENTIFYING INTERNAL BARRIERS TO WITNESSING

The greatest resistance to the spread of the gospel is within our minds and spirits. These unseen barriers are real and powerful. They can be crippling to our spiritual development and debilitating to our efforts to expand the kingdom. These are the barriers that lie within our minds.

Resistance to sharing a message from God is not unique to our time. We see Moses using the excuse of being slow of tongue, a speech problem. In the Old Testament we also see man's resistance to go to people who are different from him with God's message. Jonah did not want to go to Nineveh, so he acted in disobedience by heading for Tarshish. Yet God graciously got Jonah's attention and redirected his path for both Jonah's and Nineveh's sake.

We must continually be guided by the Holy Spirit. Paul wrote, "We demolish arguments and every pretension that sets itself up against the knowledge of God, and we take captive every thought to make it obedient to Christ" (2 Cor. 10:5). For it is the battle for the mind, the emotions, and the will that determines whether we share or hide Christ.

FEAR

I have compiled hundreds of interviews with laypersons and pastors concerning evangelism. We ask laypersons this series of questions.

Nonstaff Evangelism Survey

- What do you think when you hear the term *evangelism*?
- What do you see as the major obstacles to evangelism in your church?
- Can you communicate the evangelistic strategy of your church?
- What do you think can be done to improve your church's ability to reach lost people?
- How can the pastor/staff increase/promote the value of evangelism in churches?
- Do you think the time requirements of your church hinder your ability to develop relationships with lost people?
- What one or two things tend to hinder you from sharing your faith?
- What advice would you give me to help me lead a church in its evangelistic thrust?
- Is there anything else you would like to add?

I have learned much from reading the results and dialoging with my students about their impressions from the surveys. I discovered that fear is the number-one barrier to personal evangelism. Fears are real and imaginary, small and huge, have merit and are unfounded. Fear comes in many shades of colors, both bold and subtle.

Areas of Fear

Not all fears express themselves in the same manner. There are several different manifestations of fear.

Rejection. No one wants to feel the sting of rejection. However, in evangelism, we are not the focus of rejection, in spite of our feelings. People are primarily rejecting Jesus, not us. "Therefore, he who rejects this instruction does not reject man but God, who gives you his Holy Spirit" (1 Thess. 4:8). However, to the degree we do experience rejection, we participate in this with Christ. We need not take it personally when we present the gospel clearly and a person fails to choose Christ (Rom. 15:1–3).

Failure. Failure is feared for a variety of reasons. We can fear failure because of how it reflects on us. We also fear failure because we do not want to drive a person further from God due to our inadequacies of knowledge or skills in communicating the message. Having a biblical view of success will reduce our fear of failure.[1]

Loss of Relationship. Fearing the loss of a close relationship can keep us from sharing our faith. We should think about our actions in light of our relationships so that we become wise and sensitive in how we share the gospel. Relationships always involve some level of risk. However, as we love people, we can do nothing other than to share with people with whom we have relationships.

As we surrender our will to the Holy Spirit, the question becomes, How do I share with those with whom I have a relationship so that I do not put undue risk on the relationship? The question is not, Should I share with those with whom I have a relationship? We are wise to interact with people in a way that honors them and the Lord. We can be gracious, sensitive, and pleasant yet share the gospel appropriately.

Lack of Knowledge. Some of us struggle with sharing our faith because we are fearful of being asked questions we cannot answer. We say that we do not know enough theology or how to witness. Most lost people do not expect us to be experts on every facet of Christianity or on their religious background. Most of our worries related to information never come to pass.

One way to address this fear is to be disciplined enough to prepare. The threat of embarrassment should motivate us to learn to defend the hope that is within us. It should not keep us from sharing our faith. God can miraculously use the most feeble effort and the smallest knowledge, but He cannot use us in any way if we are unwilling to speak on His behalf.

Responding to Fear

Fear in its simplest form is a temporary loss of perspective. It is easy to focus on how someone might respond to *me*. It is also easy to forget how much people need the Lord and how much Christ desires a relationship with lost persons. How are we to respond to our own fears?

First, we can recognize that fear is natural, although we are seeking to live in the power of the supernatural. One of my favorite quotes is, "Courage is not the absence of fear but doing the very thing that you fear." I learned to share my faith among my teammates and fraternity brothers in college. Sometimes with fear and trembling I had the privilege of sharing Christ and seeing some of my friends radically surrender their lives to Christ.

Second, we can recognize that fear is not from God but a tool of Satan. We do battle against the forces of hell when we share our faith. When fear comes, acknowledge it and claim victory over it in the power of the Holy Spirit.

Third, love will disperse fear. Paul told young Timothy, "For God did not give us a spirit of timidity, but a spirit of power, of love and of self-discipline" (2 Tim. 1:7). And John wrote, "There is no fear in love. But perfect love drives out fear, because fear has to do with punishment. The one who fears is not made perfect in love" (1 John 4:18). Fear is dispersed when we love someone who is lost and headed for a Christless eternity.

Fourth, fear should drive us to a greater dependence on God. Remember, evangelism is about God, who chooses to use us. Reliance upon the Holy Spirit in prayer is always the position to maintain. We are never stronger than when we have bowed our spirits in dependence upon God to do what we cannot.

Fifth, fear should increase our desire to become more skilled in sharing Christ. My eldest daughter is a perfectionist. Her drive to get it right helps her now and will help her in the future. However, it creates frustration when she is learning a new skill. She wants to be perfect the first time. But playing volleyball and softball this year has taught her the importance of practice and repeated drills to perfect a skill. Several times early in the two seasons when she was having difficulty perfecting new skills she indicated she wanted to quit. Thankfully, she heeded my advice that what she needed was patience with herself and repeated practice with the skills to perfect them. Though still somewhat impatient with herself, she has disciplined herself to extensive practice so that she might perform well. Fear can be used to drive us to develop sensitivities and skills in sharing the greatest story ever told.

RELATIONAL DISTANCE

A common reason given for not sharing the gospel relates to the relational distance between the Christian and the lost person. The tendency is to play both sides of this excuse. We behave a lot like Goldilocks. She slept in one bed and said it was too hard. She slept in another bed and said it was too soft. She slept in a third bed and said it was just right. In sharing our faith, our tendency can be to say that a person is either too close to us relationally or too distant. It seems as though we are looking for the "just right" person with whom to share the Christian message, which in reality does not exist.

We often hesitate to share with those who are relationally close to use. To evangelize people who know us well, our lifestyle needs to be credible and the relationship clear of unresolved baggage. There are also people who are not close to us relationally but need Christ. With these people we need to take the initiative to close the distance between the lost person and us. Any small act of kindness helps to close the gap.

FALSE STEREOTYPES

Giving too much validity to stereotypes can erect barriers to our participating in evangelism. It is possible to think too highly or too lowly of evangelists and have it impact our view and participation in evangelism.

Too High (Professionals, Perfection and Positive Models)

Not Professional. It is easy to think that we will leave sharing the gospel with the professionals. Biblically, evangelism is not just for professionals. Laypersons have access to people whom professional ministers do not. If you don't reach the people within your sphere of influence at home, work, neighborhood, and other places, who will?

Not Good Enough. If we waited until we were good enough in our behavior or in our approach, we would never share Christ. Lost people do not expect us to be perfect; they expect us to be honest with our successes and failures. They want us to be authentic.

Not Possessing Positive Traits of Evangelistic Role Models. You do not have to possess the attributes and gifts of Billy Graham to share Christ. You do not have to be an extrovert, meet strangers well, have a booming voice, be courageous in every circumstance, or speak powerfully or eloquently before a crowd to tell God's story in your life. Sharing Christ involves faithfulness to report for service in the Lord's army.

God desires to use you, which includes the good, the bad, and the ugly parts of you. I am still amazed that God would use me, the guy with a speaking problem as a third and fourth grader, to draw someone to Himself.

Too Low (Negative Models)

Poor Public Models. Like many we surveyed, when you think of evangelism, you may have negative mental images of people whom you never want to emulate. You can reach people for Christ by being yourself. You can invite people to Jesus without being pushy, arrogant, obnoxious, overbearing, or preaching at people. Do not let a poor role model or public model keep you from sharing Jesus.

ISOLATION

Without relationship, typically there is no influence. Isolation from the very people we are seeking to win to Christ is a barrier to evangelism. Barna said, "We tend to associate with other Christians and thus have few significant relationships with nonbelievers. We struggle with evangelism because we are isolated from the very people God has called us to influence."[2] We must go to the world of lost people and not wait or expect them to come to us. It is our responsibility to take the initiative to enter into their presence to share.

Christians have become isolated for several reasons, none of which are acceptable. We often isolate ourselves because we want to insulate ourselves from the negative influences of people without Christ. Jesus, however, entered into our world. We also isolate ourselves out of benign neglect. We get caught up doing church work, attending church socials, and playing sports on church teams. But we neglect the church's purpose, leaving little time for building relationships with those who are in desperate need of Christ.

Let's face it together. We often become isolated because we are selfish. It is easier to live around Christians and not enter into the messy lives of those who do not speak our church language. It takes emotional energy and time, even what appears to be wasted time. It takes mental energy. It takes doing things with people we don't even like and who do things that violate the teachings of Scriptures. We often presume upon God's understanding because He knows our intentions and all the great things we are doing for the church. The problem is that our good intentions never take the gospel to one lost person.

Isolation is a particular danger to those who work in Christian environments, such as a Christian business, school, church, or seminary. One of my students reflected upon his experiences interviewing lost people. He said, "This process has led me to think about my own perceptions of those around me. Because I spend an enormous amount of my time around believers, I sometimes forget just how off base people in our society are. I have learned that I need to be disciplined to build relationships with my neighbors in an effort to show them the love of God. My mission field is the block on which I live. My neighbors need to see, hear, and understand the truth of God's mercy and grace. This has been a life-changing experience."[3]

Christian vocations are dangerous to relational perspectives. Most Christians, including pastors, staff members, seminary employees, and various other parachurch vocational ministers, are disconnected from the very people we say we are trying to reach. I have worked in Christian environments for over sixteen years. We are in danger of not even knowing the questions, yet we say we have the answers. God have mercy on us and push us out of our communes and into the paths of people who desperately want to hear the message of life.

OTHER INTERNAL BARRIERS

Several internal barriers hinder our efforts: (1) Spiritual gift—some want to use the excuse that they do not have the spiritual gift of evangelism. Everyone gets the privilege of sharing the great news. (2) Time—some say they do not have the time. Everyone has twenty-four hours in a day. Schedules are full, but we do not live to serve our schedules; our schedules are to be used to help us set priorities. (3) Age—I am too old or too young. Precious people of all ages are effectively and faithfully sharing what Jesus has done in their lives.

Two particular factors, apathy and insecurity, contribute to the other internal factors. Mental and emotional apathy in a Christian is a dangerous state. It will surface all types of internal excuses for not sharing one's faith. Insecurity also enhances other barriers. Maturing Christians need to develop a positive self-image based on their identity in Christ.

There are many more barriers to witnessing.[4] However, when there is a will, there is always a way to share. Personal evangelism is a matter of the will, not just the intellect or emotions. Emotional feelings and intellectual reasons should support our will, but they are not the primary force behind our evangelism. Active obedience to the leadership and direction of the Holy Spirit compels us.

REDUCING INTERNAL BARRIERS TO WITNESSING

USING PROPER MOTIVATION FOR WITNESSING

The highest level of motivation for evangelism is love for God. We should desire to expand His glory on the earth and to all the peoples of the earth out of a deep love for the one who extended love to us in spite of our unworthiness. For the short-term we can use methods that are "less than" at best. Guilt, fear, shame, obligation, and other forms of manipulation usually work for a short season but do not produce a lifelong and consistent witness.

There is much to learn from the evangelistic motivations of the early church. Michael Green discussed three primary factors that motivated the early Christians to share their faith in Jesus Christ. (1) The main motive for evangelism was a sense of gratitude toward God. Green stated, "These men did not spread their message because it was advisable for them to do so, nor because it was the socially responsible thing to do. They did not do it primarily for humanitarian or utilitarian reasons. They did it because of the overwhelming experience of the love of God which they had received through Jesus Christ." Early Christians also shared their faith (2) out of a sense of responsibility and (3) out of concern for lost people around them. Sharing Jesus was a matter of privilege and obedience for the early

Christians. They knew if they did not share their faith, the gospel would not spread.[5]

USING REALISTIC AND SUSTAINABLE SYSTEMS

Over an extended period of time, people must do evangelism within realistic and sustainable systems. Most major evangelistic campaigns or strategies require more of people than they can deliver while taking care of the other major areas of their lives. This may explain why we often have spikes in statistics like baptisms, whether in a denomination, region, or local church. Most evangelistic systems are not reasonably sustainable for most church members over the long haul. These include such approaches as revivals, crusades, and weekly cold calling.[6]

Using a term over and over does impact the understanding of the term over time. I am afraid that we see church in terms of a place to go. This is far from the biblical concept of church. The church is not a place to go, but something that Christians are. We are the church. Therefore, where we go the church goes.

If we are really to reach people for Christ by developing quality relationships with lost people, we will have to rethink the schedules of our church organizations. Our church schedules can easily prevent us from being the church as we invest time going to multiple meetings at the church building. We too easily create systems that do not support evangelism. Evaluate whether your church's systems and strategies are supporting those who are willing to share their faith or keeping them excessively busy so they have no time to share.

It is a trap to equate faithfulness to God with faithful attendance at all the activities of the church. Most church systems use their most mature and faithful church members to do church work rather than to do ministry outside the building. Churches need systems that elevate the roles people play in the lives of lost people by honoring evangelists and supporting their efforts. Coaching a Little League team may be the most spiritual activity in a Christian man's week.

Participating in a PTO may be of great service to the kingdom in a mother's week.

Ron Hutchcraft reminded us that "people are drowning while we have lifeguard meetings, sing lifeguard songs, and go to lifeguard committee meetings." His exhortation to us is "to get off the beach and into the water and there are more in the water than there are on the beach by far."[7]

EVANGELISTIC PROGRAM THAT MAKES SENSE TO CHRISTIANS

Much of what churches do to encourage and enhance personal evangelism actually hinders their efforts. Harold Bullock described a church approach to personal evangelism that makes sense to the members of Hope Community Church in Ft. Worth, Texas.

- Follow the leading of the Holy Spirit.
- Act in integrity in all situations.
- Maintain positive relationships with family, neighbors, and coworkers over the short and long term.
- Deal with people according to the person's distance from the gospel.
- Use an approach that piques the interest of nonbelievers.
- Avoid looking awkward and inappropriate in social situations.
- Team with other members to minister to and include nonbelievers in social and church activities.
- Invite to church events peole who can handle the "threat level" of the event.[8]

SHALLOW LOVE FOR JESUS AND LOST PEOPLE

A student asked Pastor Adrian Rogers for advice on how to lead a church in evangelism. Rogers said, "Your zeal is never any greater than your conviction. You can cheer others with your enthusiasm or their loyalty to the church or put them on a guilt trip for a while, but the only thing that will have a lasting effect is their love in the Lord Jesus Christ. It's not even a love for souls that sends people out; it's the love of Jesus that sends people out."[9]

The highest level of motivation for sharing our faith is love. We need not be "guilted" into sharing our faith. We need not be tricked or forced into telling others of Christ. We need a heart transplant. We need to develop a deeper love for God first and then choose to love people, even the unlovely, because Christ first loved us.

Love is a verb. Love has caused us to *do* many things we would not do otherwise. It causes us to learn things we did not want to learn. It has caused us to give of our emotions, time, money, sweat, and tears in situations that would not normally move us. Love has motivated us to move beyond our selfishness and our comfort zones to act for the benefit of a loved one. Love provides endurance, perseverance, and passion. Love is the most powerful motivator in evangelism.

Barriers are removed when we develop a deeper love. If we have difficulty overcoming barriers to sharing Christ's gift with others, maybe we should ask God to grant us a greater capacity to love Him and others. Love, spiritual passion, and willingness to obey flow out of a vital, dynamic relationship with Christ. Personal time with God in prayer, Bible study, and fasting help us connect with God and what is on God's heart—lost people.

SPIRITUAL DISCIPLINE

There is truth in the saying, "You are what you do habitually." Our patterns in life tell the story of our priorities and values. Donald Whitney in *Spiritual Disciplines for the Christian Life* discusses the importance of making personal evangelism a spiritual discipline.

One of my daughters shared with me a quote she learned from volleyball. "If you are not consciously forming good habits, you are unconsciously forming bad ones." Find ways to include evangelism and lost people in your life as a habit. An accountability partner can help with this.

PRACTICAL DO'S

Help people discover their style of strength in personal evangelism. There are at least six biblical styles of evangelism. We do well, especially in our early efforts, to use our preferred style, recognizing that as we mature we will expand the number of styles we can use as the situation warrants.

Help people get off to a good start in sharing their faith. Encourage new witnesses to maintain contact with a witnessing mentor. This will allow for support during difficult periods, assistance with tough questions and issues, and celebration during times of harvesting. This will also help new witnesses gain perspective on success and struggles as they arise. Also, you can involve beginning or reluctant witnesses in low-risk, high-reward evangelism such as servant-evangelism projects.[10]

Combine classroom preparation with field experience. These two work together to increase the willingness of Christians to share their faith. Witnessing has a common factor with muscle development; the more you use it, the stronger it becomes and the more you desire to use it.

Apply some practical suggestions. First, develop a personal and family mission statement that includes reaching out to lost people. Second, pray for yourself and for lost people by name. Also develop a list of three to six lost people whom you begin to pray for and love to Christ. There are no substitutes for praying and loving people to Jesus.

SUMMARY OF INTERNAL BARRIERS

We cannot leave people to their own interpretations of our lives and our God without any words. Silence about Christ is not an act of love. Maturing love compels us to speak so they may hear the truth, even with our limitations, faults, and misunderstandings. If we wait until we are close to perfect in sharing the gospel or in our personal lives, we may never speak. Throughout history the Holy Spirit has used imperfect vessels to carry His message, and He continues to do so today.

In order to develop convictions about witnessing, we need to come to grips with God's command to share our faith, and then test that conviction by intentionally placing ourselves in situations where our beliefs about evangelism are confronted and thereby transformed into convictions. Without the fire of experience, our intellectual beliefs cannot develop into convictions. We do what we really believe.

McCloskey summarized what we need to do to overcome internal barriers to witnessing. He said, "If you want to develop a burden for the lost, go out and talk to the lost and find out how lost they really are. If you desire to have the crucial nature of evangelism branded on your heart, go out and do it, and you will become convinced of just how crucial it is. If you want to develop the conviction that Jesus does indeed change lives, take His life-changing message to others and see if this isn't true."[11]

EXTERNAL BARRIERS TO FOLLOWING CHRIST

Not all barriers are erected by the witness. Lost people erect barriers as well. In this section we will address some of their common barriers and ways to reduce those barriers.

JESUS' RESPONSES TO OBJECTIONS AND BARRIERS

Several times Jesus faced the barrier of demonic beings (Matt. 8:28–34; Mark 1:21–28; Luke 4:31–37, 41). Jesus would rebuke the spirit directly and verbally, and when He commanded the demons to leave the person's body, they did.

Jesus responded to the questions that people posed to Him, even the questions that were being asked mentally but not verbally (Mark 2:1–12). Jesus anticipated their questions or responded to them after they were asked. Often He responded to their questions with His questions (Mark 2:19, 25; Luke 5:33–39). He led them to discover the answers; He did not just tell them.

People came to Jesus under various circumstances. Some wanted to follow Jesus but had not counted the cost. Jesus did not let them follow Him blindly. He told them that following Him must be above all other allegiances and relationships (Matt. 8:18–22). Some came to Jesus with physical needs but left having their sins forgiven because of their faith (Matt. 8:5–13).

Jesus addressed the barriers of social pressure and cultural sensitivities in several ways. He engaged lost people in places where lost people were in control of the environment (Mark 2:14–17). At times when Jesus faced a question, He responded by quoting a source that was credible to His listeners (Matt. 12:1–9). To some objections Jesus responded with humor (Matt. 12:9–14; 23:24–26; Mark 19:24). At other times Jesus responded with a story or parable (Luke 7:36–50; Mark 3:19–30).

Jesus used different approaches as people presented objections. At times Jesus acted outside the expectations of the religious leaders in ways that increased the value of people, especially for those who were despised or socially put down, such as the handicapped, women, and tax collectors. Rarely did Jesus respond to questions and objections with a direct, logical answer. He usually used methods to help listeners determine the answer without having to give it to them.

Jesus did not answer every question. He did not force people to follow Him. He did not accept followership at the lowest common denominator (Matt. 19:16–24). He did not ask people to follow without explaining something of the cost. He let people walk away from following Him. Jesus revealed much about His identity at times, while at other times He revealed little of who He was.

Jesus responded appropriately to the context of the inquirer and the situation. He did not have a single approach; He used a variety of approaches including humor, questions, stories, parables, quotes, Scriptures, and wise sayings. He often met the nonspiritual needs (physical, emotional, psychological) of receptive persons first and then their spiritual needs.

OBJECTIONS AND BARRIERS

Barriers and objections to responding positively to the gospel come in different forms. Some objections are emotional, intellectual, or pragmatic. Other types of barriers are theological, experiential, and relational. Some objections are seen while others remain unseen. Some barriers seem to be natural concerns, while others are more spiritual in nature.

Intellectual, Emotional, and Practical Barriers

Epistemology is the field of study related to knowledge and how people come to know. We have all said, "I believe" or "I know." Many factors lead us to say we know or believe something. In chapter 4, I introduced Yandall Woodfin's three channels which impact our knowing: intuitive, pragmatic, and rational/reflective avenues and responses.[12]

Woodfin described the three channels:

The intuitive channel is characterized by an inner, immediate, experiential convincingness or compellingness accompanying a knowledge claim. The pragmatic response is distinguished by its concern for the functional effectiveness of truth in some clearly demarcated realm of activity. Rational/reflective comprehension is recognized by the presence of conceptual coherence and consistency within a given rational context, or "logical set," and also by the degree to which claim corresponds compatibly with truth in other areas of experience or fields of knowledge. There is no necessary chronological priority among these channels because a claim may enter experience in any sequence or combination; furthermore, there should be no final assessment regarding their relative value since all are essential. Responsible interpreters will no doubt continue to swing from one emphasis to another from age to age in order to maintain a proper epistemological balance.

Moreover, the three channels are unavoidably involved in every legitimate investigation of knowledge. Various aspects of response may receive more conscious attention than others at times, but the whole person is nonetheless engaged.[13]

All three channels for determining knowledge impact receiving Christ. Each channel presents an opportunity for lost persons to erect or acknowledge a barrier to giving their lives to Christ.

Intellectual/Rational. From the philosophers of the first century until today, lost people have posed intellectual barriers to following Christ. They may struggle to accept the Bible, the biblical teachings about sin, God's existence or identity, the place of Christ, or the resurrection. These and similar theological barriers fall into the intellectual category of objections.

Information. Many have not actually rejected Christ; they have just not been clearly presented with the essential claims of Christ. In America we do well to assume lost people, even those who claim some form of religion, are ignorant of the basic Christian message. As I mentioned earlier, "A lot of people are not rejecting our Christ, they are rejecting our vocabulary, they have no idea what we are talking about."[14] This is usually due to ignorance, to misunderstanding, or to our using vocabularies that lost people do not understand.

Apologetics—Defending the Gospel. One way to address intellectual barriers is to address them with logic and reasonable responses. This is referred to as apologetics. As we become experienced in sharing our faith, we will begin to learn many of the questions and the objections people are raising. As we learn the questions, we can begin to find resources, people and materials to help us address the legitimate concerns people, have about giving their lives to Christ.[15]

Apologetics were a significant part of evangelism to highly educated modern thinkers who had little Christian influence in their lives. Apologetics in an increasingly postmodern America will become even more important not just for the educationally elite but also for the masses. However, there will be significant changes in the apologetics in terms of questions and types of approaches. The questions may include: Which God, or how many gods? not, Is there a God? or, How can Jesus be the only way to God? rather than Was Jesus the Son of God?[16]

The approach of the apologist, professional and lay alike, will have to shift from propositional fact giving only to leading people to discover truth through asking good questions and then providing timely propositional truths. The approach will become much more didactic and Socratic.[17] The Christian story will need to be communicated rather than the facts of the Bible recited. With the postmodern person, the evangelist and preacher alike will have to assume a much lower level of biblical knowledge.[18]

Emotional/Intuitive. For many the barrier is not primarily information but tied more to emotions. According to Rick Richardson, "We need to address issues not just of thinking but also of feeling and imagining and committing in ways that people today can engage with and be intrigued by."[19] These emotional barriers usually relate to a hurtful relationship. Many people have felt emotional pain at the hands of a Christian or a Christian church. Others are shut down to people in general which may hinder the gospel getting to them. This often leads to a closed spirit.

The media has facilitated the change in the default response of lost people to the gospel. In the earlier part of the twentieth century, the media was generally positive toward the church and Christians. Since 1970, however, with high-profile scandals involving Christian leaders and the media enhancing the view that Christians are narrow-minded and intolerant, the default response the general public has to Christ, the Christian church, and to Christians is negative.

Most people will be loved to Jesus, not convinced to Jesus. We need to build relational bridges. This is even truer for women, who are wired for relationships. Using servant evangelism projects with strangers and acts of kindness with people you know will help to remove the emotional barriers people may have erected to the gospel.[20]

Through my own relationships I have discovered that *intellectual* arguments are not received well when the other person is involved in an *emotional* argument. Usually the emotional issue(s) must be addressed first in order to create a climate for the logical points to be heard. This is true in evangelism as well.

In modernity, Christians shared the gospel with the intentions of reaching the head first and then the heart. Most of the U.S. population will not be reached in this sequence. We need to reach the heart first and then communicate the gospel to the head.

Pragmatic. As Christians we demonstrate through our lives the truthfulness of our message. When we live without Christ making a difference, we erect practical barriers to the gospel because we are ambassadors of Christ. The opposite is also true. When we apply the values and teachings of Christ, we testify to the power of Christ. We prove that it is profitable to follow the ways of God. The experiences lost people have with us are vitally important.

Following Jesus takes a great deal of pressure off of me as the leader of and provider for my family. I know that God has and will take care of us in His perfect will. As I examine others' lives, I see how uncomplicated my life is compared to my non-Christian friends. This does not mean my life is without struggles, but to walk in the ways of God has been and will forever be the wisest way to live. I have so many areas that are not struggles for me because God has given me instructions to follow based on how He created the world to operate.

It is not enough only to live well before others, but as the pragmatic barriers are lowered, we must verbally share the hope that is within us. Richardson said: "It is right to live our lives in ways that engender interest and questions from others. But we are not to wait passively until people ask questions. We can engage them actively, asking questions ourselves and sharing our lives and stories of God at work. One of my friends calls this practice 'living out loud.' After all, how will people hear unless someone is sent who has the guts to share (Rom. 10:14–15)?"[21]

The lifestyles of lost people present barriers. They may think the Christian lifestyle is OK for someone else, but they like life the way it is for them. They enjoy living with their self-designed morals and with themselves as the final arbiters of right and wrong. In situations like this, Christians can pray and wait for a critical inflection point or change in openness.

For some, trusting Christ involves becoming ostracized from family members and friends. It means a change not only in lifestyle but also in relationships that have been built over a lifetime.

Other Forms of Barriers

Theological. Trusting Christ involves significant theological issues. When people receive Christ, they are saying no to all other gods and all other ways of being straightened out with God. They are acknowledging that there is only one God and that they are not God themselves.

Lost people have real questions about Jesus being the only way to eternal life. They have questions about the resurrection and what happens to people without Christ and why bad things happen to good people. They want to know how someone else can determine for them what is right and what is wrong. Most theological barriers are intellectual in nature but are surrounded by fears, worries, anxieties, and mistrust.

People have other theological questions and issues. They have misinformation about Christ. They wonder if sincerity is good enough, especially since Christians cannot even seem to get on the same page regarding what God expects. They want to know how they can work their way to God to make things right. They question the whole concept of hell and how a loving God could send anyone there.

Many of the questions are legitimate and thoughtful. They want to know.

Part of the answer lies in how big we see our God to be. We must answer the question, Is God able and willing to reveal Himself to those who seek Him? God is up to the task! Encourage your lost friends to ask questions, to seek, and to explore what it means to follow Jesus, as you yourself follow Jesus and His ways. Ask them to join you on your spiritual journey in following after Christ.

Seen Versus Unseen. Not all barriers are seen. The heart is wicked and self-deceived and adept at hiding motives. When we interact with lost people, some will sometimes reveal what is keeping them from following Christ, while others are either unaware of their resistance or the factors behind their resistance.

There are different reasons for hiding barriers. Lost people will often present a false barrier to see how Christians respond. If we respond well, in time they will present the real or deeper barrier. They may also present a false barrier to deflect and guard the real fears or hurts that have prevented them from receiving Christ.

Natural Versus Spiritual. Some barriers appear to be natural human responses to the gospel, while others are less obvious. Paul reminded the church of its real enemy. "For our struggle is not against flesh and blood, but against the rulers, against the authorities, against the powers of this dark world and against the spiritual forces of evil in the heavenly realms" (Eph. 6:12).[22]

Satan and his demonic beings use influences we cannot see to hinder people from responding to Christ. Satan takes actions to inflict spiritual blindness on lost people. Lost people can be influenced with apathy and ignorance, while Satan seeks to maintain his strongholds. The following passages relate to the activities of Satan.

"Those along the path are the ones who hear, and then the devil comes and takes away the word from their hearts, so that they may not believe and be saved" (Luke 8:12).

"The god of this age has blinded the minds of unbelievers, so that they cannot see the light of the gospel of the glory of Christ, who is the image of God" (2 Cor. 4:4).

"For though we live in the world, we do not wage war as the world does. The weapons we fight with are not the weapons of the world. On the contrary, they have divine power to demolish strongholds. We demolish arguments and every pretension that sets itself up against the knowledge of God, and we take captive every thought to make it obedient to Christ" (2 Cor. 10:3–5).

QUESTIONS LOST PEOPLE HAVE

The number of possible questions is enormous. In witnessing you never know how people might respond. They ask all sorts of questions. The following list is designed to stimulate thinking about some of the types of questions that are being asked.

1. How can Jesus be the only way to God?
2. How can Christianity be true if Christians live like everyone else?
3. What does Jesus have to do with my life?
4. How can I get straightened out with God?
5. Who was/is Jesus?
6. What is God like?
7. How can I find meaning and purpose in life?
8. What happens to me when I die?
9. How can I trust that what Christians are saying is true?
10. If God is loving, why can't there be more than one way to Him?
11. How do we know that Jesus of the Bible is who He said He was?
12. Aren't all religions basically the same?

Because the questions change, I encourage you to take several steps: (1) Invest time in learning some principles of responding to objections. (2) Learn some phrases that will help you get through the first few moments of the objection. (3) Learn to respond to a select few issues that you continue to have to address. In chapter 9 we will examine the training that is necessary to respond to our pluralistic culture.

OBSTACLES TO RECEIVING CHRIST

Modern	Postmodern
See Engel's scale (p. 50)	Absolute truth of Scripture
Proving the validity of Christ	Mixed up views of life and Christianity
Lack of Information	Exclusivity claim of Christ
Skeptical of existence of God	Desire to maintain existing relationships
Evolution	Image of Christian church of today
The resurrection	Too many views (conflicting)
Questioning of miracles	Evangelism approaches based in modernity
Inconsistencies in Scripture	Lack of integrity in the witness (inconsistency)
Reasons to believe	Pluralism—broader exposure to various religions
	Biblical illiteracy
	Syncretism of the religions of the world
	No common understanding of God
	Few positive Christian examples to follow

For written resources to help you respond to particular objections, I suggest you secure a copy of Bill Fay's *Share Jesus Without Fear.* For a list of thirty-six objections, see the appendix. Fay provided some suggested responses to these common objections. Also, the tool kit *Becoming a Contagious Christian* has a written and video section with ideas for responding to eight of the most common objections to following Christ.[23]

TRUTHS AND TIPS IN RESPONDING TO BARRIERS

- Most people have multiple barriers before them, not just one.
- Your initial attitude is more important than what you say in response to the objection.
- Staying connected to the lost person is more important than what you say in response to an objection.
- You do not have to have the right answer or the best answer when the question/objection is raised.
- You almost never know what objection a person may raise until you start a spiritual conversation around Christ.
- Questions often do not have *the* answer.
- You may give a good response and the person still may not respond to Jesus.
- Keep the focus on Jesus.
- Accept responsibilities for failures of other Christians and the church when appropriate.
- Keep the focus on the implications of the resurrection.
- You will love more people to Jesus than you will convince to come to Jesus.
- When you hit a barrier, take a detour around it.
- Be sensitive to the leading of the Holy Spirit.
- No does not have to be the final answer.
- When faced with one type of barrier, move to approach the person from another angle or facet of the gospel.

You may want to take the following steps as you face a barrier.

Step 1: Pray.

Step 2: Try to identify the type of barrier.

Step 3: Affirm the person's objections.

Step 4: Decide to address or delay responding to the barrier/ question/objection.

Step 5: Take a positive outlook and step forward.

Step 6: Maintain a relationship with the lost person.

For assistance in responding to these and other common questions, see my Web site www.MEGnet.org.

PRACTICAL TIPS TO INCREASE RECEPTIVITY

Some people and some geographic areas are more spiritually receptive than others. A variety of factors affect this, some of which are controllable and some of which are not. Satan and his followers are alive and active. However, Christ followers have access to the power found in Christ that is more powerful than any influence of Satan.

As followers of Christ, we cannot force people to Christ, but we can enhance the receptivity of the lost. Within the framework of a healthy friendship, we can increase receptivity. Some would argue against building friendships to share the gospel, but without relationship there is little room for influence. Richardson wrote, "It is not manipulative to build a friendship with the goal of sharing Christ. It is loving, as long as we stay committed to our friends whether they respond to our appeal or not."[24]

HOW CAN WE INCREASE RECEPTIVITY?
1. By modeling the Christian life.
2. By praying for lost people by name.
3. By seeking God's forgiveness for the sins of city or area (past and present).
4. By encouraging Christian churches toward cooperation in their common mission.

5. By having Christians and churches contribute to the larger community.
6. By clearly presenting and clarifying the gospel message.
7. By allowing people to move along in stages, if they are not responsive to large moves.
8. By learning to ask good questions to check for clarity of the message.
9. By becoming emotionally and relationally engaged with lost people!

Ways to Cultivate Receptivity with Highly Nonreceptive People

Some people are highly resistant to the gospel. For various reasons people become hardened to Christians, the church, and Christ. These situations are difficult witnessing situations. Here are a few ways to cultivate receptivity.

1. Love them with acts of kindness.
2. Pray for a receptive spirit for the lost person.
3. Ask God to remove spiritual blinders and to give spiritual sight.
4. Ask God for insights into their hearts.
5. Wait for DDDIS (critical transitional point, Divorce, Death, Divine Encounters, Illness, and Status change).

Opening Closed Hearts/Spirits

Christians can facilitate the opening of the heart to the message through their obedience and sensitivity to the Holy Spirit. Ultimately, only God opens and prepares the heart to receive the gospel.[25] However, we can help open hearts toward us, which in turn enhances the possibilities of opening hearts toward God.

I learned a valuable principle and technique from Gary Smalley's video series on parenting, *Homes of Honor*.[26] His approach for opening the hearts of children will work whether dealing with a teenager, a spouse, a friend, or even a stranger. And it applies to spiritual matters, not just human relationships.

Often a person's heart is closed due to an unresolved offense. We can offend someone, and, if it goes unresolved, the person will either quickly or over time close his heart to us. These closed spirits manifest themselves in all types of negative ways, from withdrawal to anger and steps between.

Often people have closed their hearts toward God. And, for the message and love of Christ to penetrate their hearts, they will have to open their hearts, usually to us first and then to Christ. We cannot make people open their hearts toward God, but we can be ambassadors for God to open hearts toward us and thereby make them more receptive to the gospel message. Smalley said that when a person is closed emotionally, we should take five steps. These steps help to open the heart of a closed person.

1. Become tenderhearted.
2. Increase understanding.
3. Recognize the offense.
4. Attempt to touch.
5. Seek forgiveness.

There are many different ways to open a person's spirit toward you or Christ. As we seek to do so with prayer, gentleness, and humility, we can help people become more receptive to us and Christ.

SUMMARY

We will never know it all or become completely prepared, so as the Nike ad says, "Just do it." The best learning is often on-the-job training. Jesus modeled this by giving the disciples just enough to get them started. After getting a few bumps from interacting with people, the disciples became much more willing learners. The same is true today. Just do it.

CHAPTER 9

What's Next?
Best of the Rest

GENDER SPECIFIC KEYS

MEN AND WOMEN ARE DIFFERENT. They hear, process information, make decisions, and relate differently. Men want to *do* things with their friends, while women find pleasure in *being* with their friends. Men try to solve problems, while women want empathy as they talk about their problems. Men talk to give reports, while women develop relationships with their words. Men tend to be task-driven, while women tend to be wired for nurturing and relationships. According to Jaye Martin, who directs women's evangelism ministry at the North American Mission Board, "Men tend to think and do, and women tend to share and feel."[1] This will impact how we do personal and church evangelism to these two subcultures.

The differences—mentally, emotionally, and relationally—make men and women uniquely different creations of God. We do both men and women a disservice if we treat them as though they were exactly the same, especially in how they respond to Christ. The more we learn about the different needs and thought processes of men and women, the more likely we will be to connect the gospel message to their lives.

REACHING MEN

Brian Peterson identified several things that tend to bother men. He said men: (1) are trapped in the rat race, (2) are bored, (3) are underchallenged, (4) have lost touch with their masculine core,

(5) are falling for the notion that their best years are over, and (6) are trying to be somebody other than themselves. These certainly do not characterize all men, but some of these may be used to facilitate men receiving Christ.

Men are generally more responsive to ideas and principles than to relationships. They want to get involved in solving problems and to work with their hands. And they like being involved with doing activities such as service projects, sports, and barbeques.

Men must bow their wills to Christ, but our approaches in personal evangelism should allow them to maintain control and affirm their manhood. We can do evangelism best on neutral ground or on their turf, not in a place where they feel vulnerable, such as a church building or a small group in a Christian's home, where they may feel cornered. Talk with men, not *to* them, especially not down to them as if they were children or ignorant.

Evangelism targeting men will be somewhat different from that targeting women. Men would prefer to talk about more serious topics when they engaged in or around an activity, not just sitting around talking. They enjoy banter and light conversations, so avoid being too serious in conversations for extended periods of time without levity.

Allow men space and time to reflect and ask questions about the implications of the gospel; undue pressure hinders conversion. Allow men to say no to the gospel and maintain their dignity. Let the Holy Spirit do the convicting; do not try to shame men to Christ.

Because men are problem solvers, share Christ as the only one who solves some of the particular problems they face. Gospel conversations that involve physical or mental images are more likely to connect with men.

REACHING WOMEN

In almost every method of categorizing religion and spiritual interests and activities, women rate higher than men.[2] However, this does not mean they come to Christ easily or in the same way.

The needs of women vary by age, stage of life, background, education, financial situation, experience, geographic location, and health. Connie Cavanaugh summarized the needs of women after interviews with several leaders of women's ministries. The following nine needs emerged from her research.

1. Women need to be wanted.
2. Women need companionship.
3. Women need to belong.
4. Women need parenting skills and support from other parents.
5. Women need help to improve their marriage.
6. Women need encouragement.
7. Women need emotional support.
8. Women need accountability.
9. Women need purpose and fulfillment.[3]

In personal evangelism women more easily bridge the gap and build networks with other women. Lost women are more likely to respond to another woman or a group of women who invite them into a relationship before sharing the facts of the gospel. They are likely to respond to an invitation to attend a need-oriented event with other women. The sharing of a life-changing testimony with a lost woman is an effective approach to evangelism.[4]

HOW TO WAIT AFTER A NO

Among those who study evangelism, there is a debate of sorts. Some believe that the most difficult part of witnessing is getting started or making the transition to a spiritual conversation centered on Jesus. Others believe that the most difficult part is learning when to stop or back off from a witnessing conversation. The latter involves a no in some form. God typically uses a web of people and circumstances to bring people to Himself, so you will want to guard against closing the hearts of people by how you respond to their verbal and nonverbal no.

In personal evangelism, persistence is a needed quality. Persistence implies intentionality in sharing our faith. Hassling or nagging is not persistence. As witnesses, we want to display genuine concern for the lost person, which may involve consistent care, while not being overbearing. Evangelism can be direct or confrontational without being antagonistic.

After we receive a no, there are several things we should not do. We should not take the response personally or respond with anger, disdain, or shock. We should not remove ourselves from the lost person's life. It may be after the no that people are most sensitive to you and to the message of Christ. We can't afford to send the message that we were only friends with them as long as there was a chance they would join our club.

I am an optimist. And as a church planter by personal wiring, *no* often just means "not now." Given the right opportunity or circumstance, people will choose to follow Christ. It makes sense to follow Christ. So when I receive a no, I wait for DDDIS, look for ways to clarify the message, and bring credibility to the message with my life.[5]

Rick Warren said that people are more receptive during times of transition and tension. He said, "Any time someone experiences major change, whether positive or negative, it seems to create a hunger for spiritual stability. Right now there is enormous interest in spiritual matters due to the massive changes in our world that are making people frightened and unsettled. Alvin Toffler says that people look for 'islands of stability' when change becomes overwhelming. This is a wave the church needs to ride."[6] Regarding tension, Warren said, "God uses all kinds of emotional pain to get people's attention: the pain of divorce, death of a loved one, unemployment, financial problems, marriage and family difficulties, loneliness, resentment, guilt, and other stresses. Fearful or anxious people often begin looking for something greater than themselves to ease the pain and fill the void they feel."[7] We need prayerfully and expectantly to wait for an opening and time of receptivity.

After the no, we should do the things we were doing prior to the no. We should continue to pray for spiritual sight and receptivity. We should continue to be available to answer questions, validate the message with our lives, and love on them. Be persistent, continue to love, be available; they may be watching you more intently.

We should listen to the no carefully, seeking to determine the whys behind the no. Without being judgmental, we should seek to find out the form of their objection to following Christ. Listen not only to their words, but also listen to their heart. It is first through the heart that we will reach most adults for Christ.

Bullock summarized the philosophy and strategy used at Hope. They use several phases to help their members know what to do at various stages. Their primary roles are (1) friend and curiosity builder, (2) friend and message clarifier, and (3) friend and persuader. When we get a no, we need to continue to be a friend.

FOLLOW-UP

I can vividly remember the details of bringing home my firstborn, Blakeney Lynne. Without a call button or instruction manual, Sandy and I felt butterflies as we cared for our newest family member. With the help we received from parents and in-laws, we cared for the helpless but adorable child. Blakeney could not survive without our assistance. New believers also need assistance to grow and develop into fruitful maturity.

Much of discipleship and even follow-up regretfully have bought into the nonbiblical emphasis of modernity—namely, excessive individualism. It is as if discipleship were an individual sport, that Christians were to pull themselves up by their bootstraps to grow spiritually. Evangelism today is increasingly dependent on the living examples of the followers of Christ. Poor examples of Christians make evangelism more difficult.

Probably only 5 to 10 percent of churches follow up on people after their conversion. Many people make the mistake of separating evangelism and discipleship. These two are inseparably linked biblically, and particularly in a postmodern culture.

What new Christians need more than a paper to fill out for follow-up is a person to walk with them on their new spiritual journey. No two converts have exactly the same questions or needs. A live person, not a recorded message, is what new converts need most. The best person to do follow-up is the one who led the person to Christ.

Connection is the key to follow-up. If new believers are not connected with other Christians and discipled, they typically will fall into patterns that leave them confused about what to do next. Many will simply do nothing. They will not grow in their relationship with Christ, nor will they encourage others to follow Christ.

MYTHS AND PRINCIPLES TO FOLLOW-UP

Myths	Principles
1. Follow-up is an event.	1. Follow-up is a process.
2. Follow-up is spontaneous.	2. Follow-up requires a strategy.
3. Follow-up can be within the church building alone.	3. Follow-up should be done in the context of everyday life, especially the family.
4. All new converts learn in the same way.	4. People have individual learning needs.
5. Follow-up requires only biblical content.	5. Bible knowledge with a meaningful relationship is needed.

IMMEDIATE FOLLOW-UP

The people in front of you have just received Christ. What should you do? There is no one answer, but you should do some of the following:

- Celebrate their commitment with them.
- Assure them that they made the best of decisions.

- Encourage and help them communicate with someone who they know would be supportive of their new commitment—sharing their testimony.
- Explain their need and the privilege of talking with God throughout the day (prayer).
- Schedule the next follow-up visit with them.
- Call or write them a note within the first week.
- Provide them with an overall picture of what they might expect.
- Do not bombard them with information.

You are now in your next several contacts with the new convert. You will want to cover some of the following topics.

- Baptism—finding ways to celebrate with new believers. Celebrate baptisms by throwing a party, inviting their friends, clapping, or videotaping the baptism
- Sharing their faith on a consistent basis
- Basics of reading and understanding Scripture (modern translation)
- Church involvement—assisting them in making a connection
- Discipleship matters—spiritual disciplines and basics on how to walk with Jesus daily and for a lifetime
- Carefully addressing assurance of salvation, as the Holy Spirit confirms that a person is in Christ
- Dealing with ongoing problems and sin in their lives
- Helping them find identity in Christ

Follow-up Materials

The major issue for new believers is to get them connected to a body of believers. Most Christians need assistance in following up with new converts. The North American Mission Board of the Southern Baptist Convention produced *Beginning Steps: A Seven Day Growth Guide for New Believers*. Campus Crusade for Christ, the

Navigators, and teaching churches such as Willow Creek have also developed materials for new believers. The workbooks *The Survival Kit* and *The Arrival Kit* have been used for years to help converts. These materials are now available for children and youth.

FOLLOW-UP WITH CHILDREN

I often take a quick survey of my students in the area of follow-up. I ask, "How many of you by show of hands received follow-up after you received Christ?" Typically 10 to 15 percent of the seminary students received follow-up. Because most Christians follow Christ as children, it is important to consider our approaches to follow up with them.

The method of follow-up will depend on the family situation of the child. Barney Kinard identified six types of families and suggested an approach to follow-up.

1. *Both parents are Christians.* They are eager to follow up their own kids. You can resource them to do the follow-up.

2. *One parent knows Christ.* You can help that parent follow up with his or her child. Provide resources and encouragement.

3. *Parents feel inadequate.* They will not take the steps to influence their own child spiritually and gladly give permission to another to do it. Go for it!

4. *Neither parent is a Christian* (or they are nominal in their faith). Often they have had bad experiences with church. They leave all decisions about spiritual things for the child to "make up his own mind." Work at building acceptance but plan for one-on-one discipling moments during times the child is at church.

5. *Parents may be of another religion or are adamantly against Christianity.* They may be from another country or culture. In this case you may want to send to the home someone who can relate to their situation.

6. *Parents are not biological.* Stepparents or relatives raise the child. This situation can be similar to any of the above but needs additional compassion.[8]

All children need Christian adults to encourage, support, and instruct them in the ways of Christ. The more follow-up occurs within the context of the family, the better. The church should play a supportive role, especially through group life and learning. You will want to use developmentally appropriate approaches.

FOLLOW-UP WITH YOUTH AND ADULTS

Follow-up with youth has similarities with follow-up for both children and adults. It is always best in the context of relationships. Youth need friends to model what it means to follow Jesus.

All new believers need to become connected with a group of some sort to assist them in their spiritual development. Women more readily join a group, especially a group of women. Men also need a group, but it might not be a group that sits around a table and talks. Churches will have to find creative ways to connect with men to assist them with spiritual development.

EVANGELISM TRAINING IN A POSTMODERN CONTEXT

LIMITATION OF WESTERN EDUCATIONAL MODEL OF TRAINING

A Western educational model has dominated America, where degrees and classroom lectures are the norm. This has impacted how we approach and carry out training for various ministries, including training for personal evangelism. Classroom preparation for the witness seeking to answer common questions of modernity was helpful. However, the highly rational and mental lecture approach has significant limitations for training in the twenty-first century.[9]

As America moves toward a postmodern culture, evangelism training will have to move more toward a first-century model. I am convinced that God has not prescribed a specific method for sharing one's faith or a specific method for training. However, because our culture is more like the first century than the culture of the 1950s, we must adapt our training.

When in doubt, do what Jesus did: He modeled ministry and personal relations. He shared truth with people. He gathered the disciples and worked to instill His heart and His values into them. He then sent them out two by two. After they got roughed up a little, He brought them together to encourage them, train them, and send them back out to learn from the school of experience, more commonly known as the school of hard knocks. The disciples also learned from one another's successes and struggles. There is a difference in exposure and experience.

PERSONAL EVANGELISM TRAINING GUIDES IN A POSTMODERN CONTEXT

For those involved in personal evangelism training, the question is, How will we train people to confront the increasingly postmodern context found in America? In keeping with postmodern tradition, there is no easy answer. The approach will affect the head, the hands, and the heart for a holistic approach.

Football plays are described with *X*'s and *O*'s, which indicate where the defensive and offensive players should align themselves and then move as the play unfolds. Coaches invest significant amounts of time teaching players where they should line up before the ball is snapped and where they should go as the play begins. However, much of football involves instinct. As the play unfolds, the players have to make adjustments along the way to reach the end objective of the play.

Few plays in football come off exactly as they were designed. Players must be trained through guided practice to make necessary adjustments throughout the play. The more players practice, the more easily they adjust to what the other team is doing. Personal evangelism does involve *X*'s and *O*'s, yet it involves much more if we are to be effective in our efforts to communicate effectively.

Do not look for easy training methods; they do not exist. Tom Steffen said: "Christianity is much too complex for singular solutions, no matter how good they may sound or how famous the personality that promotes them. We must learn to add (when not contradicting Scripture) new and lost tools to our ministry toolbox without using them to institutionalize the convicting power of the Holy Spirit."[10] Some insights into the areas of knowledge, motivation, and skills may be helpful as you prepare to share and train others to share their faith.

Training involves the head, the hands, and the heart. We need to put some essential information in our heads as we prepare to share our faith. Different types of witnessing encounters require various levels of information. Evangelism also calls for the development of skills as we put our hands to the task of personal evangelism. However, the most important part of personal evangelism involves the heart, not what we know or the skills we develop.

HEAD: INFORMATION ONE NEEDS TO KNOW[11]

In a pluralistic environment you will have to know the essentials of your message. You will probably experience internal struggles as you wrestle with ways to connect our message to the various backgrounds of the diverse individuals you find. The starting point for most evangelistic conversations will now need to begin at a point much before the work of Christ. Additionally, because the questions being asked of Christians are different than they were in the last third of the twentieth century, our old answers will not suffice. As a result, Christian witnesses will need to expand the amount and type of information they use to share their faith. Much of the information used in past evangelistic training will help, but it needs to be expanded.

Many lost people will struggle with the implications of the essentials of the Christian message because they do not have a Judeo-Christian heritage. We will have to help lost people see how their personal story fits into God's overall story. The message is more than information to share but a relationship we are seeking to assist in establishing.

The following represent some key areas, which will be necessary for the development of an effective base of information.

- The overall story of the Bible—from Genesis to Revelation[12]
- The uniqueness of the resurrection
- In-depth knowledge of Jesus as a person
- Repertoire of good questions
- Values, thinking patterns, and communication patterns of postmoderns
- Where to find information about various religious backgrounds and worldviews
- A strong grasp of God's message of reconciliation, void of added-on traditions or personal cultural preferences[13]
- Reasons someone would desire to receive Christ as Lord and Savior to use as conversation starters (beyond fear of hell or promise of heaven)[14]
- Terminology void of language used only in Christian subcultures, using terms that will communicate the gospel message to those with little or no Christian heritage

HANDS: WHAT SKILLS ONE NEEDS TO BE DEVELOPING[15]

Some skills need to be developed to communicate your faith. Developing the following skills will assist you in evangelizing postmodern people.

- Asking good, sensitive, open-ended, story-giving questions
- Communicating the gospel message in story form[16]
- Listening not only to words, but emotions, body language, fears, questions, and concerns
- Transitioning normal conversations into spiritual dialogue (many transitions); recognizing opportunities as they arise and assisting in the creating of opportunities
- Letting a person exit a spiritual conversation gracefully but with a hook that leaves him or her thinking about Jesus in a positive manner
- Discerning when to move ahead and when to back up (part skill and part sensitivity to the Holy Spirit's leading)
- Practicing kindness, service, and graciousness
- Connecting with people in languages they understand (music and movies are fairly universal languages)—cultural fit or adaptation
- Connecting the rational portion of the gospel presentation at the right points to where the listener can be enlightened
- Connecting a quality testimony to the listener's life
- Discerning needs, then having faith enough to ask God to reveal Himself to people through meeting those needs
- Practicing positive deconstruction (see Nick Pollard's *Evangelism Made Slightly Less Difficult: How to Interest People Who Aren't Interested*[17])
- Leading a willing person in the final moments of surrendering life to Christ
- Communicating about Christ with the motive of love

HEART: ATTITUDES AND FEELINGS TO MOTIVATE THE WITNESS[18]

Evangelistic training affects not only the head and the hands but also the heart. Evangelistic activities flow out of a vital, passionate relationship with Christ and a deep concern and passion for lost people. Below are a few tips for developing the heart component of personal evangelism.

- Read and tell the great biblical stories of God's great love for His people.
- Share testimonies of the saving and changing power of God.
- Provide as many different experiences in evangelistic activities as possible.
- Make a big deal of baptism services—invitations to lost relatives and friends, storytelling—and create a celebrative atmosphere.
- Interview lost people.
- Take note of the significant needs in the lives of lost friends.
- Have a quiet time with the evening news and newspaper on your mind about the condition of the world.
- Develop a list of lost people with whom you will begin to cultivate a friendship.
- Pray for lost people by name; prayer walk around your house.

TRAINING IMPLICATIONS: METHODS

How will churches train people to do evangelism? How will seminaries train students in evangelism? Here are some possible methods or principles.

- When in doubt, do what Jesus did. Communicate the value of evangelism, model it, give a little information about it, send out trainees with partners for practical experience, bring them back in for debriefing, offer encouragement and additional instruction, and send them back into the field.

- Mobilize a higher percentage of people by using servant evangelism projects. This safe experience will build confidence, ingrain the value of evangelism, provide encouragement from other participants, and often lead people to take more initiative in their personal relationships, and help them to become willing to take more direct approaches.
- Use extensive role playing.
- Provide as many different types of experiences as possible.
- Use visual training, including video and drama modeling.
- Provide notebooks, audiotapes, or books to help evangelists with various religious traditions or worldviews, along with most common objections to the gospel.
- Locate resources to help with particular religions or cultures.

Shifts in Training Methods

Modernity: Christian Age (Less like These)	*Postmodernity: Post-Christian Age (More like These)*
Classroom-based	On the job
Information transferred	The process of study
Deductive	Inductive
Knowledge = competency	Knowledge + experience + coaching = competency
All at once	Gradual
Top-down information	Meet-in-the-middle information

One-time training	Multilevel training
General	Highly specialized
Large groups	Mentoring
Presentations	Dialogue
Audio/some visual	Multisensory
Hourly settings	Retreats + application
Product emphasis	Value, process emphasis
Individual focus	Group/cooperative
For mature	For everyone, even new believers
Teacher authority	Relational authority
Sermons	Watching examples
Lectures	Role playing
Reasoning	Intuition and perception

Keys to Effective Evangelism: Motivation, Skills, Head Knowledge

Modernity	Postmodernity
Ask for a decision in every encounter	Breaking down barriers to Christ and clarification
Assuming trust	Building trust
Doctrine of heaven, hell and justification	Experience of adoption, love, meaning
A large room and a good evangelist	People with a story to share
Prayer and knowledge	Prayer, wisdom, and passion
Telling the plan of salvation	Displaying God's plan in multiple ways
Bible	Bible and current events
The right answers	Some key questions
Self (maybe a partner)	A group, team, or family
Emotional appeal	Relational testimony

CONCLUSION

People need the Lord. And many are ready to receive Him when they hear the gospel in such a way that they can understand it and in a way that it makes sense to follow Christ. The average person is far from an accurate understanding of Christ. But Ron Hutchcraft reminded us, "People are more ready, because the things that have made them lost, have made them ready. They don't know who they are ready for, but they are ready for something."[19]

No easy solutions exist to seeing America turn its collective heart toward Christ. There are no easy solutions to sharing our faith effectively in our increasingly postmodern context in America. It will take men, women, and children who passionately love Jesus and lost people who are willing to take whatever measures necessary to communicate effectively the greatest story ever told in the history of mankind. Like Jesus, we must be safe persons for lost seekers as we share our dangerous, life-changing message.

Linda started out in this book as a college student in a religion course with an antagonistic attitude toward Christians, especially Christian ministers. A loving and gentle pastor provided a safe environment for her to air her belief that God did not exist. Because Sam Williams trusted God to reveal Himself to a searching college student, Linda received Christ.

Paul Harvey was the master of "the rest of the story." And now the rest of the story of Linda Bergquist. She grew in the Lord, and Sam invited her to join his church staff at Del Cerro Baptist Church in San Diego, California. She accepted and developed into an outstanding Christian minister. It has been said of Linda that she has the best church-planting mind in California. Her husband Eric is a graphic designer, and together they have served the Lord through various church-planting ministries in San Diego, Mexico City, and now San Francisco. What began with a closed mind and a faithful Christian, ended up developing a church-planting strategist who has impacted thousands through her ministry.

No one is too far from the reach of God's merciful hand. Trust God. Be intentional and faithful to share. And watch the Lord draw all people to Him. Jesus said, "But I, when I am lifted up from the earth, will draw all men to myself" (John 12:32).

"I pray that you may be active in sharing your faith, so that you will have a full understanding of every good thing we have in Christ" (Philem. 6).

Constructing a Testimony

S HAPING A PERSONAL TESTIMONY may be the most powerful tool available to the willing witness. A testimony is effective in all cultures, especially the postmodern culture the church is now facing in America. Your life story is often interesting to others, even to those usually unwilling to talk about religious matters.

Stories have a way of breaking down barriers. People usually turn off their critical-thinking skills and drop their guards when listening to a story.

THREE MAJOR COMPONENTS OF A TESTIMONY

1. Life before Christ (front)
2. Coming to know/trust Christ (middle)
3. Life after Christ (back)

(See Acts 22:3–15: Paul's life.)

Two Major Kinds of Testimonies

- Salvation—focus on how you came to trust Christ.
- Situation (present impact)—focus on how Jesus is impacting your life in relation to typical human needs, problems, and issues.

Do's Shaping Your Testimony

- Write what your life was like before you came to k1112now Christ.
- Write how you came to know you were lost and how you came to see Jesus as the forgiver and leader of your life.
- Write out the major one or two positive differences/changes Christ is making in your life.
- Write in understandable language, removing religious terms that would not be understood.
- Try to develop your testimony around one major theme with supporting information.
- The testimony should be prepared to be shared in about three minutes if shared without dialogue.
- Keep your testimony on point without too many details that distract people from seeing Christ.

Testimony Don'ts

- Don't embellish details or worry that your testimony is not exciting enough to share.
- Don't use too many Scriptures (one to three are probably in order).
- Don't feel that you have to share all your testimony at once if the situation warrants a delay.
- Don't be negative about other religions or in any matter if possible.

Sharing Do's

- Learn to ask people questions about themselves. This will usually lead to the lost person's asking you about yourself.

- Learn to share your testimony from any starting point front, middle, back, or middle, back, front, and even back, front, middle.
- Focus on how your story connects with the lost person, not just on telling your story.
- Be natural and authentic, not someone you are not.
- Practice sharing your testimony with Christian friends, get feedback, make adjustments.
- Close in such a way as to lead the person to Christ, not away from Him if they do not receive Christ in that setting.
- Share in the confidence of Christ as you relive your experiences.

Gospel Illustrations to Share Your Faith

THE FOLLOWING ILLUSTRATIONS are provided to assist you in remembering and dialoguing about the essential elements of the gospel message. A visual in your mind and in the mind of the lost person aids in comprehension.

AROUND THE BASES

Use a baseball diamond to illustrate four major facets of receiving Christ.

First base: UUnderstanding God's plan for our lives
Second base: Understanding our broken relationship with God
Third base: Understanding the work of Christ on the cross
Home: Understanding how to get home, receiving Christ

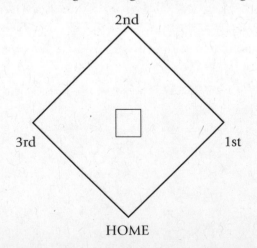

POWERBAND BRACELETS

Use powerband bracelets with beads. This illustration involves a piece of string leather and colored beads. The black bead stands for sin, the red bead for the blood of Christ, the white bead for the purity that comes with forgiveness, the blue bead is for the waters of baptism, the green bead illustrates Christian growth, the knot illustrates the end of life, and the gold bead represents heaven.

Knot: Beginning of life (you are born).
Black: Sin is a part of the world, your world.
Red: Christ died to remove the sin.
White: New life is pure after Christ removes the sin.
Blue: Baptism shows the world that Christ is in your life.
Green: Grow in your love relationship with Christ.
Knot: End of life, you die.
Gold: You will be in heaven after you die.

THE BRIDGE

One of the most popular illustrations is that of drawing out the bridge. The diagram is drawn as the gospel is explained. Below is the final diagram that is drawn.

God wants to have a relationships with us, but mankind and God are separated by sin. All our efforts cannot bridge the gulf between us. We deserve separation from God which results in eternal death. However, Christ came to bridge the gap by dying for our sins. We must move over to God's side by receiving Christ through faith, repentance, and surrendering our will. This will prevent eternal separation from God and give us eternal life.

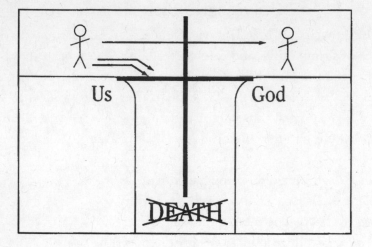

OTHER OPTIONS TO SHARE

Use a "lifeline" illustration, using paper representing the barrier of sin that separates us (below) from God (above). Punch a hole in a piece of paper representing the lifeline of Christ that has broken through the barrier and given us access to God.

Make a chart using "Do" and "Done." Illustrate that all other religious groups operate by how much mankind can put in the "Do" to please God, which is never adequate, but Christianity is only based on what Jesus has "Done." Christ did for us what we could never do.

A marked New Testament is always a good option in sharing our faith. See Bill Fay's *Share Jesus Without Fear* for details on this approach.

Common Objections

B ILL FAY'S LIST OF COMMON OBJECTIONS. His book has
a script for possible responses to these objections.

1. A Christian hurt me.
2. Cults are the answer.
3. God cannot forgive me.
4. How can a loving God send someone to hell?
5. How can I know the Bible is true?
6. How do I know I have enough faith?
7. I can't live the Christian lifestyle.
8. I don't believe in God.
9. I don't believe the resurrection took place.
10. I want to think about it.
11. I'm a good person.
12. I'm a member of another world religion.
13. I'm God.
14. I'm having too much fun.
15. I'm Jewish.
16. I'm not a sinner.
17. I'm not good enough.
18. I'm not ready.
19. I'm not sure I'm saved.
20. I've always believed in God.
21. I've done too many bad things.
22. I've tried it, and it didn't work out.
23. My beliefs are private.

24. My friends will think I am crazy if I accept Jesus.
25. The argument never stops.
26. The church only wants my money.
27. There are many paths to God.
28. There are many religions in the world.
29. There are many translations of the Bible.
30. There are too many errors in the Bible.
31. There are too many hypocrites in the church.
32. What about my family?
33. What about those who never hear the gospel?
34. Why does God let bad things happen?
35. You can't possibly know what truth is.
36. You must think you're better than me.

Readiness Scale[1]

Readiness Scale					
Level	**4** **Cynic**	**3** **Skeptic**	**2** **Spectator**	**1** **Seeker**	**Receives** **Christ**
Characterized by	*Hostility.* Not interested or open to being influenced.	*Disbelief.* May be slightly open, but plagued by doubts.	*Indifference.* May be open to ideas, but not motivated to apply anything personally.	*Interest.* Growing degree of openness; wants to know the truth and follow it.	
Suggested Approach	Ask questions to try to get at the reason for their hostility.	Ask questions to try to diagnose the source of their doubts (misinformation, lack of answers to their questions, underlying "smokescreen" issues).	Try to help them think about matters of ultimate importance: Why they're here, what their purpose in life is, where they stand before God.	Ask questions designed to identify the barriers that are keeping them from trusting Christ.	
Sample Question	"You seem pretty negative toward spiritual matters, has something happened to make you feel angry toward God/Christians?"	"You clearly have doubts about the Christian message. Can we talk about some of your questions?"	"It's so easy to get caught up in the daily grind without ever asking what it all means. Do you ever think about where God fits into your life?"	"What would you say are the main issues keeping you from committing your life to Christ?"	
Your Response	Listen carefully, empathize where possible; try to help them rethink their response to whatever happened.	Listen carefully, try to answer their questions, help them start actively looking into the evidence for Christianity.	Encourage them to not wait for tough times or tragedy to think about these matters. Illustrate from your own experience that following Christ makes sense *now*, as well as for eternity.	Correct misinformation, try to answer any lingering questions, show them that the benefits of following Christ far outweigh any costs, move them toward crossing the line of faith.	
Notes	• This scale refers to openness to influence, not to discussion or relationship.	• A person may be very religious, but still be a cynic, skeptic, etc. in how they view or respond to Christ and the Gospel message.		• People do not necessarily progress through each of these areas; they can move from any one of them to any other, including directly to receiving Christ.	

Next-Steps Growth Assignments

1. Interview fifteen people to gain information and insights on their thoughts and feelings toward Christ and His church.

- Five interviews of non-Christians under age thirty-five
- Five interviews of dechurched people—had strong background, but not active in last three years
- Five interviews with lost people who are a lot like you

The more lost people you interview, the better. After each interview, write a thoughtful reflection of your experience. You may want to include selected significant quotes, a summary paragraph on each interview, what you learned about people, what you discovered about yourself, or what you need to learn about lost people.

You should ask for the time from the persons in order to interview them, with the objective being simply to learn how people see religious things. The primary purpose is not to convert the person or even to share the gospel message. The purpose is to learn what people are thinking about religious matters.

If the person seems receptive to the gospel and you think he or she would like to talk further, you can say, "Thank you for your time in completing the interview. You seem to want to discuss these matters in more detail. If you would like to talk further, I am available now, or we can set an appointment for a later time."

Ask, "I am doing a personal research project (or public opinion poll) and need your help. I am seeking to learn how people see religious things. Will you take a few minutes to help me by sharing some of your opinions?"

You can interview people you know, neighbors, business associates, people in malls, or people in places where lost people typically hang out. People you do not know, if approached in a nonconfrontational manner, will usually give you the most honest answers.

Take the approach of a learner and inquirer, not a salesman. Do not try to convince them or debate with them, but simply record on a notepad their answers. If they ask your opinion, gracefully decline, saying that you do not want to influence their answer. If after the interview the person asks you to tell about your beliefs, listen to the Holy Spirit and either set another time to get together for that purpose or go ahead and share. If they feel you are conning them into a sales opportunity, you will not get their truest feelings and thoughts.

The following represent questions the student should ask:

- How would you describe your religious background and church involvement?
- To you, what is God like? Describe God. (If they don't believe in God, don't ask the next two questions but ask, To you, what is important in life?)
- What do you think is important and unimportant to God?
- What do you think it takes to be straightened out with God?
- Describe what the term *Jesus Christ* means to you.
- From your perspective, what are the major problems of churches today?

On the value of the assignment and what he learned, a student said, "These interviews have also taught me how badly people need God. These interviews have changed my way of thinking. They have given me a real perspective of my mission field, not a perceived perspective. Hearing the beliefs of others will help me perform ministry geared to reaching a lost world."[1]

2.   Develop an impact list of five to ten lost people. Ask God to give you a passion for Him and lost people.

3.   Learn the fifteen Scriptures from the list in chapter 5 related to sharing your faith.

4.   Complete a servant evangelism project. (See *Conspiracy of Kindness* by Steve Sjogren in the bibliography.)

5.   Locate an evangelism partner from your church (prayer partner and mentor). Tell him or her of your desire to be an active witness and that you need encouragement and prayer support.

6.   Write the story of Jesus in a two-minute format.

7.   Write the story of the Bible in a four-minute format.

8.   Write out your personal testimony, edit it several times, learn to say it easily, and then practice communicating it with a Christian friend.

9.   Attend a church service or two that is radically different from yours, preferably one of a completely different culture or a non-Christian religion. Note feelings you had from the time you prepared to go until you return home. Reflect on how guests probably feel when they attend your church services.

10. Ask God to help you personally to lead someone to a faith in Christ in the next three months. Keep praying about this and keep sharing Christ.

Personal Evangelism Bibliography

Aldrich, Joseph C. *Gentle Persuasion.* Portland, Ore.: Multnomah Press, 1988.

____. *Life-Style Evangelism.* Portland, Ore.: Multnomah Press, 1981.

Atkinson, Donald A., and Charles L. Roesel. *Meeting Needs, Sharing Christ: Ministry Evangelism in Today's New Testament Church.* Nashville: LifeWay, 1995.

Barna, George. *Evangelism That Works: How to Reach Changing Generations with the Unchanging Gospel.* Ventura, Calif.: Regal Books, 1995.

Beougher, Timothy K., and Alvin L. Reid. *Evangelism for a Changing World.* Wheaton: Harold Shaw Publishers, 1995.

Boursier, Helen. T. *Tell It with Style: Evangelism for Every Personality Type.* Downers Grove, Ill.: InterVarsity Press, 1995.

Bridger, Francis. *Children Finding Faith.* London: Scripture Union, 1988.

Celek, Tim, Dieter Zander, and Patrick Kampert. *Inside the Soul of the New Generation: Insight and Strategy for Reaching Busters.* Grand Rapids: Zondervan, 1996.

Clark, David K. *Dialogical Apologetics: A Person-Centered Approach to Christian Defense.* Grand Rapids: Baker Books, 1993.

Coleman, Robert E. *The Master's Way of Personal Evangelism.* Wheaton: Crossway Book, 1997.

____. *The Master Plan of Evangelism.* Old Tappan, N.J.: Revell Company, 1989.

Dale, Robert D. *Evangelizing the Hard-to-Reach.* Nashville: Broadman, 1986.

Daniels, Danny. *Experiencing God's Evangelism: How to Go Verbal with Your Faith.* Purpose Paradigms, 1999.

Eisenman, Tom L. *Everyday Evangelism: Making the Most of Life's Common Moments.* Downers Grove, Ill.: InterVarsity Press, 1987.

Engel, James, and Wilbert Norton. *What's Gone Wrong with the Harvest?* Grand Rapids: Zondervan, 1975.

Fay, William. *Share Jesus Without Fear.* Nashville: Broadman & Holman, 1999.

Ford, Kevin Graham. *Jesus for a New Generation: Putting the Gospel in the Language of Xers.* Downers Grove, Ill.: InterVarsity Press, 1995.

Green, Michael. *Evangelism in the Early Church.* Grand Rapids: William B. Eerdmans Publishing Company, 1970.

Griffin, E. *The Mind Changers: The Art of Christian Persuasion.* Wheaton: Tyndale, 1976.

Hawthorne, Steve, and Graham Kendrick. *Prayer-Walking: Praying on Site with Insight.* Orlando: Creation House, 1993.

Henderson, David W. *Culture Shift: Communicating God's Truth to Our Changing World.* Grand Rapids: Baker Books, 1998.

Hewitt, Hugh. *The Embarrassed Believer: Reviving Christian Witness in an Age of Unbelief.* Nashville: Word Publishing, 1998.

Hunter, George. *How to Reach Secular People.* Nashville: Abingdon Press, 1992.

Hybels, Bill, and Mark Mittelberg. *Becoming a Contagious Christian.* Grand Rapids: Zondervan Publishing House, 1994.

Hybels, Bill. *Christians in the Marketplace.* Wheaton, Ill.: Victor Books, 1982.

Johnson, Ronald W. *How Will They Hear If We Don't Listen?* Nashville: Broadman & Holman, 1994.

Keefauver, Larry. *Friends and Faith: How to Use Friendship Evangelism in Youth Ministry.* Loveland, Colo.: Group Books, 1986.

Kelley, Charles S., Jr. *How Did They Do It?: The Story of Southern Baptist Evangelism.* San Francisco: Insight Press, 1993.

Kennedy, D. James. *Evangelism Explosion.* Wheaton: Tyndale House Publishers, 1983.

Kramp, John. *Out of Their Faces and into Their Shoes: How to Understand Spiritually Lost People and Give Them Directions to God.* Nashville: Broadman & Holman, 1995.

Leavell, Roland Q. *Evangelism: Christ's Imperative Commission.* Nashville: Broadman Press, 1979.

Little, Paul. *How to Give Away Your Faith.* 2d ed. Downers Grove, Ill.: InterVarsity Press, 1988.

Long, Jimmy. *Generating Hope: A Strategy for Reaching the Postmodern Generation.* Westmont, Ill.: InterVarsity Press, 1997.

McCloskey, Mark. *Tell It Often—Tell It Well.* Nashville: Thomas Nelson, 1992.

Metzger, Will. *Tell the Truth: The Whole Gospel to the Whole Person by Whole People.* Downers Grove, Ill.: InterVarsity Press, 1984.

Miles, Delos. *How Jesus Won Persons.* Nashville: Broadman, 1982.

_____. *Introduction to Evangelism.* Nashville: Broadman, 1983.

_____. *Overcoming Barriers to Witnessing.* Nashville: Broadman, 1984.

Packer, J. I. *Evangelism and the Sovereignty of God.* Downers Grove, Ill.: InterVarsity Press, 1961.

Petersen, Jim. *Living Proof: Sharing the Gospel Naturally.* Colorado Springs, Colo.: NavPress, 1989.

Phillips, Timothy R., and Dennis L. Okholm. *Christian Apologetics in the Postmodern World.* Downers Grove, Ill.: InterVarsity Press, 1995.

Pippert, Rebecca Manley. *Out of the Salt Shaker and into the World.* Downers Grove, Ill.: InterVarsity Press, 1979.

Pollard, Nick. *Evangelism Made Slightly Less Difficult.* Downers Grove, Ill.: InterVarsity Press, 1997.

Reid, Alvin. *Introduction to Evangelism.* Nashville: Broadman & Holman Publishers, 1998.

Robinson, Darrell W. *People Sharing Jesus.* Nashville: Thomas Nelson, 1995.

Smith, Glenn C. *What Christians Can Learn from One Another About Evangelizing Blacks.* Wheaton, Ill.: Tyndale House Publishers, 1988.

Sjogren, Steve. *Conspiracy of Kindness.* Ann Arbor: Servant Publications, 1993.

_____. *Servant Warfare: How Kindness Conquers Spiritual Darkness.* Ann Arbor: Vine Books, 1996.

Strobel, Lee. *Inside the Mind of Unchurched Harry and Mary.* Grand Rapids: Zondervan, 1993.

Thompson, Oscar W. *Concentric Circles of Concern.* Nashville: Broadman, 1981.

Towns, Elmer L. *A Practical Encyclopedia: Evangelism and Church Growth.* Ventura: Regal Books, 1995.

Watson, David. *Called and Committed: World Changing Discipleship.* Wheaton, Ill.: Harold Shaw, 1982.

Wimber, John. *Power Evangelism.* New York: Harper and Row, 1985.

Wright, Tim. *Unfinished Evangelism: More Than Getting Them in the Door.* Minneapolis: Augsburg, 1995.

See www.MEGnet.org for a more extensive bibliography.

VIDEO-BASED TRAINING MATERIALS

Alpha Course
Becoming a Contagious Christian. Zondervan
Family to Family. NAMB (LifeWay)
Living Proof. NavPress
Ministry Evangelism. LifeWay
People Sharing Jesus. Thomas Nelson
Share Jesus Without Fear. LifeWay

Helpful Web Sites and Internet Evangelism

www.Web-evangelism.com

www.Gospel.com

www.thegoodnews.org

www.powertochange.com

www.thekristo.com

www.wuzupgod.com

www.billygraham.com

www.gospelcom.net

www.desiringgodministries.com

Endnotes

INTRODUCTION

1. Kent R Hunter, *Foundations for Church Growth: Biblical Basics for the Local Church* (Corunna, Ind.: Church Growth Center, 1994), 100.

2. Yosef Abramowitz, "Taking on the Southern Baptists," in *Moment*, December 1999, 34–35.

3. *On Mission*, March-April 2001, 11.

4. Cathy Lynn Grossman, *USA Today*, "Charting the Unchurched in America," http://www.usatoday.com/life/2002/2002-03-07-no-religion.htm, 7 March 2002.

5. Rick Richardson, *Evangelism Outside the Box* (Downers Grove, Ill.: IVP 2000), 42–43.

6. Will McRaney's presentation "This Cannot Be Your Father's Evangelism and Why" at National Conference for Church Leadership, Ridgecrest, North Carolina, June 2001.

7. Bill Easum stated in a personal conversation after his address at the American Society for Church Growth annual meeting in Pasadena, California, July 9–11, 2000.

8. Harold Bullock introduced these three categories to the author: *attraction*, getting people to events; *projection*, sending workers out; *media*, radio, TV, Internet, etc.

9. W. Oscar Thompson Jr., *Concentric Circles of Concern* (Nashville: Broadman, 1981), 157.

10. Conversion can be viewed as a part of the process toward regeneration or be used synonymously with regeneration. People can be converted, believe parts of the gospel, along the process toward salvation by

regeneration. An example would be, the lost person comes to believe in the deity of Christ without then immediately receiving Christ. Additionally, the more common use of the term *conversion* is to describe the moment of regeneration and salvation. At different points in the text, I use conversion to describe both.

11. "Forgiver and leader" is a phrase that is growing in popularity among younger Christians as the term "Christian" means less and less in the U.S.

12. Harold Bullock, introduction section of conference notebook "How Church Works II: Evangelism and Discipleship," January 31-February 2, 2002.

CHAPTER 1

1. See Job 5:9; 9:10; 11:7–9; Pss. 145:3; 147:5. Also see the argument in *No One Like Him* by John Fineberg.

2. Fisher Humphreys, *The Nature of God* (Nashville: Broadman, 1985), 76.

3. Luke 18:7; Romans 2:4; 8:28; 9:17; 11:22; 2 Corinthians 5:5; Colossians 1:5; 1 Thessalonians 5:8; Titus 3:4.

4. See the latter part of chapter 1 and chapter 3 for discussion of salvation.

5. See 1 Peter 3:18 and Matthew 5:45.

6. Several parts of the section on the Old Testament were influenced by interviews with Dr. Archie England, an Old Testament professor at New Orleans Baptist Theological Seminary.

7. Adapted from an unknown source.

8. Fisher Humphreys, *Thinking About God*, 126.

9. Parts of the outline of this section were taken from *Continued Witness Training Apprentice Manual*, Section I, 2.

10. Also see Mark 6:7 and Matthew 10:1.

11. Christopher B. Adsit, *Personal Disciple-Making* (Orlando: Campus Crusade for Christ, 1996).

12. See Ephesians 4:17–19 and Matthew 24:43–44.

13. See 1 Corinthians 2:7–16; Ephesians 4:17–18; and Romans 2:1–12.

14. Tom Steffen, "Flawed Evangelism and Church Planting," in *Evangelical Missions Quarterly* 34 (1998): 430.

15. Selected passages include Genesis 15:1; 20:3; 28:12; 31:10; 37:5; Judges 7:13; 15; 1 Samuel 3:15; 1 Kings 3:5; Ezekiel 12:22–23; Daniel 2:19; Matthew 1:20; 27:19; Luke 24:23; Acts 2:17; 9:10–12; 10:17–19; 16:9–10; 18:9; 26:19; Revelation 9:17.

16. Here is a link to a helpful and easy-to-read explanation of the scale: http://www.teachhealth.com/#stressscale.

17. Tom Steffen, "Flawed Evangelism and Church Planting," 430–31.

Chapter 2

1. Rebecca Manley Pippert, *Out of the Salt Shaker*, 2nd ed. (Downers Grove: IVP, 1999), 133.

2. J. I. Packer, *Evangelism and the Sovereignty of God* (Downers Grove, Ill.: Inter-Varsity Press, 1961), 85.

3. Select related passages: Ezekiel 3:17–21; Ephesians 4:1–16; 2 Timothy 4:1–5.

4. Richardson, *Evangelism Outside the Box*, 48.

5. D. Martyn Lloyd-Jones, *The Presentation of the Gospel* (London: Inter-Varsity Fellowship, 1949), 6–7.

6. See appendix for graph in Appendix 3 on different types of lost people.

7. G. William Schweer, *Personal Evangelism for Today* (Nashville: Broadman), 113–15.

8. Interview with an anonymous person by Dale Funderburg as reported in a paper January 2002, 1.

9. Will Metzger, *Tell the Truth: The Whole Gospel to the Whole Person by Whole People*, 2d ed. (Downers Grove, Ill.: IVP, 1984).

10. For additional information on defending the faith and apologetics, I would refer you to Frank Harber's Web site and ministry. He is the president of the Institute for Christian Defense. Some of his materials can be found at www.gotlife.org.

11. Ephesians 5:18; Acts 1:8.

12. Woman at the well in John 4.

13. See Donald McGavran, *Bridges to God*.

14. Interview with an anonymous person by Stephen DuVall as reported in a paper January 2002, p. 17 in paper.

15. Sermon series Stanley preached in 2001 at North Point Community Church in Alpharetta, Georgia, where he is the pastor.

16. Richardson, *Evangelism Outside the Box*, 20.

17. Ibid., 26.

18. Mark McCloskey, *Tell It Often—Tell It Well* (San Bernardino: Here's Life Publishers, 1986).

19. Lesslie Newbigin, *The Gospel in a Pluralistic Society* (Grand Rapids, Mich.: Eerdmans Publishing, 1989), 232–33.

20. J. I. Packer's *Evangelism and the Sovereignty of God* is an excellent resource to examine for insights on the interplay between God's involvement and our role in salvation and evangelism. The four major sections of the small book are: (1) divine sovereignty, (2) divine sovereignty and human responsibility, (3) evangelism, and (4) divine sovereignty and evangelism.

CHAPTER 3

1. Tom Steffen, "Flawed Evangelism and Church Planting," *Evangelical Missions Quarterly* 34 (1998): 434.

2. Several recommended resources for further study on the subject: Newbigin, *Foolishness to the Greeks: The Gospel and Western Culture*; Will Metzger, *Tell the Truth: The Whole Gospel to the Whole Person by Whole People*; Mark McCloskey, *Tell It Often—Tell It Well*; Paul Little, *How to Give Away Your Faith*, 2d ed. (Downers Grove: Ill.: Inter-Varsity Press, 1988); Newbigin, *The Gospel in a Pluralistic Society*.

3. Interview with an anonymous person by Stephen DuVall as reported in a paper, January 2002, 16.

4. Lesslie Newbigin, *The Gospel in a Pluralistic Society*, 144.

5. Steffen, "Flawed Evangelism and Church Planting," 433–34.

6. Harold Bullock, "How Church Works II" conference.

7. Lesslie Newbigin, *Foolishness to the Greeks: The Gospel and Western Culture* (Grand Rapids, Mich.: Eerdmans, 1986), 4. *Foolishness to the Greeks* explores the impact of Western culture on our understanding of

the gospel. A term that Newbigin prefers to use is "contextualization." By contextualization, he means, "the placing of the gospel in the total context of a culture at a particular moment, a moment that is shaped by the past and looks to the future" (p. 2). Newbigin attempts to separate or peel away some of the influences of Western culture on the gospel in order to allow us to better understand and comprehend the gospel's meaning.

8. Steffen, "Flawed Evangelism and Church Planting," 429.

9. Newbigin, *The Gospel in a Pluralistic Society*, 222.

10. Ibid., 239.

11. McCloskey, *Tell It Often—Tell It Well*, 20.

12. Ibid., 21–26.

13. Ibid., 29–30.

14. Michael Green, *Evangelism Through the Local Church* (Grand Rapids: William B. Eerdmans Publishing Company, 1970) 34–37.

15. Review the following passages that discuss man's problem and need: Ephesians 2:1–7; 1 John 5:11–12; 2 Corinthians 4:3–4; John 3:3, 16–19, 36; Romans 1:28–32; 2 Corinthians 2:14; Ephesians 2:12.

16. Interviews with an anonymous person by Dale Funderburg as reported in a paper January 2002, 2.

17. *USA Today*, 31 October 1997.

18. Lesslie Newbigin, *The Gospel in a Pluralistic Society*, 170.

19. Rick Sharkey introduced this framework to the author.

20. Lesslie Newbigin, *Foolishness to the Greeks*, 133.

21. Ibid., 5.

22. Kent R. Hunter, *Foundations for Church Growth*, 100.

23. Lesslie Newbigin, *The Gospel in a Pluralistic Society*, 183.

24. Kent R. Hunter, *Foundations for Church Growth*, 100.

CHAPTER 4

1. Charles H. Kraft, *Communication Theory for Christian Witness*, rev. ed. (Maryknoll, N.Y.: Orbis Books, 1991), vii.

2. Several people have added much to the Christian understanding of our role through their study and writings. Two of James Engel's work have been of particular help, *Contemporary Christian Communications* (Nashville:

Thomas Nelson, 1979) and *What's Gone Wrong with the Harvest?* with Wilbert Norton (Grand Rapids: Zondervan, 1975). A few other books may help you explore this subject in more detail:
Charles H. Kraft, *Communication Theory for Christian Witness*; Robert Don Hughes, *Talking to the World in the Days to Come* (Nashville: Broadman Press, 1991); and David J. Hesselgrave, *Communicating Christ Cross-Culturally: An Introduction to Missionary Communication* (Grand Rapids: Zondervan, 1991). Also see chapter 9 in Will Metzger's *Tell the Truth* and chapters 17–19 in Mark McCloskey's *Tell It Often—Tell It Well.*

3. Charles H. Kraft, *Communication Theory for Christian Witness* (Maryknoll, N.Y.: Orbis Books, 1991), 24–37.

4. McCloskey, *Tell It Often—Tell It Well,* chapter 17.

5. Will Metzger, *Tell the Truth,* 22–23.

6. Charles H. Kraft, *Communication Theory for Christian Witness,* 16.

7. Ibid., 17–18.

8. Ibid., 18.

9. From interviews with anonymous people as reported by Eddie Gilley in a paper January 2002, 1.

10. Transcript from the Alpha course introduction video, Sandy Millar.

11. Kraft, *Communication Theory for Christian Witness,* 19, 23.

12. Harold Bullock, conference notebook, "How Church Works II," 8.

13. Ibid.

14. Ibid, 11.

15. Ibid.

16. See David Hesselgrave, *Communicating Christ Cross-Culturally* for a detailed look at the issues related to communicating cross-culturally.

17. Yandall Woodfin, *With All Your Mind: A Christian Philosophy* (Ft. Worth, Tex.: Scripta Publishing, 1980), 26. See chapter 23 in David Hesselgrave, *Communicating Christ Cross-Culturally* for tips on communicating in a culture where intuitional thinking is dominant and chapter 24 where rational thinking is dominant. Modernity relates more to rational thinking, while postmodernity relates more to intuitional thinking.

18. Will McRaney, "The Evangelistic Conversation in an Increasingly Postmodern America," *Journal of the American Society for Church Growth*, Vol. 12 (Winter 2001): 81–91.

19. Hugh Hewitt, *The Embarrassed Believer* (Nashville: Word Publishing, 1998), 64.

20. David S. Dockery, *The Challenge of Postmodernism* (Wheaton, Ill.: BridgePoint, 1995), 13–14. Also see an excellent article, Harry L. Poe, "Making the Most of Postmodernity," *Journal of the Academy for Evangelism*, 13 (1997–1998): 67–72.

21. Rick Ferguson's outline of his message, "Six Core Competencies Related to Evangelism," in January 2001 in New Orleans, Louisiana.

- Purpose of evangelism—Glory of God, not church growth
- Product of our evangelism—Holistic discipleship
- Presentation of evangelism—Person of salvation, not the plan
- Package of evangelism—Rational apologetics, not emotional revivalism
- People of our evangelism—Culturally sensitive and must be missiologically sound
- Price of evangelism—great personal and corporate sacrifice

CHAPTER 5

1. David J. Bosch, *Believing in the Future: Toward a Missiology of Western Culture* (Harrisburg, Pa.: Trinity Press International, 1995), 5. James Emory White, "Evangelism in a Postmodern World," *The Challenge of Postmodernism*, ed. David S. Dockery (Wheaton, Ill.: BridgePoint, 1995), 362–63. White described four marks of modernity: (1) Moral Relativism—what is morally right is dictated by the situation. Consequence: crisis in values. (2) Autonomous Individualism—everyone is personally responsible for their own destiny and accountability without higher moral authority. Consequence: lack of vision. (3) Narcissistic Hedonism—what is best for me is what I'll do. Consequence: empty souls. (4) Reductive Naturalism—truth is only that

which can be scientifically verified. Consequence: inadequate method to satisfy the soul. Thomas C. Oden highlighted four similar motifs in "The Death of Modernity and Postmodern Evangelical Spirituality," in *The Challenge of Postmodernism*, David S. Dockery, ed. (Wheaton, Ill.: BridgePoint, 1995), 27. John Dewey in *Reconstruction of Philosophy* in 1929 summarized the spirit of modernity around four central ideas: (1) natural world, (2) rational authority, (3) progressive history, and (4) scientific method.

2. James Emory White, "Evangelism in a Postmodern World," *The Challenge of Postmodernism*, 363.

3. Will McRaney, "The Evangelistic Conversation in an Increasingly Postmodern America."

4. David L. Goetz, "The Riddle of Our Postmodern Culture: What Is Postmodernism? Should We Even Care?" *Leadership*, Winter 1997, 53.

5. Will McRaney, "The Evangelistic Conversation in an Increasingly Postmodern America."

6. In contrast to modernity, Thom Wolf gave five marks of postmodernity: (1) rediscovery of the supernatural, (2) embracing of alternative authorities, (3) disillusionment with historical progress, (4) multidimensional methodologies, and (5) reconfiguring through the information revolution. See "Postmodernity and the Urban Church Agenda," oral presentation at the American Society for Church Growth Annual Conference, Orlando, FL, November 1997.

7. Thomas C. Oden, "The Death of Modernity and Postmodern Evangelical Spirituality" in *The Challenge of Postmodernism*, David S. Dockery, ed., 23–25. Oden uses the beginning date of 1789 with the French Revolution and 1989 with the collapse of Communism. Dockery in this same work on page 13 also describes postmodernism in terms of a time period.

8. David L. Goetz, "The Riddle of Our Postmodern Culture," 53–54.

9. Ibid., 54.

10. Jimmy Long, *Generating Hope* (Downers Grove, Ill.: IVP, 1997), 69.

11. William Grassie, "Postmodernism: What One Needs to Know," *Zygon Journal of Religion and Science*, vol. 32, no. 1 (March 1997): 83.

12. Teaching of Harold Bullock in various settings.

13. Lesslie Newbigin, *Foolishness to the Greeks*, 13.

14. In some ways the church in America is comprised of many smaller subculture groups of Christians. The longer we are Christians, the more difficult it becomes to see the world through the eyes of lost people.

15. See Newbigin, *The Gospel in a Pluralistic Society*, chapter 12, and David Hesselgrave, *Communicating Christ Cross-Culturally*.

16. Lesslie Newbigin, *Foolishness to the Greeks*, 1–2.

17. Brian D. McLaren, *The Church on the Other Side* (Grand Rapids: Zondervan, 2000), 11.

18. Paul E. Little, *Know Why You Believe* (Downers Grove, Ill.: Inter-Varsity Press, 1967).

19. "Mystery is very attractive to people today. But there must be events and entry points that *are* intelligible and meet felt needs." Rick Richardson, *Evangelism Outside the Box*, 23.

20. Bill Easum, 21st Century Strategies Inc. "Disciple Making Leaders," 1998, p. 15.

21. Linda Wakefield Kelley, "A Winning Team: How Four Couples Work Together to Reach Their Neighbors," *Discipleship Journal*, September-October 2000, 80–82.

22. Conclusions of Eddie Gilley as reported in a paper, January 2002, 2–3.

23. James K. Hampton, "The Challenge of Postmodernism," *Youthworker*, January/February 1999, 19.

24. George Barna, Thom Wolf, George Hunter, James Engel, and Nick Pollard in *Evangelism Made Slightly Less Difficult* all agree that the conversion process will generally take longer for the postmodern person who has experienced less influence from the Judeo-Christian tradition.

25. Hampton, "The Challenge of Postmodernism," *Youthworker*, January/February 1999, 20–21, 24.

26. The conclusion was part of a paper, "The Evangelistic Conversation in an Increasingly Postmodern America," written by the

author and published in the *American Society for Church Growth Journal,*
Winter 2001, 81–94.

CHAPTER 6

1. See Drew J. Gunnells Jr., "Counseling Children about
Conversion," *Southwestern Journal of Theology* 33 (1991): 35–41, for materials on this subject.

2. See Daniel H. Smith, *How to Lead a Child to Christ* (Chicago:
Moody Press, 1987), 55, for additional information on the subject.

3. Barth and Sally Middleton, "Am I Doing It Right?" *Evangelizing
Today's Child* 27 (2000): 8–11.

4. Drs. Paula Stringer and Sharon Thompson, "Painting Pictures of
Jesus" C–35 in Counselor Training. Dr. Stringer is a childhood education
specialist in her role as a seminary professor.

5. Summarized from Dan Padgett, "Toward Understanding Children
and Conversion," *Children's Leadership* 2 (January-March 1972): 18–19.

6. Barth and Sally Middleton, "Am I Doing It Right?" *Evangelizing
Today's Child* 27 (2000): 8–11.

7. See the following for tips on communicating with children: Drew
J. Gunnells Jr., "Counseling Children about Conversion," *Southwestern
Journal of Theology* 33 (1991): 35–41. See also Stringer and Thompson,
"Painting Pictures of Jesus."

8. Stringer and Thompson, "Painting Pictures of Jesus," C–33.

9. Stringer and Thompson, "Painting Pictures of Jesus," C–35.

10. Barna Research Group, "Teenagers Embrace Religion but Are Not
Excited About Christianity," 10 January 2000, C:\Windows\Temporary
Internet Files\OLKF216\Barna Research Online.htm.

11. Tim McLaughlin, "Who Is the Next Generation?" *Moody* 101, no.1
(2000): 17. The five marks of American teens discussed were adapted
from this article. Also see Marv Penner, "Am I an Adult or Not?"
Youthworker 17, no. 2 (November/December 2000): 24–30, for additional information.

12. Tim McLaughlin, "Who Is the Next Generation?" *Moody* 101,
no.1 (2000): 17.

13. David J. Bosch, *Believing in the Future,* 32.

14. Hesselgrave, *Communicating Christ Cross-Culturally*, 81.

15. Ibid., 188.

16. Louis J. Luzbetak, *The Church and Cultures* (Techny, Ill.: Divine Word, 1963), 60–61; quoted in David J. Hesselgrave, *Communicating Christ Cross-Culturally*, 100.

17. Clyde Kluckhohn, *Mirror for Man* (New York: Whittlesey, 1949), 23; quoted in David J. Hesselgrave, *Communicating Christ Cross-Culturally*, 100.

18. Figure related to dimensions of cross-cultural communication is from Hesselgrave, *Communicating Christ Cross-Culturally*, 164.

19. Ibid., 405.

20. See works by the father of the modern church growth movement and missionary for over forty years, Donald McGavran. These books include *Bridges to God* (New York: Friendship Press, 1955) and *Understanding Church Growth*.

21. Hesselgrave, *Communicating Christ Cross-Culturally*, 98.

22. Ibid., 108.

23. Ibid., 203.

24. There are other ways Muslims seek to work their way to heaven. Muslims must completely surrender to Allah, do more good deeds than bad, and keep the five pillars of Islam: daily public recitation of the Shahadah, perform salat (daily ritual prayers) five times a day, give alms, fast during Ramadan, and at least once in one's life make a pilgrimage to Mecca, either personally or by proxy. Regardless, salvation in Islam is through works, not grace.

25. Newbigin, *Foolishness to the Greeks*, 5–6.

CHAPTER 7

1. Thom Wolf in his oral presentation, "Postmodernity and the Urban Church Agenda," at the American Society for Church Growth Annual Conference, Orlando, FL, November 1997 made the case for asking the lost person to consider the possibility of the resurrection and then the implications for their life if true. C. Norman Kraus in *An Intrusive Gospel? Christian Mission in the Postmodern World* (Downers Grove, Ill.: IVP), 19, asserted: "By implication, postmodern presuppositions

challenge traditional evangelism as cultural arrogance. They throw suspicion on a service motivation as disguised self-serving. . . . Thus whether we agree with these postmodern implications or not, they demand a change in attitudes, modes of communication and definitions of witness and service." We can and should communicate directly with postmodern people about the implications of a decision, but initially the emphasis will be consideration and allowing the Holy Spirit to work.

2. This material was first presented in a paper, "Evangelism in an Increasingly Postmodern America," ETS Regional Meeting in New Orleans, 26 March 1999, and later appeared in the *ASCG Journal*, "The Evangelistic Conversation in an Increasingly Postmodern America."

3. Ronald W. Johnson wrote a book that deals with the importance of listening, *How Will They Hear If We Don't Listen* (Nashville: Broadman & Holman, 1994).

4. The word *reach* is used in this book to mean "evangelize" or "convert."

5. Interview with an anonymous person by William T. Higginbotham as reported in a paper January 2002, 3.

6. Interviews with an anonymous person by Dale Funderburg as reported in a paper January 2002, 1.

7. Richardson, *Evangelism Outside the Box*, 36.

8. Ibid., 51.

9. For a detailed explanation of this role and approach, see Nick Pollard's *Evangelism Made Slightly Less Difficult* (Downers Grove: Ill., Inter-Varsity Press, 1997).

10. Charles H. Kraft, *Communication Theory for Christian Witness*, 129.

11. Bill Fay in *Share Jesus Without Fear* (Nashville: Broadman & Holman, 1999), 69, has a list of commitment questions: (1) Are you a sinner? (2) Do you want forgiveness of sins? (3) Do you believe Jesus Christ died on the cross for you and rose again? (4) Are you willing to surrender your life to Jesus Christ? (5) Are you ready to invite Jesus Christ into your life and into your heart?

12. See the appendix for a Readiness Scale.

13. William Fay, *Share Jesus Without Fear*, 146.

CHAPTER 8

1. See chapter 5 for discussion of success.

2. George Barna, *Evangelism That Works*.

3. Tim Passmore as reported in a D.Min. paper, 30 January 2002, 5.

4. Delos Miles devoted an entire book to the subject of internal barriers, *Overcoming Barriers to Witnessing* (Nashville: Broadman, 1984).

5. Michael Green, *Evangelism in the Early Church* (Grand Rapids: Eerdmans Publishing Company, 1970), chapter 9.

6. Concept from Harold Bullock at "How Church Works II." These approaches can be a part of an overall church strategy, but a strategy cannot be limited to these type components.

7. Ron Hutchcraft, "Communicating the Message to Our Culture," from video of North American Conference for Itinerant Evangelists, 1994.

8. Harold Bullock, conference notebook "How Church Works II," 21.

9. Adrian Rogers in an interview report by Ruben R. Raquel, 2 February 2002.

10. See Steve Sjogren, *Conspiracy of Kindness* (Ann Arbor: Servant Publications, 1993).

11. McCloskey, *Tell It Often—Tell It Well*, 255.

12. Yandall Woodfin, *With All Your Mind*, 22.

13. Yandall Woodfin, *With All Your Mind*, 22–23.

14. Ron Hutchcraft, "Communicating the Message to Our Culture."

15. Several outstanding ministries and individuals who are devoted to defending the Christian faith can be located on the internet. Frank Harber's www.defendingthefaith.com is an example.

16. McRaney, ASCG Paper, "Evangelism in an Increasingly Postmodern America."

17. For a discussion of Socratic evangelism, see George Barna's *Evangelism That Works* (Ventura, Calif.: Regal Books, 1995).

18. McRaney, ASCG Paper, "Evangelism in an Increasingly Postmodern America."

19. Richardson, *Evangelism Outside the Box*, 23.

20. See Steve Sojgren, *Conspiracy of Kindness,* for details on how to do servant evangelism.

21. Richardson, *Evangelism Outside the Box,* 27–28.

22. Other verses which relate: John 8:44; 13:2; Matthew 13:38–39; 2 Timothy 2:25–26.

23. (1) Don't all the religions basically teach the same things but just use different names for God? (2) As long as people are genuinely sincere, what difference does it make what they believe? (3) Isn't it narrow-minded for Christians to think that they're right and everyone else is wrong? (4) What credentials back up the claims of Christianity? Is there any good evidence to support them? (5) What makes you so confident that the Bible is true? It has so many authors, so many translations, and was written over so many years—there must be mistakes! (6) How do you know that God exists? (7) If a loving and powerful God really exists, why doesn't He do something about all of the evil in the world? (8) What about innocent people who suffer, like little children? Why doesn't God do something to help them?

24. Richardson, *Evangelism Outside the Box,* 27.

25. "One of those listening was a woman named Lydia, a dealer in purple cloth from the city of Thyatira, who was a worshiper of God. The Lord opened her heart to respond to Paul's message" (Acts 16:14).

26. This technique is also located in the first chapter of Gary Smalley's book, *The Key to Your Child's Heart.*

CHAPTER 9

1. Quoted by Connie Cavanaugh, "Evangelism to Women," *On Mission,* July–August 2001, 33.

2. Barna Research Online, March 2000; The Gallup Organization, October 2000; and Focus on the Family, 1998.

3. Quoted by Connie Cavanaugh, "Evangelism to Women," 33–35.

4. For tips to reach women through your local church and its events, see "Tips for Reaching Women" in "Evangelism to Women" *On Mission,* July-August 2001, 35.

5. Divorce, Death, Divine Encounters, Illness, and Status Change.

6. Rick Warren, *The Purpose-Driven Church* (Grand Rapids: Zondervan, 1996), 182.

7. Ibid.

8. Barney Kinard, "Rethinking Follow-up of Child Converts," *Evangelizing Today's Child* 27 (2000): 11–13.

9. For a review of several of the most popular personal evangelism training materials, see my Web site www.MEGnet.org. Materials will be reviewed in terms of costs, strengths, limitations, and how the materials can be purchased.

10. Tom Steffen, "Flawed Evangelism and Church Planting," 434.

11. McRaney, ASCG Paper, "Evangelism in an Increasingly Postmodern America."

12. Pollard, *Evangelism Made Slightly Less Difficult*, 105–107, provides a compact version of how to do this.

13. Only when evangelists have enough familiarity and are comfortable with the message can they focus on the person with whom they are sharing and can listen to the Holy Spirit.

14. As a starter list, consider desire for inner peace, hope, joy, acceptance, or removal of individual dependence, guilt, rejection, or loneliness. The witness will have to consider what the legitimate reasons are for desiring a relationship with the living God.

15. McRaney, ASCG Paper, "Evangelism in an Increasingly Postmodern America."

16. Pollard, *Evangelism Made Slightly Less Difficult*, 70. "Two major characteristics of postmodernism are of particular importance to us in evangelism: (1) the emphasis on questioning and (2) the displacement of propositional truth in favor of stories. If we are to be effective within this postmodern culture, then our evangelism must involve the appropriate use of questions and stories." Also see pages 111–17 for insightful helps in storytelling.

17. Ibid., 44: "The process is *deconstructive* because I am helping people to deconstruct (that is, take apart) what they believe in order to look carefully at the belief and analyze it. The process is *positive* because this deconstructing is done in a positive way—in order to replace the false belief with something better. . . . The process of positive

deconstruction recognizes and affirms the elements of truth to which individuals already hold, but it also helps them discover for themselves the inadequacies of the underlying worldviews they have absorbed."

18. McRaney, ASCG Paper, "Evangelism in an Increasingly Postmodern America."

19. Ron Hutchcraft, "Communicating the Message to Our Culture."

APPENDIX 3

1. Mark Mittelberg, Lee Strobel, and Bill Hybels, *Becoming a Contagious Christian Leader's Guide* (Grand Rapids: Zondervan, 1995), 264. This scale serves to remind the witness that not all lost people are at the same point; therefore, the approach of the witness must adapt to the readiness of the lost person.

APPENDIX 4

1. Interview reported in a paper, 30 January 2002, p. 5.

About the Author

WILL MCRANEY SERVES AS A PROFESSOR of evangelism at New Orleans Baptist Theological Seminary. He also ministers through his role as cofounder of the Ministry Enhancement Group, a training and consulting group in the areas of evangelism, church growth, and leadership development. He specializes in developing contextualized growth strategies and has done extensive research and speaking on approaches to reaching the changing culture. He gained pastoral experience in both established and new churches with both traditional and contemporary styles after learning to share his faith while an SEC baseball and football player.

To arrange for a live presentation of the material found in *The Art of Personal Evangelism* or to request a list of materials or conference topics led by Dr. McRaney, contact:

Ministry Enhancement Group
241 Westwood Dr.
Mandeville, LA 70471
985-871-0940
E-mail: mcraney@aol.com
Internet: www.MEGnet.org